Congressional
Politics
in the Second
World War

Congressional Politics in the Second World War

by ROLAND YOUNG

COLUMBIA UNIVERSITY PRESS
NEW YORK, 1956

COPYRIGHT © 1956 COLUMBIA UNIVERSITY PRESS, NEW YORK
PUBLISHED IN GREAT BRITAIN, CANADA, INDIA, AND PAKISTAN
BY GEOFFREY CUMBERLEGE: OXFORD UNIVERSITY PRESS
LONDON, TORONTO, BOMBAY, AND KARACHI

Library of Congress Catalog Card Number: 56-6007
MANUFACTURED IN THE UNITED STATES OF AMERICA

Contents

Congressional
Politics
in the Second
World War

Introduction

Introduction

THIS VOLUME tells the story of Congress during the war years of 1941–45. During the war, Congress made a multitude of legislative decisions on converting the economy from peace to war and on organizing the energies of the nation toward the high goal of survival. Although there were some precedents for fighting a war, there were no automatic standards to be applied in making these decisions, and Congress was continually compelled to break new ground in solving the perplexing political questions brought on by the war. There was often a real choice of policy alternatives in making many types of decisions, as, for instance, in allocating the burdens of the war and in anticipating the effect on the postwar economy of wartime decisions. The politics of war were more complicated, and at times more intense, than the politics of peace. Various conflicts in the government and in the civilian economy came to a head in Congress, although not all were necessarily resolved there, and some, of course, were never resolved.

At the beginning of the war, it was widely believed that Congress need not, or should not, play a very important role in fighting a war. A modern war required that the President be given the power necessary to direct the civil and military establishments. The necessity for speed and secrecy in making decisions would prevent Congress from performing all of the functions it would normally perform in peace. To bolster the belief that Congress would be placed in a subordinate position once war was declared, one could refer to historical instances of congressional behavior as well as to contemporary examples of moribund legislatures. The Continental Congress had not made an exemplary record during the Revolutionary War, and the achievements of that war have ordinarily been attributed to Washington, to the volunteer army, and to public-spirited individuals rather than to the Congress.

During the Civil War, President Abraham Lincoln performed a number of acts which he believed to be unconstitutional (but necessary to save the Constitution), and he secured the consent of Congress after he acted rather than before. Also, Lincoln expanded the concept of President as Commander-in-Chief so that the office may be thought to have power independent of Congress. President Wilson was granted considerable powers during the First World War, and he emerged as the war leader, quite eclipsing the role played by Congress. The example of some other legislatures after the First World War did not inspire faith in their behavior during a crisis. The reality of numerous dictatorships showed that free institutions did not necessarily remain free and that a defeated enemy did not necessarily wish to adopt liberal institutions. One was tauntingly reminded that the last war had not made the world safe for democracy. Despite forebodings on the future of legislative bodies, however, it was clear that the Axis dictators considered representative legislatures to be a threat to totalitarianism and that one of the prizes of the war was the continuance of free, deliberative legislative assemblies.

Once war came, Congress quickly adjusted itself to the conditions of war, and it was by no means the anachronism which many —including some of its own members—predicted it would be. Issues were raised which needed to be resolved politically, and, as before the war, the President and the government agencies continued to ask Congress for funds and for authority. The President was given great powers, but he was not a dictator, and Congress did not become a rubber stamp in delegating power. The relationship with the President and the numerous war agencies raised many problems, for though it was agreed that the prosecution of the war came within the province of the President, Congress did not wish to delegate all authority over domestic issues to the expanding bureaucracy. A wartime President was expected to have more power, to be able to act without certain congressional restraints, but once this major premise was granted, the allowable sphere of congressional action had still to be determined.

A pattern of politics prevailed which was in many ways similar to that of the prewar world. In some areas of policy, the influence of the President was preponderant. The President emerged as the over-all planner of political and economic action, and the role of Congress was that of altering, amending, objecting, and substituting. The grand strategy of the war, to take one example, was almost totally executive in concept, and even the execution of the war strategy was not seriously attacked in Congress. There were other areas of policy where the interests of the President and of Congress were not in harmony and where each attempted to persuade the other to follow its leadership. Labor policy and farm policy illustrate this point. Labor policy tended to be executive in origin, but this policy was periodically challenged by articulate segments of Congress who wished to enact into law their own theory of labor relations. However, the only major labor legislation enacted during the war was the so-called Smith-Connally Act of 1943, and this over the veto of the President. Farm policy tended to be congressional in origin, but the President frequently challenged Congress on such issues as the parity price of farm crops, the content of the parity formula, the sale of surplus commodities, and the use of consumer subsidies. The President was not always able to secure congressional support for his policies, notably in the field of taxation and labor relations, while, on the other hand, Congress was often dissatisfied with the use made of delegated power, notably in the field of price control. The Chief Executive had great power, which was partly balanced by the considerable increase in the number and scope of investigating committees.

In the period between the great wars, Congress gave some thought to the problem of how to fight another war, and several attempts were made to enact special legislation which would come into effect in the event of a war. The popular phrase for this legis-

lation was "Take the Profits out of War," but in reality the proposals went somewhat further and often included provisions for
controlling prices, allocating manpower, and mobilizing industry.

In the early 1920s, legislation to "minimize" war profits, as the
phrase went, was sponsored by the American Legion and was
known in Congress as the Capper-Johnson bills. In 1930, Congress
created a War Policies Commission (with Dwight D. Eisenhower
acting as Secretary), which was directed to study policies to be
followed in the event of war. In its final report in March, 1932, the
Commission recommended permanent legislation authorizing the
government to fix prices and to tax war profits, but no legislation
was enacted. In the 1935–39 period, the movement to take the
profits out of war became partially identified with neutrality legislation and with methods of preserving the peace, but again no
permanent legislation was enacted. These protracted discussions
developed a consensus of opinion on some of the issues to be considered in fighting a war.

A war required everyone to sacrifice something and some to
sacrifice a good deal, including, perhaps, life itself. In the rhetoric
of politics, the stereotype of inequality was the soldier contrasted
with the war profiteer or with workers whose economic position
had been greatly improved by the war. The phrase "equality of
sacrifice" was frequently used as a standard for making policy, but
its application to a concrete situation produced many ambiguities.
In one sense, equality of sacrifice implied the continuance of a
given relationship. As the war drained the country's wealth, no
one would be richer and everyone would be proportionately poorer,
having at the end of the war about the same relative economic
status as he had at the beginning. In the words of Mr. Bernard
M. Baruch, it was expected that every dollar and every man would
bear its proper share of the burden of the war.

When applied negatively, equality of sacrifice was interpreted
to mean that no one should be asked to sacrifice more than anyone
else, so that the standard was thought to be the lowest common
denominator of activity. If Mr. Y's sacrifice was compared with that

of a combat soldier, Mr. Y, of course, could never quite catch up. But if his sacrifice were compared with his competitor, Mr. Z, who was making money because of favorable administrative regulations, or even because he was in the black market, Mr. Y might well say that he should not be forced to sacrifice more than Mr. Z.

The attempt to preserve a given set of economic relationships by law was known as the "freeze," and attempts were made, for instance, to maintain the price or wage relationship which existed at a certain specific period in the past. In another sphere, it was proposed that labor unions or political parties be allowed to preserve their prewar status so that their position would neither improve nor deteriorate because of the opportunities or the exigencies of war. In administering the war economy, decisions were continually being made which affected the distribution of the burdens of war and the relative status of groups in the postwar economy. Such questions were raised as the place in the war effort of small businessmen and dollar-a-year men, the suspension of antimonopoly suits, and the time table for reconversion. In manpower policy, the sacrifice of the men in the service was continually used as a measure of judgment for other proposals. The financing of the war raised the problem of the share of the war burden which should be assumed by the present as opposed to future generations and, so far as immediate taxes were concerned, the problem of the allocation of the tax burden among various income groups. The standard of equality of sacrifice, with all of its ambiguities, was a factor in the decisions made on a wide variety of political issues.

A weakness of the equality-of-sacrifice standard was that it made insufficient allowance for the dynamics of war. The fighting of a war required necessary dislocations in the economy, and these dislocations could not always be made in an equitable ratio. Those who owned factories which were convertible to war industry, for instance, were in a more advantageous position than those owning nonessential and nonconvertible industries. Money was used as an incentive to make men move their residences, take other jobs, grow different crops, or take a defense contract, and money changed the status of people and of groups. In all, the development of a war economy required a realignment and readjustment of the productive forces of the country, and in this process many individuals and groups became proportionately better off than competitors in the same social scale and, in some cases, better off absolutely than they were before the war.

In addition to considering the immediate problems of the war, Congress had to plan for reconverting the economy to the peaceful world which lay beyond the war horizon. In the early years of the war, Congress was reluctant to consider postwar problems, believing that premature discussion would divert attention from the war. During this period the National Resources Planning Board maladroitly sent Congress two reports on expanding social security after the war; the reports were received with some hostility, and shortly thereafter the NRPB itself was liquidated. Later Congress became actively interested in postwar planning. Special postwar committees were created in each House, and these as well as some of the standing legislative committees became occupied with legislation on contract settlement, veterans' benefits, employment, and tax rates. When political issues were decided, Congressmen increasingly raised the question of the effect of the proposed policy on postwar employment.

Although the attack on Pearl Harbor united the country on an immediate policy of striking back at the enemy, the old foreign policy debates between the so-called isolationists and interventionists continued intermittently during the war. At the same time, the international position of the United States was changing with the participation in the war, and victory elevated the nation to a preeminent position in the postwar world. During the war, a new foreign policy was considered and in part adopted.

The rivalry prevailing between the two political parties also continued during the war; there was no suspension of elections, as in Great Britain, and Congress retained its partisan organizational base. The Democrats won the two war elections, although the 1942 election was very close, but the New Deal was liquidated with the blessings of President Roosevelt. Many of the votes in Congress were cast along party lines, and a series of charts has been prepared which show the degrees of party voting of the two major parties and of individual Senators and Representatives.[1]

The New Deal continued to be an issue during the war. To some, it symbolized a type of reform which was unnecessary in peace and unpatriotic in war. The New Deal should now be suspended, like other unnecessary civilian activities, it was believed, but instead it appeared that ambitious reformers were planning to entrench themselves in power. To others, the New Deal symbolized foresight in foreign policy, leadership in administration, and the supremacy of the public interest. And now conservatives were coming to Washington to run the government, achieving during the war what they could not previously achieve by popular vote.

Bureaucracy also was an issue, and in the strange semantics of politics the bureaucrat was often considered to be devoid of the attributes of wisdom and prudence with which the politician credits the average voter. The strains engendered by the dislocations, the fear, and the frustrations of war frequently found a convenient scapegoat in the bureaucrat, who could not readily talk back.

A word about the terms and method used in this study is perhaps necessary. The word Congressman is used to designate a member of either House of Congress; he may be either a Representative or a Senator. Such expressions as "Congress thought" or "Congress believed" are frequently used, although in fact the action may have been confined to a smaller group. The word Congress, in other words, is sometimes used to identify only a part of the whole body. If the small group has a significant position in the hierarchy of congressional power, its reaction may result in Congress as a whole taking some specific action, such as passing a law.

An attempt has been made to organize the considerable material

[1] See Appendix B.

around three major questions. (1) What major external events influenced Congress? These events ran the gamut from the bombing of Pearl Harbor to demands of civilians for new tires. (2) What was the reaction in Congress to these events? Sometimes Congress would study the issue and enact legislation; sometimes it would create an investigating committee; sometimes it would be inordinately passive. (3) What part was played by procedures, partisan groups, and political ideas in making the requisite decisions? The response within Congress was continually determined by the organization which existed and the procedures which had to be followed. Partisanship played a greater part in determining some types of issues than in determining others. The political ideas governing decisions were drawn from many sources, but of course during the war the concepts of fairness and justice were always compelling.

Superficially it might seem that a war would simplify the process of making political decisions by minimizing the importance of nonwar, and therefore nonessential, activities. In fact, however, the war complicated the process of making political decisions inasmuch as new standards for decisions were added and the old standards were not entirely outmoded. It is a mistake, then, to conceive of the wartime Congress as an institution which did no more than appropriate vast funds and grant great powers to the Administration. One will get a truer picture by visualizing Congress as an institution which considered simultaneously many facets of the war economy, including some of the same problems that the Administration was considering. The political fortunes of the individuals and groups who made the decisions were always at stake during the war, a circumstance which resulted in a continuation of the political competition for preferment and status and recognition and power. On the basis of the evidence presented, the reader may be able to decide for himself how well he believes Congress acquitted itself of its functions during the war. My own conclusions are given in the last chapter.

I. Congress at War

TEMPORARY UNITY

THE ATTACK on Pearl Harbor finally resolved the issue with which Congress had been concerned for so long: the United States would go to war. There surged through Congress a belief that unity was necessary if the war was to be won, and when the roll was called on the resolution stating that the United States was at war with Japan, the only negative vote was that of Rep. Jeanette Rankin (R., Missoula, Mont.), who had also voted against entrance into the First World War. As one Representative put it, in the showdown we were all for one and one for all. It was time to stop "all this idle talk and all this nagging and territorial bully ragging. It has happened." [1]

The President was considered the symbol of unity, and members who had been at odds with the Administration on foreign and domestic policy made speeches supporting him. "Out of the sky came a vicious assault by a skillful and determined enemy, and ere it was ended a representative of the Democratic Party, who was President, became our President," [2] said Rep. Clare E. Hoffman (R., Allegan, Mich.), who in the past had spoken some harsh words about the President (and was shortly to speak them again).

Pearl Harbor was, simultaneously, the force which molded unity, the ablution for past errors and dissensions, the creator of the greater goal of victory and survival to which all smaller goals

---

[1] A remark of Representative Plumley (R., Vt.); see *Congressional Record* (hereafter referred to as *C.R.*), Dec. 9, 1941, p. A5506.

[2] C.R., Dec. 16, 1941, p. 9856.

should be subordinated. Letters and wires flowed into Congress from old veterans wanting to get back into the Army, preferably with a commission. Congress, by law, authorized and directed the President "to employ . . . the resources of the Government to carry on war." Once the trumpet had sounded clearly, everyone responded.

Although Pearl Harbor created a unified resolve to win the war, it did not end the need for making political decisions, nor did it end political controversy. In less than three months, Rep. Clifton A. Woodrum (D., Roanoke, Va.), the ranking Democrat on the Appropriations Committee, was berating his colleagues for allowing partisanship to determine their decisions. "Ah," he said, referring to the attitude of Congress at Pearl Harbor, "there was unity, there was a single purpose, there was a single determination; that was to do this job and to do it right and as quickly as possible." [3] The unity of Congress, in the sense that all members agreed on policy, began and ended with Pearl Harbor. There was agreement on the issue that the war must be won, but there was no agreement on what policy should be followed in winning the war.

PARTISAN CONTROVERSY

It was widely believed in Congress that partisanship should be at least partly suspended for the duration and that parties should not take advantage of the war to advance their own position. On the other hand, it was necessary to permit a type of partisanship which would allow the parties to survive the war, for political parties were part of our free institutions for which the war was being fought. From the competitive point of view, no party or partisan wished to lose ground because of the war or to be in a less favored position once peace returned. The parties had to operate within these restrictions, and, within them, each party pressed its advantage hard.

In this struggle within a struggle, both parties had some ad-

[3] *C.R.*, Feb. 17, 1942, p. 1367.

vantages and some handicaps. The Democrats had the advantage of being in power with a strong President and of having taken a strong stand on preparedness before Pearl Harbor. They were at some disadvantage, however, in having the responsibility for running the war. They could not run the war on a partisan basis, nor could they claim partisan credit for achievements in production or for victory in arms, but they would very likely be blamed at elections for the frustrations, shortages, and dislocations caused by the war. The Republicans had the handicap of being the minority party and of having to develop a new foreign policy after Pearl Harbor. They were compelled to exercise restraint in making partisan issues of military disasters, although they could take political advantage of small-scale blunders. On the affirmative side, the Republicans could criticize reform carried into the war period and blame the Democrats for faulty administration, and they could give businessmen and the free enterprise system credit for administrative successes. The Republicans would also receive as a windfall the support of those who were tiring of the strains and injustices of war. In all, the Republicans had considerable maneuverability.

In December, 1941, the chairmen of the two national committees attempted to resolve the dilemma of supporting a nonpartisan war while leading partisan organizations. Mr. Edward J. Flynn, for the Democrats, sent a telegram to Rep. Joseph W. Martin, for the Republicans, proposing that "our combined agencies" be made available in defense preparations, in the sale of stamps and bonds, in the organization for civilian defense, and other like endeavors. Martin responded that the Republicans would gladly answer "any call to national service which may be requested by the President" and that the Republicans would not permit "politics to enter into national defense." [4] In a burst of patriotic hyperbole, a partisan publication called the exchange "the most complete adjournment of domestic politics since the formation of the

[4] The exchange of correspondence was published in the New York *Times,* Dec. 11, 1941.

two party system." Although this statement may have been relatively true, for the adjournment of politics does not happen often
or to any considerable degree, the Martin-Flynn exchange did not
contain the essential ingredients for adjourning politics. It did not,
for instance, propose a freeze in the political *status quo*, a freeze
which would have permitted the parties to have the same relative strength at the end of the war as at the beginning. No suggestion was made for suspending elections or, if there were to be
elections, of returning the same men or the same party to office.
No formula was suggested for bipartisan administration of the
government, and the exchange of views carried no implication
that political controversy was the normal method of resolving dis-
puted issues. Rather than proposing a freeze of the political *status
quo*, the statement proposed the exercise of restraint in taking
undue partisan advantage—and, in any event, such restraint may
have been "good politics." In short, no ground rules were established for "adjourning politics" or for keeping politics out of national defense.

The rule of forbearance soon ended, and the strain on the politicians for even this limited period must have been considerable.
In January, 1942, there was a lusty partisan debate in the House
in which it was implied that fan dancers were being used in the
civil defense program. This meant that the politicians were preparing for the elections; State primaries were not far off, and
politicians were naturally testing suitable political issues. In February, Mr. Flynn himself made what some considered to be a
partisan appeal by stating that nothing short of a military defeat
would be more disastrous for the country than the election of a
Congress hostile to the President. The response to Mr. Flynn's
statement was unfavorable, and the President in effect corrected
him by stating that Congressmen were needed who would back
up the war regardless of party.

The Administration had attempted to introduce a note of bipartisanship in the government by naming Mr. Henry Stimson
and Mr. Frank Knox to head the War and Navy Departments, but

a corresponding bipartisan organization of Congress was not attempted. It would have been difficult to achieve, and it was very likely unnecessary. Congress carried on during the war under its old method of organizing the two chambers and their committees according to parties. At the time of Pearl Harbor, the Democrats held a substantial majority in Congress with 65 Senate seats and 263 House seats, but the division did not accurately reflect partisan opinion on any subject other than who was to organize each House. On questions of domestic policy some Democrats voted with Republicans, and on questions of foreign policy some Republicans voted with Democrats.

The internal organization of Congress remained under the nominal control of the Democrats, although the latter did not maintain effective control over all committees or over all roll-call votes. The following list shows how the most important policy positions were distributed in the party organization and in the major standing committees and investigating committees. The floor leaders and the chairmen and ranking minority members of committees are noted, together with classification within the party.

The classificatory system has been developed from an analysis of party-votes, which are defined as those in which a majority of one party is opposed by a majority of the second party. In preparing this material, each member was given a score based on the percentage of times he agreed with the majority of his own party on all party-votes, and the scores were then plotted from zero to one hundred. The scores were then divided into three groups of roughly the same size, and the members were given the classification of the group in which they fell. In general, the members in Group I may be termed strong party supporters; those in Group II, moderate party supporters; and those in Group III, mild party supporters. Inasmuch as many Eastern Republicans voted with the Democratic majority on some issues, such leaders as Senator White and Speaker Martin fall into the category of Group II. Similarly, many Democrats from the South voted with the Republican majority, placing them in Group II or Group III. Members casting fewer than twenty party-votes have been classified "Inc." (for inconclusive). A complete classification of congressional membership is found in Appendix A.

HOUSE

	Group	Democrats	Group	Republicans
Speaker	Inc.	Rayburn, Texas		
Floor Leaders	I	McCormack, Mass.	II	Martin, Mass.
Agriculture	III	Fulmer, S.C.	II	Hope, Kan.
	I	Flannagan, Va.		
Appropriations	III	Cannon, Mo.	II	Taber, N.Y.
Banking and Currency	II	Steagall, Ala.	II	Wolcott, Mich.
	I	Spence, Ky.		
Foreign Affairs	I	Bloom, N.Y.	I	Fish, N.Y.
			II	Eaton, N.J.
Judiciary	III	Sumners, Tex.	I	Guyer, Kan.
			II	Hancock, N.Y.
Labor	I	Norton, N.J.	III	Welch, Calif.
Military Affairs	III	May, Ky.	II	Andrews, N.Y.
Naval Affairs	II	Vinson, Ga.	II	Mass, Minn.
			III	Mott, Ore.
Rules	I	Sabath, Ill.	I	Fish, N.Y.
			I	Allen, Ill.
Ways and Means	II	Doughton, N.C.	II	Treadway, Mass.
			I	Knutson, Minn.
World War Veterans	III	Rankin, Miss.	II	Rogers, Mass.
Acts of Executive Agencies (Smith)	III	Smith, Va.	II	Hartley, N.J.
Defense Migration (Tolan)	I	Tolan, Calif.	II	Curtis, Neb.
Postwar Economic Policy and Planning (Colmer)	III	Colmer, Miss.	I	Fish, N.Y.
			II	Gifford, Mass.
Postwar Military Policy (Woodrum)	III	Woodrum, Va.	II	Andrews, N.Y.
Seizure of Montgomery Ward & Co. (Ramspeck)	I	Ramspeck, Ga.	II	Dewey, Ill.

	Group	Democrats	Group	Republicans
Small Business (Patman)	I	Patman, Tex.	I II	Halleck, Ind. L. Hall, N.Y.
Un-American Activities (Dies)	III	Dies, Tex.	I III	Mason, Ill. Thomas, N.J.

SENATE

	Group	Democrats	Group	Republicans
President		Wallace, Iowa Truman, Mo.		
President pro tempore	Inc. III	Glass, Va. McKellar, Tenn.		
Floor Leaders	I	Barkley, Ky.	II II	McNary, Ore. White, Me.
Agriculture and Forestry	III II	Smith, S.C. Thomas, Okla.	II II	McNary, Ore. Capper, Kan.
Appropriations	Inc.	Glass, Va.	II I	Nye, N.D. Bridges, N.H.
Banking and Currency	I	Wagner, N.Y.	III	Tobey, N.H.
Education and Labor	I I	Thomas, Utah Murray, Mont.	III I	La Follette, Wis. Taft, Ohio
Finance	III	George, Ga.	III II	La Follette, Wis. Vandenberg, Mich.
Foreign Relations	II	Connally, Tex.	Inc. II	Johnson, Calif. Capper, Kan.
Judiciary	III III	Van Nuys, Ind. McCarren, Nev.	III II	Norris, Neb. Danaher, Conn.
Military Affairs	III I	Reynolds, N.C. Thomas, Utah	III	Austin, Vt.
Naval Affairs	III	Walsh, Mass.	II III	Davis, Penn. Tobey, N.H.
National Defense (Truman)	I II	Truman, Mo. Mead, N.Y.	I	Brewster, Me.
Postwar Economic Policy and Planning (George)	III	George, Ga.	II	Vandenberg, Mich.
Small Business (Murray)	I	Murray, Mont.	II	Capper, Kan.

CONGRESSIONAL ORGANIZATION

Although the President assumed the leadership in fashioning the wartime administrative structure, Congress was not silent in proposing new plans or in criticizing old ones. The role which Congress should play in wartime was of considerable concern to some members, for it was believed that Congress might wither on the vine if it had little control over policy after laws were enacted. Three choices were open to Congress: it could organize a single committee, representing the whole of Congress, which would be made privy to administration secrets; it could create several investigation committees interested in various facets of the war; or it could carry on as before, depending largely on the existing committee structure of exacting effective control.

The plea for a single committee, "a liaison committee representing the United States Congress," was advanced by Senator Arthur H. Vandenberg (R., Grand Rapids, Mich.) immediately after Pearl Harbor. "It would very well be a meeting place for satisfying the sense of responsibility which Members of Congress inevitably feel, which may not otherwise be too easily satisfied unless there is some such official instrumentality by way of link between these two branches of government," [5] he explained. Neither this plan nor any of the similar plans was adopted. The Vandenberg proposal left unanswered the important political questions of who would represent Congress, how such representatives were to be chosen, and the power they would have to speak for Congress or to direct administrative officials. Such questions were difficult to answer in any event, but as it was, a good many committees already in existence had some jurisdictional claim over the war agencies which they would have been loath to relinquish.

Multiplication, not contraction, was in order. Instead of centralizing control in a single war committee, Congress dispersed control over a wide number of standing committees and newly created investigation committees. During the war, also, the State, War, and Navy departments revealed information to relevant legislative committees which was not revealed to the whole Congress or to the public. In addition, the President held weekly "free and

[5] *C.R.*, Dec. 9, 1941, p. 9543.

open discussions" with the political leaders of the House and Senate, and Speaker Sam Rayburn once told the House that "these are not blowpulling conferences." [6]

The proliferation of investigation committees was one of the singular characteristics of the war Congress. The emphasis on investigation, on the control of policy after the passage of an Act, was a spontaneous congressional reaction, as it were, to the increasing number of activities with which the administrative branch was concerned. At the beginning of the war, the major investigation committees were the Truman Committee (Senate Special Committee Investigating the National Defense Program), which was interested in questions relating to production; the Tolan Committee (House Committee on Inter-state Migration), which broadened its activities from migratory labor to include also general problems relating to the organization of production; the Murray and Patman Committees (Senate and House Committees on Small Business); the Maloney Committee (Senate Special Committee to Investigate Gasoline and Fuel-Oil Shortages); and the House and Senate Committees on Military Affairs and on Naval Affairs. There was considerable overlapping of committee interests inasmuch as jurisdictions were not precisely determined. Some dozen different committees were concerned with such controversial subjects as rubber production; manpower policy was considered by the Labor Committee as well as by the Military Affairs, Appropriations, Judiciary, and Agricultural Committees, and by the Truman and Tolan Committees.

This overlapping of interests resulted in some diversity among the committees themselves on the merits of any particular policy. The degree to which the administrators accepted criticism varied; not being bound by law to accept this advice, they had to make a prudent evaluation of the nature of the criticism and the strength of the political groups supporting it. An administrator might find himself in the ambivalent and somewhat embarrassing position of being supported by one committee and vilified by another. Al-

[6] *C.R.*, Jan. 6, 1943, p. 7.

though there were frequent duplications of effort, the committees spread their nets sufficiently wide to encompass most of the war activities. The actual influence of congressional investigations cannot be measured solely by their hearings and reports and by the immediate administrative reaction thereto. Every administrator knew that some day he might be asked to explain his action before a congressional committee.

ATTITUDES TOWARD CONGRESS

Throughout the war, the status of Congress was a perennial topic of debate. One of the anomalies of the early months of the war was the sharp decline of Congress in public esteem, but Congress was resilient and by the time of the elections in 1942 it was the Administration, not Congress, which was on the defensive. An episode contributing to the early decline of congressional popularity was the so-called pensions-for-Congressmen plan. Shortly before Pearl Harbor the House had passed a noncontroversial civil service retirement bill, which also extended the retirement system to members of Congress. When the Senate considered the bill in the following January, there was increased opposition, but the bill passed easily, 42–24 (73 percent of the Democrats; 43 percent of the Republicans), and it was signed by the President. Then the storm broke. It seemed to some people that Congress was demanding sacrifices from others while giving bounties to itself, and a movement known as "Bundles for Congress" soon made a farce of the episode. Congress quickly withdrew from its exposed position, and it very shortly repealed the provision by the large majorities of 75–5 in the Senate and 389–7 in the House.

Congressional prestige was also shaken as the result of the X-card episode. In an early plan to ration gasoline on the Eastern seaboard, the letter X was used on cards permitting the bearer to purchase unlimited quantities of gasoline. Following the registration in the District of Columbia, it was revealed that about ten percent of the members of Congress had requested or were given

X-cards, and as the story was played up in the press it appeared that Congressmen were selfish creatures indeed. It should be added, however, that according to the regulations governing the rationing, all Congressmen came under the category of individuals who were entitled to X-cards. They were not obliged to take them, however. There were various reactions in Congress to the episode and to the subsequent bad publicity which Congress received. Senator Robert M. LaFollette, Jr. (Prog., Madison, Wis.) thought that the incident was part of a deliberate campaign "to undermine the faith of the people in their elected representatives in the Congress," but Senator Sheridan Downey (D., Atherton, Calif.) wanted the Senate to pass a resolution waiving "any special rights, privileges, or exemptions" of its members and binding them to accept all rationing restrictions of general application. Senator Alben W. Barkley (D., Paducah, Ky.), the Majority Leader for the Democrats, was unmoved by this argument, for he thought it was unnecessary for the Senate "to pass a resolution binding the membership to be honorable men." [7] As anyone knowing the Senate could have predicted, the Downey resolution was defeated. The vote was 2–66.

There seemed to be a professional touchiness on the part of some members in implying that the President, the bureaucrats, and other detractors were attempting to undermine the dignity and authority of Congress. This attitude came out, for instance, in the debate which followed a report by Rep. Harold D. Cooley (D., Nashville, N.C.) on his unconducted and unauthorized inspection of the anti-aircraft installations on the New House Office building. Cooley told the House: "And here comes the story. We are being protected by wooden guns and decoy soldiers—believe it or not. Those guns are made of wood, and the soldiers are decoys. . . . Gentlemen, it was a gruesome sight." By making an analogy to his duck-hunting experiences, Cooley reasoned that the guns had been so placed to attract bombing planes. "When I

[7] C.R., May 14, 1942, pp. 4171ff.

put out my decoys," he said, "I expect to attract live ducks, and if I should put out wooden guns, I certainly would expect to attract live enemy planes." Rep. Hamilton Fish (R., Garrison, N.Y.) saw additional political implications, and he asked whether they had "wooden guns and wooden soldiers protecting the other two branches of the government, or whether we are just selected for this particular privilege." Another rumor, even more devastating, had it that the installations had been constructed to protect the White House, so that Congress was again slighted, not even being protected by wooden guns! Rep. Fred L. Crawford (R., Saginaw, Mich.) said that he was "not so much concerned about how many wooden guns, but how many wooden Congressmen they have got around here." [8]

1942: ELECTIONS

The year following Pearl Harbor was rife with political controversy, but during this period Congress enacted a number of laws relating to the prosecution of the war. The First and Second War Powers Acts were enacted. The draft was extended to include the eighteen-year old class. A revenue act was passed. Price control legislation was enacted, and then revised, and this in turn antagonized the farmers. Congress was concerned over strikes in industry and the forty-hour work week.

By election time of 1942, the popular support of the Administration so evident after Pearl Harbor was declining. The congressional elections were a setback for the Democrats, with the party losing heavily in both chambers. The issue of foreign policy, which had been so pronounced in the 1940 elections, was eclipsed by new internal issues. Isolationism had been "sunk at Pearl Harbor," [9] said Senator C. Wayland Brooks (R., Chicago, Ill.) in his election campaign, and, indeed, other issues were now of more immediate concern. There was the question of the management of the war, and there was public dissatisfaction over price control, rent control, and gasoline rationing; over the forty-hour week,

[8] C.R., Feb. 23, 1943, pp. 1230–31.   [9] C.R., April 21, 1942, p. A1465.

strikes, and the wage rate being paid to defense workers; over the loss of farm labor to the city, the lack of farm machinery, and the ceilings on farm prices. In all, there was dissatisfaction with the increasing social unbalance brought on by the war, and it was not too difficult to identify individuals and groups who were improving their relative position in society because of the war.

The Democrats maintained control by a thin margin, having enough votes to organize Congress but not enough to determine all policy, and during the session the Democrats' majority in the House fell to two. The 1942 election brought into office a number of Congressmen who were loudly opposed to "bureaucracy," which became the collective noun symbolizing obnoxious restrictions, and some members were so carried away with their theme that they advocated the elimination of bureaucracy in its entirety. With the change in the relative strength of the parties, it became harder for the Administration to defeat amendments which it did not want and easier for the opposition to create investigating committees. Old domestic issues were revived, and a Republican leader, Rep. Charles L. Gifford, of Cotuit, Mass., told the House that it was necessary to "win the war from the New Deal." [10]

The election shook the Democrats, and some, surely, indicated that there was some basis for Republican charges. Rep. Sam Rayburn (D., Bonham, Tex.), who was reelected Speaker of the House, laid down a rule for the Administration to follow. "Before determinations are reached or proposals are announced," he said, "those in positions of responsibility upon the Hill must be consulted." He "trusted and believed" that this would be done.[11] According to a leader of the Southern Democrats, Rep. Eugene Cox, of Camilla, Ga., the new Congress should recapture what delegated powers it could, and those which could not be recaptured should be defined. "Government by bureaucrats," he said, "must be broken, and broken now." [12] Such talk was more than empty rhetoric, and it implied, indeed, a resurgence of congressional in-

[10] C.R., Jan. 6, 1943, p. 6.   [11] C. R., Jan. 6, 1943, p. 7.
[12] C.R., Jan. 6, 1943, p. 10.

terest in what bureaucrat made what kind of decision on administering the war. In administrative results, the year 1943 was notably fruitful; records were set in mobilization, training, and production, and there were military successes as well. However, while these achievements were taking place, the decisions were being made in Washington in an atmosphere highly charged with political controversy.

The new Congress abolished some of the more vulnerable New Deal agencies. The Works Progress Administration, the Civilian Conservation Corps, and the National Youth Administration, which had been created in the depression to provide jobs and otherwise assist recovery, were obvious targets, and they were all liquidated in 1943. The Rural Electrification Administration and the Farm Security Administration survived, but they were faced with continual political attacks.

The biggest prize was the National Resources Planning Board, a staff agency in the White House, which was also terminated by Congress. The Board had been created initially by the President, and it had never enjoyed the strong support of Congress. Its unpopularity in Congress increased in 1943 when it submitted an ill-timed report on expanding the social security system after the war. The report, it was felt, was full of the political clichés of the past decade, as when the President told Congress that "we must not return to the inequities, insecurity, and fears of the past, but ought to move forward toward the promise of the future." [13] Congress wanted to get on with the war, and it surely had no desire at that time to start debate on a new scheme of social security. Rep. Hugh Peterson (D., Ailey, Ga.) commented that the proponents of the program were "turning heaven and earth" to fasten such panaceas on the American people while the people's thoughts were turned primarily toward winning the war.[14] Congress not only rejected the plans proposed by the NRPB; it also liquidated the agency by refusing to supply it with funds.

[13] *C.R.*, March 10, 1943, p. 1792.   [14] *C.R.*, March 18, 1943, p. 2197.

Partisanship continued in some types of appointments, the most controversial of which was probably the nomination in 1943 of Edward J. Flynn, the Chairman of the Democratic National Committee, as Minister to Australia. The nomination of such a partisan figure as Mr. Flynn would have been controversial in any event, but it was given an additional fillip by the awkward manner in which Mr. Flynn preceded the White House in making the announcement. The nomination was a rich gift to the Republicans, and they made the most of it. The public was reminded that Mr. Flynn was national chairman of his party and boss of the Bronx. The hearings conducted by the Foreign Relations Committee of the Senate renewed and reviewed the charges that bricks owned by the City of New York had been used in paving what Flynn's opponents called his "Antique Belgian Court" and what Flynn called his parking lot. In all, the committee heard testimony from an assortment of witnesses more learned in the machinations of Bronx politics than in the diplomatic problems of the Antipodes. After the committee had reported the nomination favorably, Flynn requested that it be withdrawn.

The years 1943 and 1944 were also busy legislative years. The draft was extended to include fathers, another revenue measure was passed, price control was continued, subsidies were debated, a labor measure was passed, and Congress was well along with its own postwar planning. A bill on soldier voting consumed a good deal of Congress' time and energies, for again elections were not far off and they had to be anticipated.

The pending November elections dominated political thinking in Congress in 1944, and the commanding issue was the possibility that President Roosevelt would be elected for a fourth term. Senator Ellison D. (Cotton Ed) Smith, of Lynchburg, S.C., said he wanted to get a "decent" President by nominating Senator Harry F. Byrd (D., Berryville, Va.). Smith, who came to the Senate in 1909, was most disparaging of President Roosevelt, and he told the Senate that he had served with five Presidents and "the thing we have got." [15] Some Republicans thought that the war effort was

[15] C.R., Dec. 9, 1943, p. 10517.

being used as a vehicle for advancing the political fortunes of the Commander-in-Chief, and Senator Rufus C. Holman (R., Portland, Ore.) charged that the Army training film, *A Prelude to War*, contained fourth-term propaganda. "References to war, oppression, combat, and so forth," he said, were "only window dressing and stage scenery for the cleverly organized campaign material." [16] Speeches, documents, and administrative decisions were searched for overtones of election propaganda, and the prolonged controversy over the Soldiers' Voting bill was primarily concerned with the effect of G.I. votes on the election.

THE FINAL YEAR

The election of 1944 was a victory for the Democrats, for they reelected President Roosevelt, gained some twenty-five seats in the House, and held their own in the Senate. The major issues facing the new Congress were an odd mixture of war measures for the immediate present and peacetime measures for the immediate future. In its eagerness to press the war effort to its maximum, Congress all but enacted mandatory labor legislation, but the victories in Europe made this unnecessary. Price control was extended, and certain postwar measures were passed. A number of international commitments were made, including membership in the United Nations.

The new session also had its quota of controversial partisan issues, some of which involved presidential nominations. Shortly after Congress reconvened in January, 1945, the President created a political tremor by nominating Henry Wallace, the outgoing Vice President, to be Secretary of Commerce and simultaneously removing Jesse Jones from the position. All of the election controversies of 1944 and of prior elections were continued and footnoted in the subsequent debate on the Wallace nomination and on the bill removing the lending powers from the Department of Commerce. In a letter asking Jones "to relinquish this present post for Henry," the President reviewed the contributions of Wallace

[16] *C.R.*, Feb. 8, 1943, p. 674.

in the 1944 campaign (and, by silence, the conspicuous noncontribution of Jones). Henry Wallace, the President said, deserved "almost any service he can satisfactorily perform," and Wallace believed that he could do "the greatest amount of good in the Department of Commerce." There was no intention of making Jones unemployed, for, indeed, there were "several ambassadorships which are vacant—or about to be vacant," and if Jones were interested in such work, he should "speak to Ed Stettinius." Jones's reply was too gruff to commend him for a diplomatic post, which he said he didn't want anyway. He did not agree that "Henry" was qualified for any job "which carried with it the vast financial and war production agencies within the Reconstruction Finance Corporation and its subsidiaries." [17]

It seems doubtful that the Senate would have approved Wallace's nomination had a vote been taken immediately, but the first item of consideration was the bill introduced by Senator Walter F. George (D., Vienna, Ga.) to remove the Federal Loan Agency from the control of the Department of Commerce. Wallace's friends opposed the bill in the Senate, viewing the whole procedure as a slap at Wallace, but their position was made more difficult by the statement of the President that he would sign the George bill and by the statement of Wallace that he still wanted the job, even with the lending agencies removed. So the George bill was passed, 74–12 (78 percent of the Democrats; 98 percent of the Republicans).

In the House, the Republicans believed that Wallace could not be confirmed if the George bill were defeated, so the partisans switched sides, with the supporters of Wallace now active proponents of the George bill. The bill barely squeezed through the House; the motion to consider the bill was passed, 202–192, and the motion to recommit was defeated, 196–204, the winning vote in both cases being supported by 90 percent of the Democrats and less than 2 percent of the Republicans. On the final vote, the various groups united, for diverse reasons, to pass the bill, 400–2.

[17] *C.R.*, Jan. 22, 1945, p. 365.

After the George bill was safely law, Wallace was confirmed, 56–32 (90 percent of the Democrats and 29 percent of the Republicans).

The new Congress saw a change in Administration, with Vice-President Truman succeeding to the presidency after President Roosevelt's death in April, 1945. During the remaining few months of the war, there appeared to be no conspicuous difference between the policies of the two presidents. In the 1945 session, Congress approved several important international commitments, the nexus of which was the United Nations, and it continued its interest in preparing legislation to reconvert the economy to a peacetime basis. By September, 1945, the war was over, and Congress was anxious enough to consider again the many controversial domestic issues which had been partly suspended during the war.

2. Conversion and Control

WITH THE COMING of the war, Congress was faced with an expanding range of activities. Additional legislation was needed on the subjects of price control, taxes, profits, manpower, and production. Committees were increasingly active in examining the adequacy of defense agencies and the conversion of the economy to a wartime basis. Members of Congress were importuned to see that local interests and talents were considered when war contracts were let or commissions awarded. With all of this increased activity, however, the President maintained a strategic position for organizing the country to wage a total war. Senator Joseph C. O'Mahoney (D., Cheyenne, Wyo.) once went so far as to say that war was "an executive function; it is not a legislative function," [1] which is perhaps an exaggeration overlooking the fact that the powers and policies of the President, and of the numerous government agencies, were subject to the constant surveillance of Congress. Nevertheless, it is surely true that a modern war has to be administered, and the behavior of Congress during the war period was geared to this inescapable fact.

THE ORGANIZATION FOR WAR

Shortly after Pearl Harbor, Congress enacted the First and Second War Powers Acts, which were designed to increase the President's power to reorganize the government as he saw fit and to enforce regulations on controls over priorities. The First War Powers Act was in all essentials identical with the so-called Over-

[1] *C.R.*, Jan. 26, 1942, p. 623.

man Act of the First World War, and the persuasive argument was made that the bill merely gave the President "the same powers that were given to Woodrow Wilson in the last war." In philosophizing over the reasons for giving the President such considerable powers, Rep. Hatton W. Sumners (D., Dallas, Texas) concluded that Anglo-Saxon governments were not plagued with dictators because they "instinctively" sensed the conditions which required "a quicker pick-up and a stronger power." [2] There were time limitations on the Act, and it was to terminate six months after the end of the war or earlier by action of either Congress or the President. It passed both chambers without a record vote.

Congress was more deliberate in enacting the Second War Powers Act, and it completely rewrote the preliminary draft which had been framed by a special cabinet committee created to coordinate departmental requests for war legislation. The Act was an omnibus measure covering a score of items, including such diverse topics as increasing penalties for priority violations and granting free postage for soldiers. Most of the titles of the Act were to remain in force until December 31, 1944, or they could be terminated earlier by either the President or Congress.

The answer to the question of how the government should be organized for war was conditioned by the experiences of the First World War and by the development of the defense agencies in 1940 and 1941. The War Industries Board of the First World War served as a model for the type of agency which could coordinate the economy with the least degree of governmental coercion. The fact that government agencies sometimes exercised power not specifically granted by law may be explained by the rationale used in creating the War Industries Board in 1917. The War Industries Board had no specific power granted by law and no authority for existence other than a letter from President Wilson, followed by an Executive Order. The purpose was not to create a presidential dictatorship but rather to secure a maximum amount of voluntary compliance in accordance with President Wilson's belief

[2] C.R., Dec. 16, 1941, p. 9858.

that "the highest and best form of efficiency is the spontaneous cooperation of a free people." Mr. Bernard M. Baruch, the Chairman of the Board, has written that the power of the Board "depended in large measure upon its ability to demonstrate its effectiveness in accomplishing the common purpose and the willingness of other agencies to be assisted by it, together with the voluntary support of the business interests of the country." The committees of Congress discussed legislation to give the Board larger legal powers, but "the general conclusion was that the Board was accomplishing its purpose well enough without further legislative powers." [3] In the Second World War, also, agencies were created which had very sketchy legal authority for their existence or their actions.

The organization of the government for war was also conditioned by the gradual development of a system of controls in the prewar period. Agencies which were initially advisory in character were later given further power from the President's pool of delegated authority, or, in some cases, Congress would create new agencies specifically based on law. A National Defense Advisory Commission had been created in May, 1940, which in turn was based on an Act passed in 1916. This agency was the nucleus from which developed such war agencies as the War Production Board, the Office of Price Administration, and the Office of Civilian Defense. The government was able to centralize the direction of defense production through its control over the flow of raw materials, a power given by Congress in 1940. As a further sanction, the government could take possession of plants when defense contracts were refused or orders disobeyed; the Reconstruction Finance Corporation could assist construction through loans, and it was itself authorized to build defense plants.

This prewar development of agencies and testing of administrators resulted in a relatively smooth transition of the economy to a wartime basis. However, it also meant that Congress was

---

[3] Bernard M. Baruch, *American Industry in the War: A Report of the War Industries Board* (New York: Prentice Hall, 1941), p. 27.

never called upon to establish an over-all organizational plan for administering the war; its attention was focused on particular agencies rather than on the totality of the war bureaucracy. The administrative system which actually developed was monstrous. It is difficult now to reconstruct an adequate image of those great monoliths of power, with their polysyllabic titles shortened to initials, holding the stage for a period and then being replaced or outstripped by some new and grander combination of authority. Very often the effective channels of power had little relation to the diagrammatic charts of organization or even to the Executive Orders creating the agencies.

Congress rarely protested when the President created a specific war agency, one explanation being that it was understood that the war agencies were temporary; a specific statute might imply that the agency had a greater degree of permanency than Congress wished. When the President created the Office of War Mobilization in lieu of supporting a similar plan contained in the Kilgore bill then before Congress, Senator Claude Pepper (D., Tallahassee, Fla.) said that while many would have preferred the agency to be created by Congress, the sponsors of the legislation were "concerned about results and not honors and not even technique." [4] A species of consent was in fact achieved by the authorization of funds for the agencies, and in 1944 Congress tightened this control by providing that all agencies which had been in existence more than a year had to receive their support from specific congressional appropriations. The test for Congress was how the agency functioned, and it could influence its behavior by creating a new agency or a commodity czar or by controlling funds, prices, subsidies, and personnel.

At the time of Pearl Harbor, the dissatisfaction with the defense organization was so general that for a time it appeared that Congress itself might create a new agency by legislation. The criticism of the Truman Committee was documented at length when its chairman, Senator Harry S. Truman (D., Independence, Mo.)

[4] C.R., May 28, 1943, p. 5068.

made his first annual report on January 15, 1942. The report spoke
of the "disappointing record" of the Office of Production Management and of the "ineptness" of its officials.[5] However, the President had removed the nettle of the Truman report two days
previously by creating the War Production Board, the chairman
to be Donald Nelson, a businessman who came to Washington in
1940 to help manage the National Defense Advisory Commission.
The creation of the new agency and Mr. Nelson's appointment
silenced congressional criticism for a time, and good relations
were established between Mr. Nelson and the Truman Committee.
Mr. Nelson wrote after the war that the investigations of the committee were conducted "fairly and objectively and in a thoroughly
business-like way" and that he enjoyed meeting the committee
"even when it made me perspire a trifle." [6] Mr. Nelson remained
chairman of the WPB until August, 1944.

The creation of the War Production Board set the general pattern of war controls over the economy, although two administrative superstructures were later created. In general, control was
organized around various functions of the economy, such as transportation, rather than around specific commodities, such as rubber, steel, or cotton. A functional organization bore no party label,
but under the stress of war it became the object of partisan debate,
with many groups insisting that the ongoing system be replaced,
or supplemented, by controls over specific commodities. Measured
by the total war production of American industry, the War Production Board performed its job well, and it was operating smoothly
at the end of the war. However, the agency was continually involved in controversy because of the nature of the policy decisions
it had to make, and the civilian reputations of its personnel were
highly expendable.

The two administrative superstructures were the Office of Economic Stabilization, created in October, 1942, and the Office of

---

[5] *C.R.*, Jan. 15, 1942, pp. 380ff.
[6] Donald M. Nelson, *The Arsenal of Democracy: The Story of American War Production* (New York: Harcourt Brace, 1946), p. xiii.

War Mobilization, created in May, 1943, both of which were headed by former Members of Congress—James Byrnes, who had been a Senator from South Carolina, and Fred Vinson, who had been a Representative from Kentucky. Like the WPB, these new agencies were created after Congress had persistently called attention to the lack of coordination among various war programs. As an example of the lack of coordination, the Military Affairs subcommittee pointed to the recurring conflict between the three competitive programs—100-octane gasoline, rubber, and escort vessels. The proponents of these programs, the subcommittee said, had aired the controversy in the public press "at least three times within the past six months and many more times before congressional committees." [7] The Kilgore plan, which would have created a new agency to resolve such disputes, was not enacted, but elements of it were included in the order creating the Office of War Mobilization.

CONTROLS OVER POLICY

Whatever rationale may have been used in delegating power to the President, in actual practice Congress did not accept completely the thesis that running a war was solely an administrative matter, and it attempted in various ways to imprint its influence on policy. Congress was perhaps less concerned with broad principles of administrative organization than with the manner in which the economic position of certain groups and commodities was being affected by the war. Farm groups wanted more agricultural equipment; consumers wanted a greater share of production; food producers wanted assistance, and so did the small businessman. These disconsolate groups, with or without a just grievance, appealed to Congress when buffeted by the bureaucrats.

These appeals did not necessarily constitute inadmissible appeals for favoritism, for the perfect formula for utilizing the skills of all and balancing their respective needs had not been achieved. Some fairly objective standards existed, but it was also possible

[7] *C.R.*, May 28, 1943, p. 5065.

to place different emphases on different goals, and political appeals could be made on this basis. The same appeal to, and the same sanction over, the legislator was available both to the saint and to the sinner, to the rightly aggrieved and the seeker of special favors. In evaluating congressional criticism, it was always pertinent to ask: What is back of this? Is the criticism meritorious or synthetic? Are special groups asking Congress to advance particular ends? Why? Happy was he who could advance a proposal which simultaneously identified patriotism, the best interests of the nation, and his own economic interests.

The position of several economic groups was worsened during the war, and in some cases this worsening could be attributed to decisions made by unsympathetic bureaucrats. The small business group is a case in point. There was real fear in Congress that small business might be liquidated by the war measures, and Congress was continually vigilant in its behalf. Special committees were created; government agencies were constantly reminded of the usefulness of this group; and special legislation assisting small business was enacted. In 1942 the Senate committee found that small business was "facing bankruptcy and chaos along a wide front," and to remedy this situation Congress created a Smaller War Plants Corporation with a capital of $150 million. The five directors were to be men "deemed to be familiar with the problems of small business." [8]

Economic assistance was also given to the 44,000 automobile dealers whose business suddenly became expendable on January 1, 1942, when the OPA stopped the sale of all cars. After inquiry, the Small Business Committee of the Senate reported that the dealers had been struck "a sudden and terrific blow" and were faced with "the specter of bankruptcy and ruin." [9] A conference was at once arranged between Leon Henderson, the Price Administrator, and the officials of the National Automobile Dealers Association; some thirty-six Senators attended this conference, which is an indication of the political sensitivity of the subject.

[8] S. Rept. 1044, Feb. 5, 1942.   [9] S. Rept. 279, Part 3, Feb. 25, 1942.

Legislation was immediately introduced authorizing the RFC to lend money to automobile dealers with their frozen inventory as security, and the bill passed without controversy.

An attempt was also made to assist small newspapers by compelling the government to purchase advertisements for bond sales from them. The bill sponsored by Senator John H. Bankhead (D., Jasper, Ala.) provided that the Secretary of the Treasury should spend $25,000,000 in newspaper advertising, at least half of which was required to be placed "with weekly, semi-weekly, tri-weekly, and monthly newspapers." The Treasury opposed the plan, and many Republicans did also, the latter believing that the subsidy might, just might, be a method of gaining support for the Democrats in the country press. The Senate adopted the bill, 40–35 (68 percent of the Democrats; 29 percent of the Republicans), but the House did not consider the legislation.

Farmers also wanted help, for manpower was leaving the farm for the draft and for industry, and farm machinery was in short supply. Here was a clear conflict between the desires of the farmers and the desires of industry and the Armed Services. In taking up the case for the farmers, the Truman Committee reported that the lack of farm machinery had endangered the 1943 goals for the production of food. By considering farm machinery as "semi-essential," the Office of Civilian Supply had "gambled dangerously and unwisely with our nation's food supply," and the committee recommended that the office be headed by someone who would "fight for materials for essential civilian programs." [10] Throughout the war, the farmers remained dissatisfied with the quantity of farm machinery produced, although, as will be seen, special legislation was enacted to preserve the farmers' dwindling labor supply.

Civilian groups also complained that their needs were not being properly considered. Senator Francis T. Maloney (D., Meriden, Conn.), who acted as spokesman for enterprises dealing with civilian supply, claimed that these enterprises had been drained of materials and manpower and were unable to compete with big

[10] S. Rept. 10, Part 2, Jan. 21, 1943, pp. 1ff.

business. Maloney proposed that Congress create a civilian agency which would be a claimant of equal rank with the Army, Navy, Lend Lease, and other agencies in the allocation of scarce commodities. The bill had the support of a number of trade associations, and it was passed by the Senate without a record vote. However, when the President created the Office of War Mobilization in May, 1943, the Maloney legislation was dropped.

When some program was not doing particularly well, it was frequently proposed in Congress and elsewhere that a "czar" be created to establish greater order and secure better results. The creation of a "czar" meant, in general, that a single agency with a strong administrator would be given all regulatory powers over the particular commodity concerned. However effective czars might be for developing particular programs, they were not useful for coordinating several programs or for allocating scarce items among competitors. Czars were proposed, in particular, to administer programs for food, petroleum, and rubber.

The creation of a czar for rubber in 1942 followed a prolonged and complicated controversy revolving around the shortage of the rubber supply. A number of issues were involved which, in the ordinary course of events, would have been decided over a period of time by several different agencies. At this particular time, however, there was a special urgency about the problem. Supplies of raw rubber from the Pacific had been cut off, and the production of synthetic rubber was not enough to meet military demands, much less the demands of restless civilians wanting new tires. A number of people in and out of the government demanded rubber—now. Questions were raised: Who had failed to stockpile natural rubber? Was the production of synthetic rubber being retarded because of patent agreements with the I. G. Farben industry? Could surplus grain be used for making rubber, thereby helping the farmer to get rid of surpluses? What government agencies were responsible for developing the rubber program? Rubber became the political conversation piece of the day, and, as one could anticipate, a number of congressional committees became interested. Mr. Nelson has written that he explained the rubber situation to seventeen different committees: "The last committee which got into the picture," he said, "was the Coinage Committee —why, I shall never know." [11] (Note to Mr. Nelson: Perhaps the Coinage Committee was interested in the rubber dollar.)

The Truman Committee found that the rubber program was the responsibility of a number of government agencies, and it recommended, in effect, that a czar for rubber be created by giving one person "full power to take all necessary action to provide such rubber as is necessary to the war program." [12] Another approach was taken by the Senate Committee on Agriculture, which saw an opportunity to help the farmer by compelling rubber to be made from wood or grain alcohol. The Senate authorized the committee to spend $5,000 to investigate the subject, and the committee took up the job with zest, hearing an amazing constellation of experts and near experts. According to the views of this committee, the devil of the piece was the dollar-a-year-men in the Chemical Branch of the WPB who opposed the expansion of industrial alcohol plants because it would put their firms at a competitive disadvantage after the war.

Legislation was introduced to create a czar for rubber, with specific directions to provide an adequate supply of rubber by using alcohol as the base material. This bill, designed to help the wheat farmer, met with little opposition in Congress, and it was passed by both Houses without a record vote. The President vetoed the bill, and his message contained the salty observation that "by legislative fiat, the manufacture of synthetic rubber is ordered in quantities large enough to satisfy any and all civilian needs." [13] There was no attempt to override the veto.

The President then named a committee composed of Bernard M. Baruch, James B. Conant, and Karl T. Compton to study the problem of rubber supply, and the subsequent report of this committee

[11] Nelson, *Arsenal of Democracy,* p. 297.
[12] S. Rept. 480, Part 7, May 26, 1942, p. 57.   [13] *C.R.,* Aug. 6, 1942, p. 6752.

in September, 1942, ended the public aspect of the controversy. On the basis of the recommendations of the Baruch Committee, a Rubber Director was created, with power independent of the War Production Board. William M. Jeffers, the President of the Union Pacific Railroad, was named Rubber Director, and he proceeded with his new job with great vigor; by December, the Truman Committee was complimenting him on his successes. But if rubber were given priority over competitors for the same raw materials, what would be the effect on the production, say, of 100-octane gasoline and of escort vessels? The Truman Committee took a second look at the wisdom of creating a czar for rubber with independent authority, and it recommended that the War Production Board be reintegrated as a decision-making board around whose table all rival claimants would sit. Moreover, the committee suggested, members of the Board should feel individually responsible for their particular program and collectively responsible for the entire program.

Many administrative decisions on the conduct of the war affected partisan interests, and none more than the wartime status of projects sponsored during peacetime by the New Deal. To generalize broadly, the political question now was whether these projects could assist in prosecuting the war or whether their opponents could now label them "unpatriotic" as well as undesirable. In the early months of the war, an issue arose over the extent to which the Rural Electrification Administration should continue building power lines for farms. The REA had been a contentious political issue since its creation, and now with the war on and copper in short supply, the opponents of the REA had a new weapon of attack.

The War Production Board ruled that the REA could finish those projects which were more than forty percent completed at the time of Pearl Harbor. This ruling did not satisfy some critics in Congress. Rep. Thomas D. Winter (R., Girard, Kan.) went so far as to say that in some countries the firing squad would be the fate of government officials who continued "to sabotage our national defense efforts." [14] After investigating REA, a House Military Affairs subcommittee concluded that WPB officials had shown "a reckless disregard for the conservation of critical war materials" and that the REA had been misleading the public by propaganda. It also questioned whether the "impractical, theoretical, pseudo-intellectuals who are already planning our foreign and domestic, economic, social and political state" could insure victory.[15] On the other hand, some members of the committee argued that much of the confusion would have been obviated had Mr. Nelson or representatives of the REA been given an opportunity to testify, and one member daringly congratulated the REA for its "whole-hearted cooperation" in furnishing power for war production. The locus of the controversy then shifted to the debate on appropriations, and in the end Congress appropriated the funds for REA requested by the Bureau of the Budget.

CONTROLS OVER PERSONNEL

Just as the government decided to create new war agencies to administer the war rather than rely on old-line departments, so also it decided to rely for staffing on temporary appointments rather than on the career civil service. This new personnel, recruited primarily from civilian life, brought zest to the task, but some were also ambitious and often impatient with government procedures and with the necessity for coordinating policy within and without their own agency. There was often a struggle for power among the wartime personnel, policy becoming identified with specific individuals and changes of policy with attempts to remove key individuals from positions of authority. Some decisions affected the postwar world as well as the administration of the war, and various groups wished to protect their competitive position by having decisions made by individuals who were sympathetic with their interests.

One controversial aspect of personnel policy concerned the em-

[14] *C.R.*, Jan. 29, 1942, p. 866.   [15] H. Rept. 1873, March 5, 1942.

ployment of dollar-a-year men, a general term applied to a select group of businessmen who worked for the government without compensation and who were not obliged to sever their fiscal connections with their own business. Groups within Congress and within the government had conflicting views on the use to be made of these experts. The controversy came to a head when a WPB official, Robert R. Guthrie, resigned after publicly charging that certain dollar-a-year men in the War Production Board had delayed the conversion to war production of the consumer's durable goods industry and the textile industry. Guthrie's charges were subsequently investigated by the Truman Committee and the Military Affairs Committee.

The Truman Committee supported Guthrie, finding that he was correct in criticizing certain dollar-a-year men for "the slowness with which curtailment orders were issued by the Bureau of Industry Branches." On the broader issue of using the services of dollar-a-year men, the committee raised the question whether these men might determine policy "in the light of their past experiences and convictions," and it recommended that the men be paid regular government salaries and dissociate themselves from companies obtaining large defense contracts.[16]

The House Committee on Military Affairs was more tolerant of the dollar-a-year-men. While believing that Guthrie was "sincere," it thought that the controversy over conversion showed only that those who offered technical advice had strong convictions. At such a critical period in history, the committee did not think it possible to depend "solely upon government career men and college professors without practical experience in industry." It opposed the constant sniping at the dollar-a-year-men, and it did not see why a successful businessman "desiring to contribute to the Nation's war effort, becomes an overnight threat to national security when he goes to work for the government for a dollar a year." [17]

[16] S. Rept. 480, Part 8, June 18, 1942, p. 20; S. Rept. 480, Part 5, Jan. 15, 1942, pp. 7ff.
[17] H. Rept. 2272, June 23, 1942, p. 8.

Mr. Nelson also defended the employment of the dollar-a-year men, saying that it was otherwise impossible to obtain the type of executive that was needed. Many of these men had incurred financial obligations, he said, which made it difficult for them to adjust abruptly to a far lower salary scale. However, he would not allow the dollar-a-year men to make decisions directly affecting their own company; preference would be given to those, equally trained, who would take the job on a regular government salary rate.

Other personnel disputes during the war also affected policy. Mr. Nelson later quarreled with Ferdinand Eberstadt and Charles E. Wilson, both vice chairmen of the War Production Board, and when Mr. Nelson resigned in 1944 a conflict was raging over the question of the resumption of the manufacture of civilian goods. In the Office of Price Administration, Leon Henderson, the Price Administrator, was replaced by former Senator Prentiss Brown, and Brown by Chester Bowles. There was a major and embarrassing public dispute between Vice-President Henry A. Wallace, who was also head of the Board of Economic Warfare, and Jesse Jones, the head of the RFC, over priority purchases abroad. The list of wartime disputes over policy on the part of strong personalities is long.

In Congress, Senator Kenneth McKellar (D., Memphis, Tenn.) pointed out that the heads of many important war agencies had not been confirmed by the Senate. The imposing list included the heads of almost all the important war agencies. On the basis of the Senate's failure to control the appointment of these men, and on other more political grounds, McKellar proposed that the Senate confirm the nomination of all federal employees receiving $4,500 or more annually. The Senator's proposal, if adopted, would have gone a long way toward giving Democratic Senators control over most war jobs. The President, however, opposed the bill under the theory that the head of an agency was responsible for the success or failure of his program. He differentiated this from the McKellar proposal which, he said, "presupposed congressional responsibility for the operations of executive agencies." [18] Despite the President's objections, the Senate passed the McKellar bill, 42–29 (81 percent of the Democrats; 28 percent of the Republicans). The bill was not voted on in the House, for there was no wish to place the control of the bureaucracy in the hands of Democratic Senators.

In all, Congress kept busy during the war. The ordinary business of Congress had to be attended to, and there were extra demands on time from the expanding committee activities. In many cases, individual members were expected to act as special pleaders, say, for a constituent who wanted a captain's commission, or a sewer project contract, or an airport, or a housing program, or a new war plant. The whole structure of federal-state-local relations was shaken by the vast array of people who wanted the government and their Congressman to do something for them, and it may be presumed that Congressmen were persuaded to do things for which some lobbyists were paid money. The line between the public interest and the private interest became blurred.

CONTROLS OVER MONEY

Congressional control over the purse strings was at times strained during the war, for Congress had the task of granting enough money to fight the war successfully and at the same time of preventing waste and of husbanding the nation's resources. In actual practice, Congress distinguished between different types of money bills. Those for military purposes only were relatively noncontroversial, so far as public debate was concerned, and the objects of expenditure were not itemized in any detail. Those for war agencies were controversial to a degree, and they were carefully scrutinized. Those for nonwar civilian agencies, and especially those created during the New Deal Administration, were given the most sedulous attention, and Congress abolished some of these agencies by cutting off supply.

When all sums are added, it is clear that Congress was generous

[18] *C.R.*, Feb. 17, 1942, p. 1366.

in appropriating money for the conduct of the war. The military expenditures for the fiscal year 1941 were $6.1 billion; for 1942, $26.0 billion; for 1943, $72.1 billion; for 1944, $87.0 billion; for 1945, $90.0 billion, and for 1946, $48.5 billion. In appropriating such vast sums, Congress was seldom in a position to consider in detail the minutiae of relatively small expenditures or to compare new estimates with past expenditures. Indeed, military requirements were so fluid that Congress could not determine gross amounts with any finality, and an extraordinarily large number of supplementary and deficiency bills were enacted.

Congress had little enough intimate knowledge on how effectively military appropriations were spent, but it does not follow that Congress appropriated whatever was requested or that it ended its interest once appropriatons were made. Investigations could be used, and, in particular, committees investigated the costs of the construction of Army camps, the Canol project for producing oil in the Arctic, and the Alaska Highway. Moreover, the fact that funds were appropriated annually tended in time to provide precedents for guiding Congressmen; past performance could be measured when requests for additional funds were made. As in peacetime, "understandings" between departments and appropriation committees developed on how funds were to be spent, even though these informal agreements were not a formal part of the written bill.

The need for caution in generalizing on the degree of congressional control over military appropriations is borne out by the fiscal history of the Manhattan Project, which produced the atom bomb. Congress had a delicate and difficult role to play here, for the development of atomic weapons required such a degree of secrecy that even the mention of an over-all appropriation for an unidentified object might be the telltale. Congress was far more aware of the project, or that "something was going on," than the public records indicate. The congressional committees discovered that funds were not being used for purposes stated in the appropriation acts, and administrators were asked to explain why. As a result of this inquiry, a group of Congressmen were given confidential information on the project which created the political support necessary for its completion.

In describing how the House handled appropriations for the Manhattan Project, Rep. Clarence Cannon (D., Elsberry, Mo.), the Chairman of the House Committee on Appropriations, has written:

The Manhattan Appropriation was slipped into the Military Appropriation Bill under guise of engineering and other appropriations.

It was not until we analyzed the estimates that we discovered a large discrepancy in the form of exorbitant request for money beyond the possibility of use for the purposes designated. When we called General Marshall before us he refused to tell us what the money was for but finally explained that it was for experiments which both Germany and America were working on and that if Germany solved the problem first, Germany would win the war; if the United States solved it first, the United States would win the war. Under this vague explanation we appropriated in the next two years or more a little over two billion dollars and Members of the Subcommittee did not know specifically how the money was being used and no one else in the Committee or the Congress knew anything about it at all. It was hidden in the several appropriation bills and was not made public until the bomb was dropped in Japan.

When the amount reached two billion dollars and the problem had not yet been solved we refused to appropriate more. The Secretary of War came to see me personally and wanted to take me down to Oak Ridge where the work was under way. I refused to go but agreed to go if four other members of my subcommittee could accompany me. After visiting Oak Ridge we provided further funds but with great doubt as to the eventual success of the experiment. The news that the bomb had fallen was a great relief to the five men on the House Committee who alone were aware of the object of the experiment.[19]

A similar story has been written by Senator Styles Bridges (R., Concord, N.H.), a member of the Senate Committee on Appropriations and its ranking Republican in the latter part of the war.

The manner in which the funds were provided for the atomic development during the war period was extremely interesting and probably one of the most unusual things which has ever occurred in our nation insofar as Congress is concerned. I happened to be one of the

[19] From a letter to the author.

few United States Senators who had knowledge of the project and in turn took the leadership in providing for the necessary appropriations. I understand that there were four or five such Congressmen in the House of Representatives. I think the total number of Senators who had knowledge of this was five, but when one of these members, Senator McNary, died, former Senator White was informed of this project as he succeeded Senator McNary as the Republican Floor Leader. My understanding of the situation, as I recall, is as follows:

In late 1942, Secretary of War Stimson called for a highly secret conference in his office consisting of two Republican Senators and two Democratic Senators. I was called as one because I was the ranking Republican member of the War Department Sub-committee on Appropriations and at this conference besides Secretary Stimson and the four Senators there were one or two other men who were high in the initial research of this project. These Senators were sworn to secrecy and told of the Atomic Project, the progress Germany had made in this field, and the possibility that the side which achieved successful results in the development of the atomic bomb might have the deciding factor in the winning of the war. We were advised from time to time insofar as our government was aware of progress by the Germans. I remember in the middle stages of the war that I was very much worried about the German progress and the danger of their success.

These Senators were asked to take the leadership in providing the appropriations by not identifying the various sums which went into this project by including the amounts under various headings and to vouch for the necessity of doing this to our colleagues in our respective parties without disclosing to them in any way whatsoever the purpose for which they were to be used except to say they were for a very vital matter.

In my judgment this secret was one of the best kept secrets in the history of our country, and certainly members of the Senate and members of the House who cooperated in this matter never indicated by word or suggestion in even the most remote manner anything about the Manhattan Project. The first time that I spoke of the matter was the day following the dropping of the atomic bomb on Hiroshima. I think the development of the Manhattan Project in which the money was provided by Congress in such complete confidence was one of the best examples of the functioning of our democratic processes in an emergency.[20]

[20] From a letter to the author.

MONEY FOR THE WAR AGENCIES

The appropriation of funds for the war agencies raised no special procedural problems for Congress: secrecy was not involved, the broad purposes of expenditure were apparent, and standards of criticism relating to organization, personnel, efficiency, and purpose were fairly well established. During the debates on funds for war agencies, partisans often seized the opportunity for gilding their peacetime conflicts with war-inspired arguments. The war agencies were frequently vulnerable to political attack, especially if their activities created domestic political issues, and they had no "clientele" which could come to their support. Domestic agencies could build up such political support, but war agencies could do it far less easily.

The Office of Civilian Defense is an example of an agency which was especially vulnerable politically. Its greatest usefulness depended on bombs falling, at which time the agency would become indispensable functionally and probably invulnerable politically. In the meantime, while waiting for the bombs to fall, the OCD was placed in the equivocal position of having to ask for funds for events which it hoped would never occur. A peacetime army is faced with a similar problem. The OCD relied on voluntary participation and, for whatever reason, attracted to its leadership a number of talented and vigorous personalities who were politically controversial. These leaders included Fiorello La Guardia, the mayor of New York City; James M. Landis, a former chairman of the Securities and Exchange Commission and lately Dean of the Harvard Law School; and Mrs. Franklin D. Roosevelt.

The Office of Civilian Defense was only one of the agencies which had difficulty securing funds from Congress. The Office of Price Administration ran into various kinds of trouble, and it was especially difficult for it to secure funds for price enforcement. The Office of War Information faced difficulty securing funds for its Civilian Branch, which eventually was reduced to carrying on a very modest program under specific limitations. The War Manpower Commission was not popular. In 1944 Congress provided that all war agencies of whatever nature receive their supply from Congress; the Committee on Fair Employment Practice wound up its affairs the following year when it was not given funds.

The debate on funds was frequently concerned with administrative personnel who, for one reason or another, were unpopular with some members of Congress. This interest in personnel raised a number of questions about the control which Congress may rightly exercise over individuals whose policy it dislikes. Congress can invite administrators to testify before its committees, and it can reduce funds for any reason whatever—including dissatisfaction with personnel. Can it go beyond this, however, and set up standards of employability which those currently holding office cannot meet? Can it remove people from office by specifically naming them in legislation, or would this procedure violate the constitutional injunction against bills of attainder?

In 1942 the House became interested in the possibility that subversives were employed by the Office of Civilian Defense, but its interest was diverted by the physical fitness programs being carried on by the agency. This became the object of a good deal of buffoonery. The butt of Congress's heavy-handed humor was Miss Myris Chaney, a friend of Mrs. Roosevelt and a dancer, who was employed in the physical fitness program of the OCD. Rep. John Taber (R., Auburn, N.Y.) called the attention of the House to a picture in the press of Miss Chaney performing what someone had named "the Eleanor Glide," and political wits chose to identify a physical fitness program with fan dancing. Rep. Leland M. Ford (R., Santa Monica, Cal.) rose to the opportunity by offering an amendment which prohibited the payment of funds for instruction "in physical fitness by dancers, fan dancing, street shows, theatrical performances, or other public entertainments." The House adopted the amendment, and it appeared in the final Act.

The Democratic leaders in the House were not amused at this parliamentary pettifoggery, but they had not had sufficient control over their party organization to stop it. Rep. Clarence Cannon, who was chairman of the Democratic Steering Committee as well as of the Appropriations Commitee, told his Democratic colleagues, many of whom had been absent on the vote, that the Republicans had "handed us a Pearl Harbor." With no issues at stake, he said, the Republicans had ended the debate "with one of the cleverest coups and one of the most effective political appeals to the country that has been seen in the House in the last twenty years." Their only purpose in offering the amendment was "to gain advantage in the congressional elections this fall." The responsibility for "the success of the Republican blitzkrieg" lay with the Democratic members of the House, who had not been present to vote at the proper time.[21] In the end, the OCD received all the money it had requested; the Republicans, no doubt, picked up some votes.

A more serious debate occurred in 1943 when Congress attached a rider to an appropriation bill removing three federal employees —William E. Dodd, Jr., Robert Morse Lovett, and Goodwin B. Watson—from their jobs. The debate reveals how various crosscurrents of interest affect the decisions of Congress. The issue here was not only the type of employees who should work for the government (and whether the specific employees fell within that category) but also the prestige of the House Committee on Appropriations, the prerogatives of the House and Senate, the relevance of the constitutional provision regarding bills of attainder, and the political advantage or disadvantage resulting from the incident.

The episode which finally resulted in the removal of Dodd, Lovett, and Watson may be said to have started with a speech made on February 1, 1943, by Rep. Martin Dies (D., Orange, Tex.), the Chairman of the Committee on Un-American Activities. The speech, a fulsome, oratorical blast at what Dies called crackpot bureaucrats in the government, was made, one may imagine, with the end in view of persuading the House to continue the committee. In order to "make crystal clear" what he meant by "irresponsible, unrepresentative, crackpot, radical bu-

[21] *C.R.*, Feb. 17, 1942, p. 1366.

reaucrats," Dies listed some forty individuals who had "wormed their way into this bureaucratic set-up," including one individual who, according to Dies, "advocated the practice of universal nudism in office and factory." [22]

Dies did not give the House a clear indication of the action he believed it should take on these forty individuals; the list was not definitive, he said, and was offered as a sample of the thousands of crackpot bureaucrats then working in Washington. However, a movement developed to remove the forty from office forthwith. Representative Cannon opposed such sudden action, saying that the whole proceedings had the appearance of "a lynching bee," and he asked that the Appropriations Committee be permitted to sift the evidence and give the accused an opportunity to be heard.[23] Cannon's request was granted, and subsequently Rep. John H. Kerr (D., Warrenton, N.C.) was named chairman of a subcommittee which was directed to examine any allegation that federal employees were unfit to hold office because of their present or past "association or membership" in subversive organizations. The creation of the Kerr subcommittee no doubt prevented the House from removing the forty individuals without further ado, but it also created a situation where the recommendations of the subcommittee would carry extraordinary influence and could not readily be ignored. Kerr, who had twice voted against continuing the Dies Committee, was respected by his colleagues for his fairness and open-mindedness.

When Dies made his charges, the House was considering the appropriation bill for the Treasury and Post Office, and it happened that one William Pickens, named on Dies's list, was employed by the Treasury Department. Rep. Joe Hendricks (D., DeLand, Fla.) reasoned that if funds were granted to the Treasury Department without specific reference to Pickens's employment, Pickens might be allowed to retain his job without his case being considered by the Kerr subcommittee. To avert this, Hendricks offered an amendment removing Pickens from his job, and the amendment was

[22] C.R., Feb. 1, 1943, pp. 474ff.   [23] C.R., Feb. 5, 1943, p. 655.

adopted. This turned out to be most embarrassing. The Pickens who had been removed with such haste turned out to be a Negro leader whose job was to stimulate bond purchases among Negro organizations, and he was not to have a chance to defend himself because of the happenstance that the House voted appropriations for his agency first. Representative Martin, the Republican leader, asked the House to reconsider its action, saying that "all against whom charges have been made will be given a hearing—all except one, William Pickens, a colored man." Representative Hendricks, of Florida, insisted that no question of racial discrimination was involved. Indeed, he said that he "got in the habit of saying 'Mr. Pickens' and made that statement on the floor two or three times, which is evidence to you that I did not even know he was a colored man and did not care about it." [24] In the face of these developments and clarifications, the House retracted and deleted the Pickens amendment.

Following the Dies charges and the Pickens episode, the Kerr subcommittee heard testimony from various individuals and eventually concluded that only three of the original forty should be debarred from federal employment. Representative Kerr offered an amendment to the so-called Urgency Deficiency Appropriation bill removing Dodd, Lovett, and Watson from the pay roll. This was adopted, 318–62 (74 per cent of the Democrats; 93 percent of the Republicans).

The Senate was not especially interested in the personnel controversy raised by Representative Dies, and it did not accept the removal amendment. The Senate was later asked for an expression of opinion by the conferees, and it voted 69–0 to delete the amendment. The House conferees, however, refused to drop the removal amendment; they stuck to their position in successive conferences, and gradually wore down Senate resistance. Some Senators were willing to accept the position of the House inasmuch as funds were needed to carry on government activities in the new fiscal year. Others were persuaded to vote for the conference report because

[24] *C.R.*, Feb. 8, 1943, p. 704.

an amendment was reinserted limiting the use of the President's emergency funds. Still other Senators believed that the removal amendment was unconstitutional, that Congress had no right to remove government employees from office by naming their names in legislation, and that a principle of this nature was not a proper subject for legislative compromise.

Once the House had showed that it was adamant on the subject, Senator Kenneth McKellar (D., Memphis, Tenn.), who was in charge of the bill on the Senate floor, asked that the amendment be accepted, for if the Senate did not yield "there would be no bill." McKellar became angry when the Senate continued its opposition, and after the fourth conference he told his party leaders that "as a member of the organization" he thought he had a right "to expect that when the conference committee brought in a report we would receive help from the organization on our side of the Senate." [25]

In the early stages of the dispute, an amendment limiting the use of the President's emergency funds had been dropped, but it re-appeared in the fourth conference report. According to Senator Barkley, the conferees hoped that by clipping the President's wings they could muster enough votes to adopt the conference report "with no change whatever in the manner of dealing with these three men." [26] Senator Bennett C. Clark (D., University City, Mo.) thought the proposal was "the most barefaced attempt to trade votes that I think I have ever witnessed in this body." [27] A number of Senators objected to the removal amendment on constitutional grounds, and there was continued criticism that the method of re-moval constituted a bill of attainder. In explaining his opposition, Senator Joseph C. O'Mahoney (D., Cheyenne, Wyo.) quoted from the Constitution of the State of Wyoming: "Absolute arbitrary power over the lives, liberty, and property of freemen exists no-where in a republic, not even in the largest majority." [28]

Following the fifth conference, the elusive formula was at last found. The names of Dodd, Lovett, and Watson must be submitted

[25] *C.R.*, June 25, 1943, p. 6409.   [26] *C.R.*, June 29, 1943, p. 6729.
[27] *C.R.*, June 29, 1943, p. 6733.   [28] *C.R.*, July 2, 1943, p. 7014.

by the President to the Senate for confirmation by November 15; otherwise the three would be permanently prohibited from drawing federal salaries. The President could not use his emergency funds for projects which had been rejected by the House or Senate or by the committees on appropriations thereof. This was merely saying negatively, and less politely, what had been said in the original Act of 1941, which required the purpose of the expenditure to have been approved. The Senate accepted this formula, and the report was adopted by a vote of 48–32 (53 percent of the Democrats; 70 percent of the Republicans). Excluding the first unanimous vote, thiry-five Senators consistently opposed the report and twenty-two consistently favored it; of the latter, ten were members of the Committee on Appropriations.

In the end, the Supreme Court declared the provision removing the three men to be unconstitutional. In the case of *United States v. Lovett,* the Supreme Court said that legislative acts "that apply either to named individuals or to easily ascertainable members of a group in such a way as to inflict punishment on them without a judicial trial are bills of attainder prohibited by the constitution." [29]

[29] 328 U.S. 303 (1946), at p. 315.

3. Work or Fight

THE SIMPLE PHRASE, work or fight, expressed the alternatives which were open to most men during the war. In developing public policy, however, Congress had to create some administrative patterns which would give meaning to the work-or-fight alternative. In general, it had to set the standards for allocating the available manpower among competitive claimants, and, in part, to determine the conditions under which civilians would work. Initially, there were various strands of manpower policy which were considered and developed separately, but as the war progressed the strands became increasingly intertwined. In 1940 it was possible to have an independent policy for the draft, but by 1945 the draft was but part of a more comprehensive manpower policy.

Congress did not develop all manpower policy, although it was constantly reviewing the policy of the government and of the private employer and, on some occasions, modifying it. The Administration was able to have an independent civilian labor policy, and one which Congress did not necessarily approve, because the effectiveness of the policy depended less on specific sanctions and more on the voluntary acceptance of the program by the parties concerned. However much Congress disliked some phases of the program, it could not readily substitute a policy of its own because of the probable necessity of overriding a presidential veto. As time went on, it became increasingly difficult for the Administration to follow a policy which relied on voluntary cooperation. Directives tended to have the force of law, however tenuous a claim they may have had to constitutional legality, and Congress was continually advocating stronger legislation. In the latter part of the war, the Administration finally supported mandatory work-or-fight legislation, but Congress was no longer sure that a strong policy of such a nature was desirable, and the legislation was never enacted.

Three major agencies were created to administer manpower problems: the Selective Service System, in 1940, to administer the draft; the War Manpower Commission, in 1942, to coordinate and develop the domestic supply of manpower; and the War Labor Relations Board, to resolve labor disputes and determine the conditions of work.

SELECTIVE SERVICE AND LABOR

A policy on manpower began to develop in 1940 when Congress passed the Selective Service Act. The preamble of the Act enunciated the principle that the "obligations and privileges" of military service should be "shared generally" according to "a fair and just system" of selectivity. This standard was adhered to throughout the war, and it provided an effective method for supplying the armed service with manpower and for binding the nation to the war. All regions of the country and all draft boards within neighborhoods were to be treated equally; all subject to the jurisdiction of the Act were to share alike.

However, a number of questions remained which were not specifically answered in the Act itself or by applying the principle of equality of obligation. For instance, what was the remaining obligation of those who were rejected for military service? In selecting individuals to be called, it was necesary to establish some type of deferment categories and draft eligibilities, and this raised additional questions of values and need. What should be the deferment priority for men with dependents, for those over age or under age, and for those working in war plants or on the farm? If a man with dependents were drafted, had the government any obligations toward his dependents? Again, the question was asked whether the government could compel a man to work as well as to fight. Some claimed that the civilian worker should be treated no differently from the soldier and should be compelled to work where he was told for as long as he was needed. Others claimed that the civilian worker should remain free, that the principle of free labor rather than forced labor was an issue of the war which should not be sacrificed in fighting the war.

Initially, the problem of settling strikes and other types of industrial disputes had little relation to the draft, so far as legislative policy was concerned, but as the war progressed various aspects of manpower policy were seen to be interrelated, and likewise the wage rate was a factor in price stabilization. When war began, there was no well developed administrative policy for handling labor disputes in defense industries, but various individuals and groups in Congress were offering a potpourri of plans. Earlier in 1941, the President had created the National Defense Mediation Board, with a membership selected to represent the interests of the public, of labor, and of industry, and it operated throughout most of the year. However, in the fall of 1941, the United Mine Workers called a series of intermittent strikes in the so-called captive mines. The Board decided not to recommend the adoption of the union shop, one of the issues of the strike, whereupon the two labor members representing the Congress of Industrial Organizations withdrew. Henceforth the Board was ineffective and for all practical purposes ceased to exist. The President, however, supported the Board's decisions, and he stated that "the Government of the United States will not order, nor will Congress pass legislation ordering, a so-called closed shop." [1] The striking miners eventually won their point. A three-man arbitration board was appointed, and it announced on the day of Pearl Harbor that, by a 2-1 decision, it recommended that the contracts contain a union shop clause.

Congress was vastly annoyed, to put it mildly, by the coal strikes, and although the swirling events of Pearl Harbor tended to ob-

[1] Committee on Records of War Administration, *The United States at War* (Washington, D.C.: Bureau of the Budget, 1946), p. 191.

scure the significance of the closed-shop decision, this latter event was unfavorably received. The captive-mine strike, which followed other unsettling labor disputes, helped to persuade the leaders of the House that labor legislation should be passed at once. The vehicle at hand was the Smith bill, which proposed to regulate strikes and the union shop. As for strikes, the prevailing belief in Congress was that they were indefensible and should be outlawed, but no bill actually outlawing strikes was seriously considered. The Smith bill proposed, instead, that strikes be regulated by requiring "a fair, democratic strike election by secret ballot" before any strike was called. The unstated assumption of this provision was that workers were often compelled to strike by unrepresentative labor leaders. Inasmuch as the strike weapon could be used in organizing defense plants, it proposed, in effect, that the status of labor remain constant by freezing the existing closed-shop agreements. Labor would be allowed to keep its organizational gains, but it would not be allowed to expand. The Smith bill passed the House by a relatively large margin of 252–136 (54 percent of the Democrats; 81 percent of the Republicans).

The Senate was less anxious to pass labor legislation than the House, although several Senators were pressing for a vote on the Connally bill, which would have permitted the government to seize a strike-bound plant under the expectations that normal operations would be carried on while the dispute was being settled. However, the events of Pearl Harbor added a new element to the considerations. With a war on, perhaps labor would be less inclined to strike, and Senator Barkley further suggested that the Administration should be given time to develop a wartime labor policy. He was supported by Senator Elbert D. Thomas (D., Salt Lake City, Utah), the chairman of the Senate Committee on Education and Labor. So the Senate did not then take any action on the Smith Bill, the Connally bill, or analogous legislation.

The President did act. He called a conference at which management and labor were asked to set up procedures and establish rules for regulating their wartime relationships. The conference recommended the creation of the National War Labor Board. Its jurisdiction was not precisely determined, but it eventually included the prickly issues of union security and wage rates. Like the old Mediation Board, it also had representatives from labor, industry, and the public. The representatives of labor and industry agreed that there would be no strikes and no lockouts during the war. The NWLB had no independent power to enforce compliance with its orders, but compliance could be strongly suggested as long as all groups continued to participate. Senator Thomas (of Utah) acted as associate moderator of the conference, and throughout the war Thomas supported in Senate debate the principles of voluntary cooperation laid down at the Washington meeting.

The pattern of wartime labor relations was set at the Washington conference, although for some months various groups continued to demand that Congress "do something about labor." Shortly after the conference, Senator Thomas called attention to a letter in which the U.S. Chamber of Commerce had urged its local units to "become aggressive in calling Congress' attention to desirable labor legislation." The letter did not analyze proposals currently before Congress, "as this might be confusing." Thomas denounced the letter as a "confusion-engendering document" the purpose of which, he believed, was to break down voluntary agreements and to substitute government by fiat.[2] Following the Washington conference, the major decisions on labor policy were made by the National War Labor Board, but Congress was always in a position to comment on the decision and, given the right conditions, to formulate a different policy by legislative action.

One such issue was the closed shop, which had wrecked the efforts of the prewar Mediation Board. The new War Labor Board resolved the issue for the duration by the ingenious device of the "maintenance of membership clause." Under a contract containing this clause, a worker was not obliged to join a union as a condition of work, but he was compelled to maintain his membership in the union for the duration of the contract. The theory on

[2] *C.R.*, March 25, 1942, p. 2910.

which this clause was based was similar to the "freeze" on labor organizations found in the Smith bill. The vote was 8–4, with the industry members in the minority, but these members were somewhat mollified by the inclusion of a fifteen-day "withdrawal period" during which workers could leave the union. There was no singular reaction in Congress to this decision, and no attempt was made to overturn it.

The issue of wage rates was another item of labor conflict. The effective decision here was the Little Steel formula, which allowed wage increases up to fifteen percent. This corresponded with the increase in the cost of living between January, 1941, and May, 1942. Under this formula, labor would receive as much real income as it had received in a base period, provided the cost of living remained stable. The Little Steel formula was continued as the official wage standard for the duration, although in the latter days of the war the interpretations placed on it were very broad. Congress accepted the Little Steel formula and no effort was made to overturn it directly: it was more interested in the forty-hour week controversy and in the dispute over the rate of wages to be paid railroad employees.

The forty-hour week was established by Congress in 1938 as part of a policy of spreading work. When the policy was continued into the war period, however, a strenuous but unsuccessful attempt was made to persuade Congress to amend the law. Some of the virulence of the campaign was due to the mistaken assumption that the law prohibited anyone from working more than forty hours per week, whereas the law merely provided that overtime rates would go into effect after forty hours. The Mississippi House of Representatives, for instance, was apparently misinformed on the provisions of the law when it complained to Congress in a petition that the forty-hour week was impeding the manufacture of arms and munitions "necessary for our armed forces to defend our country." The inevitable comparison with the soldier was made, and one constituent wrote to his Congressman suggesting that if labor wasn't satisfied, "why not send them to the front lines on soldiers' pay?" A more legitimate complaint against the forty-hour week was that it required bonus payments for overtime work, a fact stressed by Rep. Howard W. Smith (D., Alexandria, Va.). Overtime payments were a penalty on the employer, he said, and this meant that war production work which required overtime payments was a burden on the taxpayer. "Who dares to contend," he asked, "that the Congress should penalize all of the American people in our desperate crisis, in order to preserve the social gains of an organized minority? Who dares to contend that the American workman is less willing to sacrifice than our soldiers at the front line at $21.00 a month with no overtime?" [3]

The question Congress had to decide was whether the overtime provisions hampered or assisted the production of war goods. Initially, the overtime provisions served as an inducement for civilian workers to take defense jobs. An industry with a defense contract was more concerned with securing labor than with the cost of labor, and it could outbid the civilian goods industries. Later, overtime provisions would have had less effect on the supply of labor, but in the meantime the overtime provisions had become established as part of the wage scale. Mr. Nelson, the chairman of the War Production Board, told Congress that repeal of the forty-hour law would "create a widespread demand for increase in wage rates, throw the entire wage structure out of adjustment, and remove an important incentive for labor to shift from nonessential industries into war production jobs." [4]

Despite the intensity of the pressures from outside Congress, no legislative action was taken on the forty-hour law. The House Naval Affairs Committee considered at length a bill repealing the law, but it decided that the bill would create labor unrest by changing the wage scale and did not report the bill back to the House. In February, 1943, the President issued an Executive Order establishing the minimum work-week as forty-eight hours, with overtime payments for work in excess of forty hours. The agitation

[3] *C.R.*, April 13, 1942, p. A1348.   [4] *C.R.*, Nov. 10, 1942, p. A4008.

for repealing the law died down gradually and disappeared completely after 1943.

Another wage question in which Congress became involved related to the wage rate of the nonoperating railway employees. It is not necessary here to describe the complicated administrative proceedings which preceded the conflict in Congress. We may begin with the situation after Mr. Vinson, the Director of Economic Stabilization, had rejected the recommendation of the President's Emergency Board that railroad employees be granted a flat increase of eight cents an hour. The railroad workers then decided to ask their friends in Congress to make an independent decision in the matter by raising the wage rate through legislation. Senator William Langer (R., Bismarck, N.D.) led off with a calumnious personal attack on Vinson, whom he called "the most hated man in America today." [5] Senator Truman went to the support of the railroad workers by introducing legislation to grant them the eight cent an hour increase which had been rejected by Mr. Vinson. The Senate proceeded to pass the resolution by a vote of 74–4, even though Vinson protested that the Administration would be forced to abandon the Little Steel formula for settling wage disputes. When the House failed to act on the Truman resolution, it appeared that there would be a nationwide railway strike, beginning December 31, 1943. No strike occurred, however, for on the 27th the President authorized the War Department to take possession of the railroads and to operate them. (A Special Emergency Board later settled the wage dispute and the government relinquished control of the railroads on the midnight of January 18, 1944).

Another labor issue which troubled Congress was absenteeism, a new word introduced into the congressional vocabulary in 1943. Although absenteeism was not confined to the shipbuilding industry, the interest of Congress in the subject seems to have been caused by the concern of the Navy and the Maritime Commission

[5] C.R., Nov. 16, 1943, p. 9569.

over its effect on the production of ships. The House Naval Affairs Committee was told that absenteeism was taking "a death toll of twenty destroyers for every one that we lost to the strikes." The reaction of many Congressmen was to draft the shirkers; the Selective Service was a "potent disinfectant for this type of vermin," one member said.[6] However, the Naval Affairs Committee did not report back such legislation when it was learned that many of the offenders were women for whom the work-or-fight would not be a "potent disinfectant." Absenteeism had many causes: illness, accidents, inadequate housing and transportation, employment of older workers, housekeeping difficulties for women, improper scheduling of materials, and overindulgence in strong drink. Absenteeism, as it turned out, was a word without a precise meaning that could be used for various ends. In a slogan contest conducted by an aircraft company the inspired winner admonished: "You can't spell Victory with an absent T."

Many members of Congress seemed willing enough to drop the issue of absenteeism after the Labor Department asked for $337,-000 to investigate its causes. This item was stricken from the appropriation bill, and the Secretary of Labor, Miss Frances Perkins, was accused of being "more concerned about social gains than in winning the war." [7] The House Labor Committee then stepped into the picture; after finding that there was very little "willful" absenteeism, it sponsored legislation to direct the Secretary of Labor to investigate the major causes of absenteeism, "beginning with illness and industrial accidents." [8] The Rules Committee would not grant a rule for a bill of this nature, and subsequently the bill was stricken from the Consent Calendar. After the Committee on Labor and the Department of Labor began to think of absenteeism as a reason for promoting social reform, many Members of Congress lost interest, and little was heard of the topic for the remainder of the war.

[6] Rep. Lyndon Johnson (D., Texas), in C.R., Feb. 26, 1943, p. A829.
[7] Rep. Jed Johnson (D., Okla.), in C.R., Feb. 26, 1943, p. 1371.
[8] H. Rept. 405, May 4, 1943.

THE SMITH-CONNALLY ACT

As we have seen, agitation for legislation to regulate or prohibit strikes had continued spasmodically since the prewar period, with the Senate more reluctant than the House to consider such legislation. In the late spring of 1943, however, further strikes on the part of the United Mine Workers caused a most unfavorable reaction in Congress; resistance crumbled, and the War Labor Disputes Act—known popularly as the Smith-Connally Act—was passed. There was a considerable hostility in Congress against John L. Lewis, the mine leader, and the hostility was increased after Lewis told a Senate committee that he did not consider the no-strike agreement binding "in any case that the War Labor Board did not do equity." [9] The miners ignored the request of the President that they return to work, and they also ignored an order of the War Labor Board commanding them to do so. By May 1 some 400,000 miners were on strike and coal production had virtually ceased. The President then directed the Secretary of the Interior to take over and operate the mines, but the miners stayed out of the shafts until June 23, when they were instructed by union officials to return to work. (The mines were returned to private operation on October 12, 1943.)

Shortly after the strike began, the Senate took up the bill proposed earlier by Senator Tom Connally (D., Marlin, Tex.). The bill, it will be recalled, authorized the government to seize strikebound plants. The Connally bill was not especially appropriate for the situation, but the decision to consider this legislation was dictated by the internal arrangement of Senate power. The Connally bill was before the Senate, having been reported previously by the Judiciary Committee, and there was little reason to suppose that the Committee on Labor and Education would report out any new legislation.

The inconclusive Senate debate on the Connally bill was largely concerned with the question of the appropriateness of the legislation. Why, indeed, should Congress pass a bill authorizing the

[9] *C.R.*, April 29, 1943, p. 3767.

President to do what he had already done? Senator Robert A. Taft (R., Cincinnati, O.), for instance, argued that the President had power to take over the mines under Section Two of the Second War Powers Act; if this interpretation was correct, the Connally bill would be unnecessary. On the other hand, Senator Tydings (D., Havre de Grace, Md.) argued that the President's action was not legal, and he proposed an amendment "confirming and validating" the President's seizure much as an earlier Congress had legalized the actions of President Lincoln.[10] This amendment was defeated. The best argument of the proponents of the bill was that the bill would strengthen the authority of the government by giving the government more specific power. The bill was passed, 63–16, with the support of 75 percent of the Democrats and 86 percent of the Republicans.

The House was elated when the Senate passed the Connally bill, for this meant that labor legislation would now be enacted. There was no specific, single plan then before the House; rather, there was a series of plans which had been proposed from time to time by various committees. Jurisdiction over the Connally bill was given to the House Military Affairs Committee, and this committee suspended the hearings it had been holding on manpower legislation and reported out an amended bill by a vote of 21–0.

Rep. Mary Norton (D., Jersey City, N.J.), the Chairman of the Labor Committee, asked the Speaker why the bill had not been sent to her committee, and she was told that it came under the jurisdiction of the Military Affairs Committee because it amended the Selective Service and Training Act. Later, Mrs. Norton was refused time to speak against the bill, and, being very much irritated, she stated that there were "just a few people in this House" who were attempting to use "pretty dictatorial tactics." [11] The mood of the House was so unsympathetic with the behavior of labor and labor leaders that it wanted to prevent the so-called "friends of labor" from controlling the legislative proceedings. The bill was reported under an open rule, a procedure which

[10] *C.R.*, May 5, 1943, p. 3990.   [11] *C.R.*, June 3, 1943, p. 5338.

allows any type of amendment to be offered from the floor. Passions ran high during the subsequent debate. Those who opposed the legislation emphasized the great increase in war production which had taken place, for which labor was given generous credit; those who supported the legislation emphasized the prevalence of strikes and shutdowns—and the coal mines were not then in operation—and contrasted the sacrifices made by labor with those made at Guadalcanal.

The bill as finally enacted authorized the government to seize strike-bound plants and to regulate strikes by supervising pre-strike plebiscites. The War Labor Board was given a legal base. The election laws were amended by prohibiting labor organizations from contributing directly to political campaigns. The bill passed the House 233–141 (54 percent of the Democrats; 72 percent of the Republicans).

The President vetoed the bill. He did not believe that strikes should be sanctioned, "with or without notice"; the provisions, he believed, would stimulate unrest.[12] He also believed that preventing labor organizations from contributing to political campaigns was discriminatory; if the idea had merit, it should be extended to other nonprofit organizations also. The President also advocated, for the first time, a limited form of national service legislation by which persons up to the age of 65 could be inducted in noncombat military service. The veto made little impression on Congress, and Senator Connally said that the sections about which the President complained were "merely incidentals." The vote to override in the Senate was 65–25 (60 percent of the Democrats; 82 percent of the Republicans) and in the House, 244–108 (63 percent of the Democrats; 76 percent of the Republicans). In the House there was greater support for overriding the veto than there had been for the bill initially.

The question of the type of strike-bound plant which the government might seize came to a head in the case of Montgomery Ward and Co. The government seized the plant when the com-

[12] *C.R.*, June 25, 1943, p. 6487.

pany officials refused to obey an order of the War Labor Board, and the seizure was dramatized when soldiers were detailed to remove Mr. Sewell Avery, the chief executive officer, from his Chicago office. The removal order was carried out literally, and the press of the country carried the shocking picture of two soldiers riding Mr. Avery on their shoulders. Was this just a publicity stunt of dubious taste, or was someone stretching his authority to the point that force was actually being used?

Congress reacted quickly, with ready-made political judgments and standard proposals for investigations. Rep. Howard W. Smith (D., Alexandria, Va.) asked for a citation of the authority by which the Army could "take private property not in any way directly connected with the war effort." [13] Rep. Ray J. Madden (D., Gary, Ind.) said it was Mr. Avery's contention "that his company is not in this war" and therefore did not have to obey the orders of the government. [14] The House proceeded to create a special committee to investigate the dispute. Rep. John J. Cochran (D., St. Louis, Mo.), who disapproved of investigating committees in general, thought that the proposal to create yet another committee was "nothing less than the cheapest, dirtiest kind of politics" and that one had only to "watch the Republican vote" on the resolution to determine this. [15] All of the Republicans voted for the resolution. The vote was 300–60 (66 percent of the Democrats; 100 percent of the Republicans).

The special committee presented a divided report, with the Democrats supporting the government and the Republicans supporting Avery's defiance of the War Labor Board order. The majority said that the President followed his constitutional and legal duty in a situation which demanded "prompt, firm, and courageous action." The minority said that the seizure of Ward's property was "in direct defiance of the will of Congress and in complete disregard of the Constitution." [16] The Avery case was thereby made

---

[13] C.R., May 5, 1944, p. 4054.   [14] C.R., May 5, 1944, p. 4068.
[15] C.R., May 5, 1944, p. 4060.
[16] H. Rept. 1904, Sept. 19, 1944.

into a partisan dispute, but the implications of the case went beyond partisan advantage. The partisans making the decision had some stake in the nature of the decision made. One may question whether in this case an investigating committee was the best agency for sifting the facts and proposing more legal and less discomforting solutions for disputes of a similar nature.

MANPOWER SUPPLY AND ALLOCATION

Now let us return to the other facet of the manpower question —the adequacy of the manpower supply to meet total requirements. In the early stages of the war it was not too difficult to provide manpower both for civilian jobs and for the armed services because new supplies could be drawn from the pool of unemployment. Manpower shortages began to develop in many areas with the continued expansion of military production and the size of the armed services.

The agency responsible for establishing and coordinating manpower policies was the War Manpower Commission, which was created by the President in April, 1942, and placed under the chairmanship of Paul V. McNutt, a former governor of Indiana. The agency was not especially popular with Congress, and on one occasion the House sulkily refused to raise Mr. McNutt's salary to $15,000, commensurate with the salaries of the heads of other war agencies. The WMC did not have very much power over the internal supply of manpower and its allocation among competing claimants, and it had no power to bring military and civilian requirements into balance. The size of the manpower supply available for civilian use was conditioned by the number of men in the armed forces. Once the latter figure was determined, other manpower problems could be more readily resolved, yet the size of the armed forces was a fluctuating figure, determined by military authorities and not by the WMC or by Congress.

The WMC was faced with many maddening problems in its attempt to maintain a free labor market, and it had little authority to remedy many situations which arose. Industry would hoard manpower, even allowing it to remain idle in order to have men available for future contracts. Workers would "jump jobs," as the expression went, for higher pay, or they might quit work if they became draft-exempt with some classification such as IV-F (unfit for military service). The decentralized Selective Service System operated unpredictably, and skilled workers on farm or factory might be called to the colors, even though their services were needed to fulfill production quotas.

The war had been under way for less than a year when Congress was informed that the Army required more men. It would need a total of five million men by the end of 1942, it was estimated, and seven and one-half million by the end of 1943. If these requirements were to be fulfilled, Congress would have the devil's choice of deciding whether fathers or those eighteen and nineteen years old should be drafted first. The decision was made to draft the teen-agers, and the House Committee on Military Affairs argued that young men would make better soldiers and that their induction would least disturb the normal pattern of economic and family life.

The appropriate legislation was actually introduced by two Republicans, Rep. James W. Wadsworth, of New York, and Senator Chan Gurney, of South Dakota, who had taken the leadership before Pearl Harbor in supporting defense measures. But why was this legislation introduced by the Gurney-Wadsworth pair now that the war was on? Was the Administration floating a trial balloon and withholding its endorsement of the legislation until it could test public reaction? Senator Vandenberg hinted that this is what had happened. If it was imperative to lower the draft age, he asked, why had the movement been initiated by certain Republican members of Congress, rather than "by an official request to the Congress, from the Commander-in-Chief and from the general staffs of the Army and Navy?" [17] For his part, Senator Gurney claimed that he introduced the legislation on his own responsibility, having become convinced of its necessity after an

[17] C.R., Oct. 22, 1942, p. 8512.

inspection tour of military camps. However widely Vandenberg's suspicions may have been shared, the testimony of military leaders persuaded Congress that the measure was necessary.

The decision to draft teen-agers was made regretfully, but there was little emotional oratory of the type heard in the First World War when similar legislation was enacted. An exception, perhaps, was the speech of Senator Hiram W. Johnson (R., San Francisco, Calif.), who had been in the Senate during the earlier war. Johnson was against the draft in principle, and he now raised the acidulous question of whether it had occurred to anyone "that there might be some member of this body who had sufficient sympathy to speak for little boys?" [18]

The legislation gave members of Congress an opportunity to debate other matters associated with the draft. Rep. John E. Rankin (D., Tupelo, Miss.) wanted the bureaucrats and labor to be drafted first; they were "just as much entitled to fight this war as these eighteen-year old boys," Rankin said, and drafting them would be especially appropriate because they seemed to think that the war was "a joy ride." [19] Senator Josh Lee (D., Norman, Okla.) wished to protect the soldiers' morals by prohibiting liquor from being sold in and around military camps. Senator W. Lee O'Daniel (D., Fort Worth, Tex.) wanted to repeal the forty-hour law. Senator Tydings offered an amendment exempting farm labor from the draft. This amendment was adopted; its results will be discussed at a later point.

The most contentious issue was the proposal that all of the eighteen-year-old group be given a minimum of one year's training "before being sent out of this country to battlefields all over the world," as one Representative put it. The Senate adopted a minimum-training amendment, and so might the House had the rules permitted a vote on the issue. The War Department, however, opposed the flat requirement of a year's training, which it believed was excessive for some types of units and some kinds of replacements. The amendment was dropped in conference and did

[18] *C.R.*, Oct. 23, 1942, p. 8570.   [19] *C.R.*, Oct. 17, 1942, p. 8301.

not appear in the final Act. Once the Administration and the military leaders had endorsed the teen-age draft bill, the legislation proceeded rapidly through Congress, and it was adopted by the heavy majorities of 345–16 in the House and 58–5 in the Senate.

The decision not to legislate on a minimum training period did not put an end to the question, although the issue was never raised with regard to other age components. It came up again in 1945 under discomforting conditions. It happened that eighteen-year-old soldiers with less than a year's service had lost their lives in the Battle of the Bulge, and some parents raised the disquieting point that their sons would still be alive had a minimum training period been adopted. Congress considered and eventually adopted an amendment which provided that soldiers under nineteen would be required to have six months' training before being sent into combat.

The War Department still opposed any specific training requirement. It naturally resented the implication that young soldiers had died because they were insufficiently or improperly trained. Training was a relative matter, it was explained, and it applied to units as well as to individuals. An eighteen-year-old replacement was "safer" with a division which had been tested in combat than he would be with a green division, whether he had been trained for six months or twelve. Unexpectedly, however, the House conferees accepted the proposed Senate amendment. Word had just been received of the juncture of Anglo-American and Soviet forces in Germany, and it was believed that, under the new conditions, the minimum-training amendment would not be crippling to the armed forces.

DRAFTING OF FATHERS AND FARM WORKERS

The lowering of the draft age to eighteen failed to provide enough manpower to meet the expanding military requirements. The following year, in 1943, the Joint Chiefs of Staff raised their sights, aiming now at the target goal of 8,200,000 in the Army, making a total of 11,100,000 men in the armed forces. Congress

again had to broaden the draft components if it was satisfied that
these requirements were defendable. The new military goals were
investigated by the Senate Appropriations Committee, and it was
concluded that the request was justified. Whoever attempted to
change the plans without the most convincing evidence, said Senator Theodore F. Green (D., Providence, R.I.), a member of the
committee, was "directly responsible to the country for any failure
of such altered strategic plans and for all the disastrous consequences of that failure." [20] There was opposition, however, including that expressed by former President Herbert Hoover, but Congress inferentially approved the new plans in revising the draft
components.

It was now necessary to find another source of manpower to
meet the increased military demands, and all fingers pointed at
the pre-Pearl Harbor fathers who up to now had been given a
blanket deferment in the draft. There was some opposition to drafting fathers, especially on the part of Senator Burton K. Wheeler
(D., Butte, Mont.), who, though a nominal Democrat, had split
with the Administration over foreign policy. When Congress ad-
journed for a summer recess in 1943, legislation to regulate the
drafting of fathers was pending, although existing legislation would
permit fathers to be drafted if their deferment was rescinded. In
other words, it would be necessary to amend the law only in the
event Congress wished to prevent fathers from being drafted.

During the recess, Senator Wheeler heard that the Selective
Service System planned to rescind the deferment of fathers and
begin drafting them for military service. He asked the leaders to
reconvene Congress at once, but the leaders turned him down,
saying that the subject could be taken up when Congress reconvened in September. Wheeler took up the fight again that fall, insisting that bureaucrats and industrial workers be drafted first;
according to this classification, neither bureaucrats nor workers
appear to have been fathers. "Before American homes are broken
up, before children are driven into the streets," Wheeler said, "let

[20] C.R., March 5, 1943, p. 1012.

the slackers in the government bureaus, the bureaucrats who are demanding sacrifices on the part of the American businessmen, American mothers, and babies of the country—let the slackers, I say, be driven out of the bureaus and into the Army where they belong." [21]

Wheeler did not get very much support for his proposal to defer fathers indefinitely. Instead, Congress enacted legislation giving fathers a low draft priority; they would not be exempted completely, but they would be placed in a category which would be called last. This legislation had the support of the War Department.

If the armed services were to be expanded, it was axiomatic that manpower shortages would develop in other areas. The decentralized draft did not necessarily make allowance for the manpower needs of other claimants—indeed, an aggressive draft policy would make the conditions worse—and there was no national agency to balance the various demands. Farmers were especially hard hit, losing their hired help to the draft and to higher-paying war jobs. They appealed to Congress for help, and Congress, in turn, reacted very much as if a sensitive nerve had been irritated. Several committees held hearings and conducted investigations, there was much speechmaking, and legislation was adopted which assisted the farmer in retaining his manpower.

In the controversy over the adequacy of farm manpower, the spokesmen for the farmers were overtly hostile toward industrial labor, which was pictured as receiving high wages, being exempted from the draft, and showing their lack of patriotism by frequently going on strike. The farmer believed that there was inequality and favoritism in the policy being followed. This attitude is expressed, for example, in some doggerel which was inserted in the *Congressional Record* and which is quoted here in part. The verse tells the story of a farmer whose son and hired man had been drafted:

[21] *C.R.*, Sept. 28, 1943, p. 7846.

His hay needed raking, there was milking to do;
His tractor was broken, no mechanics to work;
In unionized factories, unions taught them to shirk;
His wife and his daughter worked early and late,
Their hands raw and blistered, from pitchfork and rake.
The loyal and honest, their faith was sore tried,
By numerous talks from a certain fireside. . . .

Although farm parity prices did not include the cost of production, a steel worker nevertheless received fifteen dollars a day, worked forty hours a week with double pay for overtime, and was provided with vacations and tires. As for the farmer—

His son would be shot if he struck for more pay,
But strikes stop production, day after day.
The farmer groaned as he lay on his bed with a sag,
For he realized a union card overshadowed his flag.[22]

The draft act contained the proviso that farm workers could be deferred if their work was found "to be necessary to the maintenance of the national health, safety, or interest," but the thousands of draft boards had not interpreted this phrase uniformly. The heart of the matter was the meaning of the word "necessary," which was variously interpreted by the draft boards. Some boards continued to draft farm workers, saying that they were not "necessary" if replacements were available or if the farmer-employer could get along without them by mechanizing the farm. In order to clarify policy and protect the pool of farm manpower, Senator Tydings offered an amendment to the 1942 draft act which provided that farm workers could be deferred who were "necessary to and regularly engaged" in farm work. This was adopted.

Despite the fact that Congress had given a good deal of attention to the problem of farm manpower, the Tydings amendment did not represent the judgment of any particular committee. It was offered late in the debate and had not been considered by a committee; no indication was given of the attitudes of the War,

[22] *C.R.*, Nov. 10, 1942, p. A4008.

Navy, or Agriculture Departments, who apparently were not consulted. Senator Chan Gurney, a Republican from the farm state of South Dakota, thought that the amendment constituted a "class deferment." He maintained that the farmers were "as patriotic as any other group in America" and were not looking for preference.[23] Others said that the amendment provided no protection against draft-dodging by requiring, say, a minimum time in which the worker would have been "regularly engaged" on the farm. These protests did not prevent the quick approval by the Senate of the amendment, which was adopted by a vote of 62–6. The amendment was later agreed to by the House and appeared without modification in the final version of the legislation. By September, 1943, some two million farm workers had been deferred from military service.

The Tydings amendment did not fully protect the supply of farm labor. The amendment protected the farm worker from the draft, but it did not prevent him from taking a war job, or quitting his farm work if classified IV-F, or enlisting. Now more drastic proposals were placed before Congress to freeze the farm worker on his job. Senator John H. Bankhead (D., Jasper, Ala.) and thirty-nine other senators introduced a bill preventing a farm worker from leaving his job without the consent of his draft board. This proposal would subject the farm worker and the soldier to the same type of criminal penalties for violating the law, but farm labor and other types of labor would be treated differently. The Military Affairs Committee, which reported the bill, said that the farmers had been given little or no consideration by local boards and that the Tydings amendment had not been administered "with understanding, sympathy, and uniformity." [24] Despite the opposition of the War Department, the Selective Service System, and the Office of Economic Stabilization, the Senate proceeded to pass the bill, 50–24 (59 percent of the Democrats; 76 percent of the Republicans). The bill was not considered in the House.

In 1945, the Selective Service System placed on the Tydings

[23] C.R., Oct. 24, 1942, p. 8644.   [24] S. Rept. 92, March 5, 1943.

Amendment a different interpretation which was less favorable to the farmers. Additional demands for military manpower developed after the Battle of the Bulge, and the Selective Service System cast covetous eyes at the prospective draftees still working on the farm. In order to give the draft boards greater authority over farm workers, the word "necessary" was reinterpreted to mean "relatively essential" when compared with other necessary functions, such as serving in the Army. Farm workers were no longer to be exempt from the draft merely because they were performing work which, in other respects, might be necessary.

Congressional committees first attempted to persuade General Lewis B. Hershey, the Director of the Selective Service System, to rescind this new interpretation, but when he refused they proceeded to consider new legislation. In the House, there was considerable support for the old Bankhead proposal of freezing all farm labor in their jobs, but this plan was eventually rejected. The bill finally passed by Congress merely reestablished the interpretation of the Tydings amendment which had been followed for more than two years. Later, President Truman's veto was upheld by the House, 177–186 (85 percent of the Democrats; 8 percent of the Republicans).

In his veto message, President Truman said that the essence of the Selective Service System was that no one be safeguarded from the hazards of war "because of his economic, occupational, or other status." The practical effect of the legislation would be to "single out one special class of our citizens, the agricultural group, and put it on a place above both industrial occupation and military service." [25] The veto message was not entirely frank. It overlooked the facts that the proposed policy was no innovation but had been the policy followed by the Selective Service System for more than two years and that the new interpretation of the Tydings amendment differed from the interpretation initially made by Congress. On abstract grounds the "special class" argument might appear to have merit, but the abolition of this "special class"

[25] C.R., May 3, 1945, p. 4153.

neither provided the farmer with manpower nor did it place the farmers, industry, and Selective Service on an even footing. Without the Tydings amendment, the farmer could not compete with industry and the draft in securing manpower. The problem of supplying farms with sufficient manpower was not solved until the war ended. In the meantime Congress considered a more comprehensive manpower plan in the form of national service legislation.

COMPULSION—NATIONAL SERVICE LEGISLATION

From the early days of the war, there was some support in Congress for adopting a comprehensive plan for controlling manpower —known as national service legislation—which would give the government power to tell a man where he should work. Much of this support was based on the abstract principle of equality of obligation, the argument being that the civilian and the soldier should be treated alike in their obligations to their country during war. However, the Administration did not give its unequivocal support to such legislation until 1945, and in the meantime it had developed a policy based primarily on the voluntary cooperation of the employer and the employee. Its limited sanctions did not extend to assigning jobs or preventing men from quitting work.

In 1942, Mr. McNutt suggested that his agency, the War Manpower Commission, be given more control over manpower, but this trial balloon was soon pricked in Congress by the labor committees, and by the end of the year it was completely deflated. The following year, the President advocated limited work-or-fight legislation in vetoing the Smith-Connally Act, but he did not press the argument, and Congress took no action on the proposal.

Within the Cabinet, Secretary of War Stimson especially was a persistent advocate of national service legislation, and he was active in persuading the President of the wisdom of this policy. At length, in his annual message of 1944, the President asked Congress to enact legislation which would prevent strikes, make available for war production every able-bodied adult, and provide a measure of

equality of sacrifice for all civilians. The War and Navy Departments and the Maritime Commission supported this policy, but the
War Manpower Commission and the War Production Board were
apathetic, being more concerned in improving current methods of
manpower control. The President did not unequivocally embrace
national service legislation, and, indeed, his request was based on
the premise that Congress would enact additional legislation on
prices, taxes, and profits. The reaction in Congress was negative;
there was not debate and no vote, and the proposal was ignored.

Instead, Congress considered ways of utilizing more effectively
the four million civilians classified IV-F in the draft. This group
was in an anomalous position. Being exempt from military service,
the IV-Fs were free to move from job to job, or even to quit work
altogether, and they were virtually free from the regulations applicable to most civilians of military age. The IV-Fs were not a
homogeneous group, the members having little in common other
than their draft-deferred status, so that it was not easy to develop
a policy applicable to this group alone. However, a step toward
developing a policy on IV-Fs was made in December, 1944, when
the War Department agreed to accept men for induction who
were below Army physical standards. Thereafter workers with
IV-F and other classifications who left their jobs without the
consent of their local draft board were declared eligible for induction. Under this policy, workers who were formerly draft exempt
now faced induction if they quit work or "jumped" their jobs. In
all, some 70,000 men were given pre-induction examinations under this policy, of whom 45,000 were actually inducted. According to the *The United States at War*, the normal procedure was to
place these job-jumping inductees in army camps "and then after
a short time offer them a chance to return to their previous jobs
as members of the enlisted reserve—an opportunity which few
men declined." [26]

National service legislation became a serious issue in 1945, and
it was almost adopted by Congress. The message of the President

[26] Page 450.

advocating the legislation was more compelling than that of 1944, and it abounded with optimism, verve, and the will to win. There was no equivocation, no suggestion that other legislation also be enacted, and the President now seemed certain that the legislation was necessary. National service legislation was to be the knockout punch, the one, final, superb civilian blow which would defeat the enemy and win the war. The soldiers, giving their all, were being killed in great numbers on all battle fronts, and now the civilians must unite for the final thrust. The legislation would give "supreme proof to our fighting men that we are giving them what they are entitled to have." [27]

The President cited an impressive list of programs which were behind requirements, owing in part to inadequate manpower controls. This included supplies of ordnance, ammunition, aerial bombs, tanks, heavy trucks, and B-29's. The cruiser and carrier programs, the rocket program, and the repair of damaged ships were all behind schedule. To clinch the argument, the President quoted a letter from the service chiefs stating that the equilibrium between Allied and enemy weapons was so unstable that it might be necessary to concentrate instantly on the production of some new weapon. This might have been a reference to the A-bomb. If the government were to concentrate quickly on producing new weapons, it would be necessary to have some authority over where labor would work; a law freezing jobs or preventing job jumping would not be enough.

Congress then debated at length the two questions of whether the standards applicable to a soldier were also applicable to a civilian worker and whether current controls over manpower were adequate. The initial reaction in Congress was favorable to the passage of the legislation. Senator Thomas, of Utah, who had helped develop and had long defended the voluntary system, was now Chairman of the Military Affairs committee, and in his new role he introduced the legislation and had charge of the Senate debate. Senator Thomas, a thoughtful and reflective man, told the

[27] *C.R.,* Jan. 6, 1945, p. 65.

Senate why he had changed his mind. Personally, he said, he had opposed and still opposed the legislation, but each Senator had more than one loyalty to which he was faithful. Sometimes it was necessary to be loyal to the committee, sometimes to the Administration, sometimes to the party. "There comes a time," he said, "when the request of certain of our leaders cannot be denied," and the appeal made by the President "was too powerful for me to resist." [28]

The issue of equality of sacrifice was brought into the discussion by Senator Josiah W. Bailey (D., Raleigh, N.C.), who said that those who believed in the compulsory principle "intend to invoke it." [29] This principle had been used with respect to more than ten million men in the services, and Senator Bailey thought this was not the time to abandon it. Other Senators, who were less convinced than Senator Bailey that the same principle was applicable, argued that civilians and soldiers should be treated differently. National service legislation went "to the very foundation of action in a free government by free citizens," said Senator O'Mahoney, one of the most forceful exponents of this position. He argued that the application of military sanctions "to individuals working for other individuals or organizations which may profit from their labor, is altogether out of harmony with our system of government." [30]

Senator Tydings took a middle position, saying that the determining factor should be the demonstrable need for manpower controls rather than some abstract concept such as equality-of-sacrifice. He found no equality of service even under the Selective Service System, for the Army accepted for induction only a percentage of those who were sent by the draft board, and all who served in the Army did not sacrifice equally. It was impossible to devise a system where the burdens of war were shared equally, although this factor should of course be considered in making decisions. For him the decisive element was found in the ques-

[28] C.R., Feb. 26, 1945, p. 1776.   [29] C.R., March 6, 1945, p. 1776.
[30] C.R., March 2, 1945, p. 1644.

tion, "How can this country arrange its affairs so as to give the men who are facing death on the battlefields the last full measure of devotion and support?" [31]

Those who stressed the equality-of-sacrifice principle appeared to be more interested in applying equal sanctions to the soldier and to the civilian than in developing and improving existing civilian controls. The legislation which was considered, for instance, was a somewhat awkward throwback to the Selective Service principles of 1940, where the emphasis was on compulsion, equality, and neighborliness, and it ignored the experiences gained during the war in developing manpower controls. The President was, in a way, the intellectual prisoner of those who had continuously advocated national service legislation. These advocates had zeal and patriotism of a high order, but they tended to be overly doctrinaire in advancing their argument. The national service legislation passed by the House reflected this doctrinaire attitude. All civilian males between eighteen and forty-five were to be frozen in their jobs or compelled to take war work when offered, and the law was to be administered by the Selective Service System, which had not heretofore had experience in handling civilian manpower requirements. The House passed the bill by a vote of 246–167 (78 percent of the Democrats; 36 percent of the Republicans).

The Senate was a more reluctant supporter of national service legislation. The Senate bill emphasized control and direction, not duress. Ceilings would be established on the number of employees who could be hired, and greater care would be exercised in directing workers to areas of labor shortage. The bill did not, however, propose to tell a man where he could work, and it was to be administered by the Office of War Mobilization and Reconversion, not the Selective Service System. The issue of compulsion, of work-or-jail, was decided in the negative when the Senate rejected the so-called Bailey amendment, 23–60 (36 percent of the Democrats; 17 percent of the Republicans). The bill then passed,

[31] C.R., March 26, 1945, p. 2764.

63–16 (88 percent of the Democrats; 74 percent of the Republicans). The opposition contained members who wanted compulsory sanctions, such as Senator Bailey and Senator Gurney, as well as those who opposed any form of national service legislation, such as Senator Homer E. Capehart (R., Indianapolis, Ind.) and Senator Albert B. Chandler (D., Versailles, Ky.)

The conference committee combined major portions of both bills, retaining the Senate provisions for manpower ceilings and controls over hiring and the House provision for freezing current job positions. The work-or-jail provision was deleted, but an ambiguous phrase was added which stated that everyone had "an obligation" to work when called upon. It was not clear whether this was a legal obligation or merely a moral exhortation. In the meantime, however, there was growing opposition to the whole idea of national service legislation on the part of business and labor groups and within Congress itself, and it was also pointed out that the approaching end of the European war would make the legislation unnecessary. The House adopted the conference report by the dwindling margin of 167–160 (74 percent of the Democrats; 20 percent of the Republicans). The Senate support also dwindled, and some Senators objected especially to the penal sanctions contained in the conference report. For instance, Senator O'Mahoney, who had voted for the initial Senate bill, sharply criticized this phase of the conference report. By including penal sanctions, he said, one individual would be given "complete authority over the movements of the men and women who have made so startling and magnificent a contribution to the winning of the war," and he thought that such delegation would be an abandonment of congressional responsibilities.[32]

In an attempt to maintain the support of the wavering Senators, Senator Thomas quoted from a letter of President Roosevelt asking the Senate to adopt the conference report. The President said that the war was still serious and had yet to be won and that there would be future temptations for workers to leave their jobs. By

[32] C.R., March 26, 1945, p. 2764.

enacting the legislation, Congress would have discharged its duty, "and the responsibility for effectively and fairly handling the manpower situation will be placed squarely on the executive branch." But the appeal was not effective, and the Senate rejected the conference report, 29–46 (46 percent of the Democrats; 31 percent of the Republicans). Of the 63 Senators who voted initially for the bill, only 20 supported the conference report, 29 opposed it, and 14 did not vote. Of the 246 Representatives who voted initially for the bill, 158 supported the conference report, 29 opposed it, 2 voted "present," and 57 did not vote. This was the end of national service legislation.

Congress was also considering special legislation to draft nurses, a proposal which failed with the collapse of support for national service legislation, but an interesting debate developed in the House over the proposition that all nurses should be granted commissions. The argument arose when Rep. Forest A. Harness (R., Kokomo, Ind.) offered an amendment which provided that no nurse be inducted "except as a commissioned officer." The proponents argued that inequality would result if those nurses meeting the required physical standards were given commissions and those who failed to meet these standards were given enlisted ratings. The solution would be to make all nurses officers. The opposition was based on less egalitarian grounds. Can an officer be drafted? Absurd. An officer's commission was something which was offered and accepted or rejected, but it could not be granted by legislation. This subtle distinction was not appreciated, and the amendment granting commissions to all drafted nurses was adopted. The bill subsequently passed the House, 347–42 (98 percent of the Democrats; 79 percent of the Republicans), and it was reported to the Senate favorably. However, the timing of the report coincided with the final defeat of national service legislation, and there was no further action on the measure.

VOTES

In enacting manpower legislation, Congress adopted the traditional political posture of keeping one eye on the ballot box and one ear to the ground. This was especially evident in the passage of the Smith-Connally Act in 1943 and the two Soldier Voting Acts in 1942 and 1944. In the Smith-Connally Act, it will be recalled, a provision was added making it illegal for labor unions to contribute directly to political campaigns, one purpose being to make electoral reprisals against candidates for Congress more difficult. Following the passage of this legislation, the CIO created a political arm known as the Political Action Committee, which action resulted in an increase rather than a decrease in the political activity of labor unions. The House Committee on Un-American Activities also became involved by preparing a study on the CIO which attempted to discredit its leadership; the study was made widely available to members of Congress for use in the 1944 elections.

The legislative controversy over the voting of soldiers was prolonged and at times acrimonious. All Congressmen were interested in the issue, for the extent to which soldiers voted might determine the political fate of the members of Congress and of the presidential candidates. The political complexion of the soldiers was not definitely known, but the age-group from which soldiers came tended to be more Democratic than Republican. It was further believed that Commander-in-Chief Roosevelt would be a popular candidate with the soldiers.

The various partisan blocs in Congress tended to support legislation most favorable to them. The Northern Democrats wanted a federal ballot, which would make it easy for soldiers to vote for the presidential candidate. The Republicans wanted a State ballot, which would give the soldiers greater opportunity to vote for State officials as well as the presidential candidate. The Southern Democrats also wanted a State ballot, so that the States would continue to regulate the standards of residence, registration, and voter eligibility.

Congress was slow in developing a policy on soldier voting, and the first Act was passed so late in 1942 that it played an insignificant part in the November elections of that year, only 28,000 soldiers voting under its provisions. The major controversy centered around an amendment waiving the poll tax, which developed into a North-South fight. The amendment was offered in the Senate on behalf of Senator Brooks, an Illinois Republican, who, as it happened, was a candidate for reelection that year. The Senate adopted the amendment 33–20 (47 percent of the Democrats; 100 percent of the Republicans). There was vocal opposition in the House, but the amendment was at length adopted, 248–53 (70 percent of the Democrats; 99 percent of the Republicans). Fifty of those who voted in the negative were Southerners, and one of their leaders, Rep. Hatton W. Sumners (D., Dallas, Tex.), the Chairman of the Judiciary Committee, said that the legislation would "strengthen the stranglehold of this great Federal bureaucracy upon the throats of the States." [33]

There was a somewhat different political alignment in 1944, for the Republicans were now less willing to waive State regulations if the result would make it easier for a Democrat to be elected President. The contest developed early, with the Senate Committee on Elections reporting a federal ballot bill a full year before the presidential elections. During the following four months, there was a vituperative and complicated debate on the prosaic subjects of administrative structures and constitutional provisions, but the most significant and immediate issue, as everyone knew, was the effect of the decisions being made on the coming presidential election. In the end, the proponents of the federal ballot were routed, and the States were allowed to determine the kind of ballot they would permit. The coalition between the Republicans and Southern Democrats was the controlling factor in both the Senate and the House, although the strength of the coalition waxed and waned on the various votes which were taken. On the whole, the effective leadership was assumed by the Southerners, who were more successful in mustering majorities than the chairmen of the two election committees, Senator Theodore F. Green (D., Providence, R.I.) and Rep. Eugene Worley (D., Shamrock, Tex.), both of whom supported the federal ballot.

[33] C.R., Sept. 9, 1942, p. 7065.

The initial skirmish in December, 1943, was easily won by the Republican-Southern coalition. The Senate approved a States' rights plan proposed by Senator James O. Eastland (D., Ruleville, Miss.), Senator John L. McClellan (D., Camden, Ark.), and Senator Kenneth McKellar (D., Memphis, Tenn.), which "requested" the States to enact absentee ballot legislation. The States would retain their authority over ballots, registration, residence, and poll-tax payments, and would prepare postal-card applications for ballots which would be distributed by the armed services. The vote was 42–37 (39 percent of the Democrats; 60 percent of the Republicans). No Southern Senator other than Senator Pepper, of Florida, voted against the amendment.

The War and Navy Departments told the Senate that the plan they had adopted was unworkable, for it would have been impossible to supply each unit with the correct number of postal cards to accommodate servicemen from the various States. The postal cards, it will be remembered, were to be supplied by the States. The Senate accepted this advice and subsequently revised the bill. The Senate continued to debate the issue, and a vast number of amendments were considered. In the end, a compromise was reached which allowed the federal ballot to be used in those cases where a qualified service voter was "beyond reach" of the absentee voting procedure prescribed by his own State.

The armed services were embarrassed during the debate by having to comment on the feasibility of plans which were supercharged with domestic politics. A federal ballot scheme would have been the easiest for the service departments to administer, but to support this plan would raise suspicions of partiality and partisanship. Senator Taft, in fact, was especially angry with the War Department, which he accused of cooperating "100 percent with the extreme New Dealers and the CIO Political Action Committee in support of a clearly unconstitutional federal ballot carrying no names except those of the candidates for President." Taft went on to say that the War Department's organization of getting out the vote extended to the smallest Army unit and was "on a scale which no political organization could possibly duplicate among the civilian population." [34]

In the House, the support for a States' rights ballot was even stronger than in the Senate. The nominal leadership was overthrown, and legislation was presented to the House which, in effect, limited federal action to "recommending" that the States pass remedial absentee-voting legislation. The bipartisan bloc, which had almost complete command in the House, was led by Rep. John E. Rankin (D., Tupelo, Miss.), who proved himself to be a skillful floor leader.

The crucial date of the House debate was February 3, a singularly tumultuous day when the House was kept in session until 10:58 p.m. to rout completely the Worley federal ballot forces. At one point, Rep. Clifton A. Woodrum (D., Roanoke, Va.), a veteran of twenty years of legislative service, scolded the House for its ill-tempered behavior. "It hurts me," Woodrum said, "to see us in the mood in which we find ourselves tonight." Complicated amendments were offered without adequate explanation, "and when some Member asked that an amendment be permitted to be reported that we might know what we were voting on, objection was made to it." It was that kind of performance which gave an opportunity to critics of the legislative process, and he concluded by saying that "the spectacle you are making here tonight is not adding to the prestige of the House of Representatives." [35]

Part of the sharpness of the debate was due to the prevailing belief that there would be no roll call vote on the federal ballot proposal. This state of affairs resulted from the so-called majority and the Republican minority favoring the same bill. A roll call would have been possible by a motion to recommit the bill under discussion and to substitute therefor the federal ballot bill. The privilege of making such a motion, however, belonged to the Republicans, as the minority party, and the Republicans did not favor a federal ballot. The sharpness of the debate increased when

[34] C.R., Aug. 15, 1944, p. 6937.   [35] C.R., Feb. 3, 1944, p. 1220.

the President sent a special message to Congress which stated that in his opinion the States' rights ballot bill was "meaningless" and "a fraud," that he had been informed it would be possible to reject the Worley bill without a roll call vote, and that he agreed with most Americans that members of Congress should be willing to stand up and be counted. In the end there was a roll call, and Representative Martin, the Republican leader, said: "We are not afraid to be counted." The motion to recommit and to substitute the Worley federal ballot bill was defeated, 168–244 (75 percent of the Democrats; 10 percent of the Republicans). The States' rights bill then passed, 328–69 (67 percent of the Democrats; 98 percent of the Republicans).[36]

With the House supporting a States' rights ballot and the Senate a modified federal ballot, it was clear that the conferees would have considerable influence in shaping the final bill. Ordinarily the selection of Senate conferees is perfunctory and stylized, but on this occasion, when the attitude of a single conferee might be decisive, there was considerable controversy over the principle to be followed in such selection. One principle was that of naming the senior members of the committee, which would have helped the States' rights ballot bloc. Another principle was that of naming the members of the subcommittee who had worked on the particular legislation, which would have helped the federal ballot bloc. Still another principle was that of electing the conferees, which would have caused considerable confusion with unpredictable results. In the end, a combination of the principles of committee seniority and of subcommittee membership was utilized, and to a degree this favored the States' rights bloc.

The bill reported by the conference was a victory for the supporters of the States' rights ballot. The federal ballot was to be allowed in a limited number of cases and then only with the consent of the State. For instance, a soldier overseas could use a federal ballot only if he had first applied for a State absentee ballot dur-

[36] C.R., Feb. 3, 1944, p. 1221.

ing a prescribed time period and if the governor of his State certified that the federal ballot was authorized. The Senate sponsors of the federal ballot bill did not sign the conference report, and Senator Barkley spoke and voted against the report. There was also some dissatisfaction in the House. All of this, however, was not enough to defeat the conference report, which passed the Senate, 47–31 (49 percent of the Democrats; 77 percent of the Republicans) and the House 273–111 (50 percent of the Democrats; 97 percent of the Republicans). The President allowed the bill to become law without his signature.

There was a semihumorous aftermath to the voting controversy when the War Department interpreted too literally a restriction on the government "sponsoring" political propaganda "designed or calculated" to affect the result of a federal election. An event which roused public interest was the conclusion of the War Department that *The Republic,* by Charles A. Beard, and *Yankee from Olympus,* by Catherine Drinker Bowen, came within the scope of the ban inasmuch as they contained favorable references to President Roosevelt. There were other incidents: an Army outfit canceled a subscription to the Los Angeles *Times* under the theory that otherwise the government would be "sponsoring" political propaganda, and under the same theory many post exchanges stopped their sale of newspapers and magazines. Congress soon revised the law by providing that sales of publications at post exchanges did not constitute "government sponsorship" and that in determining their political import, publications, broadcasts, and films should be considered "in their entirety." In advocating amendatory legislation, the Senate committee upheld the War Department, stating that the proper way of correcting bad law was through congressional action, not through administrative interpretation. Senator Taft, the author of the initial restrictive amendments, was less charitable. He wanted the War Department to revise its interpretation at once, and he went on to accuse the department of bad faith. "Many persons have suggested to me," Taft said, "that the course pursued by the War Department and its Morale Division is deliberately intended to discredit Congress in order to affect the election." [37]

The federal ballot was not a significant factor in the election itself. Twenty States certified that they would accept the federal ballot, and some 111,773 federal ballots were cast by service personnel under this program. On the other hand, it is estimated that there were more than four million State absentee ballots cast by the 9,225,000 service personnel of voting age.

[37] *C.R.*, Aug. 15, 1944, p. 6937.

4. Frozen Prices
in a Hot War

THE STEREOTYPED VIEW that Congress has little to do in wartime must be revised if applied to the subject of price control. The concern of Congress with this contentious subject was displayed over an extensive front and lasted throughout the war. Once control was established over some prices, everything seemed to be interrelated, and, like the organ, if one pressed in here, it came out there. With supplies scarce as they were, the formation of a policy on prices soon led to proposals for controlling wages and salaries, subsidizing costs, rationing scarce items, and establishing standards of quality. After Congress had established basic price policy, it was continually importuned to adjust price relationships between various economic groups and to review the administration of the law.

Prices began to rise with the expansion of defense spending. There was no price control legislation on the statute books, and the Administration, which was especially concerned with the rise in prices and its effect on the economy, attempted to maintain price stability through voluntary cooperation and what was known as "informal persuasive control." These measures were not effective, and at length on July 30, 1941, the President asked Congress to enact legislation which would permit the government to impose ceilings on prices. He did not ask that ceilings be placed on wage rates, but he did say that the wages in defense industries should not "substantially exceed" those prevailing in comparable non-defense industries.

Congress was in no hurry to enact legislation controlling prices. The rise in prices was not unwelcome to many members of Congress; indeed, Congress had been trying for years to lift the economy from the trough of the depression, and there were now signs that farm prices were at long last approaching the magical goal of parity. In any event, the need for controlling prices presented to Congress a different kind of problem which was supported by neither demonstrable need nor constituent demand. The House Banking and Currency Committee held extensive hearings on price legislation, which lasted almost until Pearl Harbor. These leisurely committee deliberations served as a type of economic seminar in which all aspects of price control were investigated. During the process a number of members developed considerable insight into the ramifications of the problem which was of assistance to them later when they assumed the leadership in the debates on price control.

Two of the controversial issues relating to price control were the extent of the controls and the standards which should be applied. Initially, the Administration believed that the control should be relatively limited and applicable to key commodities only. As the war developed, it abandoned this position for the more extensive control of all prices in a general price freeze. This policy had long been advanced by Mr. Bernard Baruch, who was guided by his experiences in controlling prices during the First World War as Director of the War Industries Board. The basic principle of a price freeze was that all prices should be held to the level existing at some representative base period. The concept of equality of sacrifice was also inherent in the proposal, as one advocate implied when he told the House that he wanted "to look into the whites of the eyes of the man who is willing to vote to take young men into the Army . . . and then is unwilling to vote to require some uniformity of sacrifice from the other groups." [1]

[1] Representative Gore (D., Tenn.), in *C.R.*, Nov. 26, 1941, p. 9150.

Despite its appeal to justice in the abstract, the establishment of a total freeze on prices raised many practical difficulties. Many groups which were not satisfied with the representative base period carried on strenuous campaigns to secure a base period more favorable to their interests. Moreover, existing legislation prevented any general freeze of farm prices, which were based on a parity relationship and not pegged to any fixed figures. The parity price of farm commodities would rise or fall with the fluctuation of other prices, and the ceiling on farm prices was based on the parity price. Similarly, the increase of farm prices would affect other costs, so that, in fact, parity helped create a spiral of rising prices. The farm groups, however, would have opposed any standard other than parity, which had become a word epitomizing the economic goals of the farm groups. In fact, no attempt was made to supplant the concept of parity itself.

The new legislation became law in January, 1942. Circumstances had altered since Congress began considering price control six months earlier, so that in many cases the provisions of the law were no longer adequate. The Act provided that the Price Administrator should give "due consideration" to the prices prevailing in early October, 1941, although for farm prices he could select the highest of four different standards, including 110 percent of parity. The Office of Price Administrator was created with a legal base, supplanting the Office of Price Administration and Civilian Supply, which had been created by the President, and subsequently Leon Henderson, who had headed the former agency, was named Price Administrator.

Mr. Henderson, a controversial figure, was considered by many Congressmen to be so pronouncedly and vocally a New Dealer that he would not take a sympathetic attitude toward the interests of business or of agriculture. His nomination was confirmed unanimously by the Senate, but many members were cool to the appointment, and earlier in the debate Senator John H. Bankhead (D., Jasper, Ala.) had suggested that many Senators might vote against price control legislation because "they do not want to entrust the administration of the bill to Mr. Henderson." [2] In defending Henderson in the House, Rep. Henry B. Steagall (D., Ozark, Ala.), the Chairman of the House Committee on Banking and Currency, said that he had revised his original opinion after listening to Henderson's extensive testimony on price control. Steagall had never seen a man "handle himself more satisfactorily or with a deeper, broader, or more complete grasp of his subject and of his responsibilities and duties." Henderson had other qualifications which appealed to Steagall. He was a veteran, a member of the American Legion, a member of the Methodist Church—"his daddy was a Methodist preacher like my granddaddy"—and, Steagall added, "a thing that does not discredit him with me,—but he belongs to the Democratic Party." [3] Henderson was confirmed without vocal opposition, but all did not share Representative Steagall's enthusiasm. During the year, the Office of Price Administration ran into many difficulties, and Henderson resigned as Price Administrator after the election reverses in November.

Prices continued to increase. By March, 1942, the price of food had risen 4.9 percent since Pearl Harbor and the price of clothing 7.7 percent; both items were approximately 20 percent higher than they had been a year earlier. The reaction of the Administration was to develop a comprehensive plan known as the General Maximum Price Regulation, which, in effect, froze the price of all consumer commodities as of March, 1942, and extended the control over rents to new areas. Subsequently, a standard for wage increases was created by the War Labor Board in the Little Steel decision. The Administration believed additional legislation was required, and the President asked Congress to assist the fight against inflation by lowering the ceiling on farm prices to 100 percent of parity and by levying additional taxes.

In view of the subsequent political developments on price policy, it may be desirable to give here a word or two of explanation on why Congress took no immediate action on price legislation, although, as will be seen, it subsequently enacted new tax legis-

[2] *C.R.*, Jan. 27, 1942, p. 725.　　　　[3] *C.R.*, Nov. 24, 1941, p. 9070.

lation. The congressional agenda was crowded, and the planned legislative program would not be upset without compelling reasons. Was a message from the President a compelling reason? Not necessarily. A request is not a command; it may not even be seriously considered unless the President continues to make his interest known. He will not rely on spontaneous action on the part of Congress, and at the least will initiate conferences with committee chairmen and party leaders so that there will be some meeting of minds on what kind of legislation might be expected. In this case, the President apparently took no further action to convince Congress that the legislation was necessary. Substantive reasons also existed to support the hesitation of Congress in lowering the ceiling on farm prices. Many Congressmen did not think that the current prices on farm commodities were too high, especially considering the rising costs of farm labor—and there was no ceiling on the cost of farm labor. The farmer, it appeared, was being unjustly blamed for rising prices, whereas prices were driven higher by increased costs, increased demand, and the availability of cash from the expanding wage bill. It was common knowledge that farm wages had skyrocketed and that the wages in defense plants were often fabulous. However, wages seemed to be sacrosanct, surely not a fit subject for legislation, and the President seemed prepared to veto any attempt of Congress to interfere with what he considered to be his prerogative.

The spring and summer of 1943 passed with Congress taking no specific action to amend the price law. Then on September 7 came the threat: the President told Congress that he would act independently if within the month Congress failed to lower the price ceilings on farm commodities to 100 percent of parity. The unexpected and even frightening message contained these ominous words: "I ask the Congress to take this action by the first of October. Inaction on your part by that date will leave me with an inescapable responsibility to the people of this country to see to it that the war effort is no longer imperiled by the threat of economic chaos. In the event that the Congress shall fail to act and act adequately, I shall accept the responsibility and I will act. At the same time that farm prices are stabilized, wages can and will be stabilized also. This I will do." [4]

The economic necessity for making such a proposal was not apparent to everyone, and in the perspective of time the threat appears to have been a rash and unnecessary challenge to constitutional procedures. Congress came within a day of meeting the President's imposed deadline, and this quick response, humiliating as it was under such goading, prevented the development of a constitutional crisis. However, the threat was not forgotten, and the episode created suspicion and distrust which continued to harass the Administration for the remainder of the war.

Surely no responsible congressional leader could have advised the President to follow the course he took, and one may well ask why the President acted as he did. The staff on whom the President relied for advice on price control was also free in giving political advice, and this group appears to have had little experience with Congress or even sympathy with the legislative process. The official administrative history of this period, published by the Bureau of the Budget, says that the President was under strong pressure to act independently of Congress and that these advisers, who are not identified, had prepared an appropriate order for his signature. He was told that it was essential to lower the ceiling on farm prices, that he had legal power to revise an Act of Congress, and that immediate action was necessary to save the economy from chaos. This questionable advice was partly based on the erroneous assumption that the President's war powers are unrestrained. A section of the Second War Powers Act was used as a legal fig leaf, the section stating that whenever defense requirements resulted in a shortage of supply, the President could allot material "as he shall deem necessary or appropriate in the public interest and to promote the national defense." This, of

4 *C.R.*, Sept. 7, 1942, p. 7044.

course, was a reference to the establishment of priorities and the allocation of war materials, not to the fixing of prices on farm commodities.

The President rejected the suggestion that he act independently and, instead, asked Congress to revise the law. Unfortunately he didn't stop there. Having accepted the advice that he had power to revise the price law independently, he made what appears to be a compromise with his advisers. The power that was said to be his would be used only in the event Congress failed to act and act adequately. He included the terms of the compromise in his message, but when stated in that fashion it appeared to be such a crude form of coercing Congress that the President received no credit for disavowing the advice that he act in an unconstitutional manner. Indeed, the explicit threat in the message was so blunt that the President appeared to be prepared to run the war by fiat rather than by law.

The President's message was bewildering to his friends and antagonizing to his opponents. The farm groups, especially, were not persuaded that the legislation was necessary; their leaders were energetic during the subsequent debate, and the mail of Congressmen was flooded with letters from farmers asking for more adequate prices. The farm groups decided to take advantage of the legislative situation by pressing for a revision of the parity formula which would include the costs of farm labor, a proposal which to many people seemed reasonable enough. However, some knowledge of the background of the controversy will help explain why the Administration opposed the plan, why labor costs had not been included previously, and why farmers now insisted on including labor costs in the parity formula. The farmers had indeed changed their position. When the parity formula was first established, farm labor was cheaper than in the base period, so that the exclusion of labor costs in the parity formula resulted in a higher parity price. Now that the cost of labor was higher than in the base period, the farm groups were anxious to include labor costs in the parity formula so as to raise the parity price.

It might be helpful at this point if a simplified illustration were given of how the parity price of farm commodities would be affected by varying the components of the parity formula.

LABOR COSTS EXCLUDED

Past Base Period
(Parity index, 375)

Actual price of wheat, $1.00 bu.
Actual price of cotton, 0.10¢ lb.

Present Pricing Period
(Parity index, 750)

Parity price of wheat, $2.00 bu.
Parity price of cotton 0.20¢ lb.

LABOR COSTS INCLUDED

Past Base Period
(Parity index, 400)

Actual price of wheat, $1.00 bu.
Actual price of cotton, 0.10¢ lb.

Present Labor Costs Decrease
(Parity index, 770)

Parity price of wheat, $1.92 bu.
Parity price of cotton, 0.19¢ lb.

Present Labor Costs Increase
(Parity index, 850)

Parity price of wheat, $2.13 bu.
Parity price of cotton, 0.21¢ lb.

The House not only rejected the President's request to lower the ceiling on farm prices, but it also passed a bill which raised the ceiling to 112 percent of parity, included the cost of labor in the parity formula, and placed a floor under farm commodities by providing that commodity loans could be made at 100 percent of parity. Some said that the bill would have increased the cost of food by as much as three billion dollars annually. The Senate, on the other hand, was more inclined to follow the suggestion of the President, and the final version of the legislation reflected the views of the Senate. The bill was handled on the Senate floor by Senator Prentiss M. Brown (D., St. Ignace, Mich.), a member of the Banking and Currency Committee, who was placed in an unenviable political position. Although facing election that November in the State of Michigan, which had considerable farm interests, Brown was nevertheless unequivocal in supporting the President's position on price control, and he even seemed to go out of his way to reprimand the leaders of the farm groups. When the content of the Senate bill was revealed, Brown told the Senate, the trains coming into Washington were "filled with representatives of the farm bloc." Brown then proceeded to criticize by name the leaders of the main farm groups, including "the able, suave, and powerful Ed. O'Neil," the President of the American Farm Bureau Federation. Brown told the Senate that "we should not turn the leadership of the legislative branch" over to the heads of the various farm groups. "They are hired by the people whose interests they serve," he said, and he asked that the Senate follow the leadership of the President, who represented no special group.[5] (P. S.: Senator Brown was defeated in November.)

The crucial votes in the Senate came on the cost-of-labor amendment. The Senate first adopted the amendment, 48–43 (51 percent of the Democrats; 57 percent of the Republicans), which showed the strength of the farm groups; the following day, as if to save the bill from a veto, the Senate modified the amendment by stating that the cost of farm labor should be given "adequate weighting." Then it passed the bill, 82–0.

The new legislation did not meet completely the standards set by the President, but it was approved, becoming the Stabilization Act of 1942, and the President said in signing the bill that "Congress has done its part" in helping to stabilize the cost of living. However, the new Act contained many equivocal phrases whose effect on the price structure was not readily apparent. Although price ceilings on farm commodities were reduced to 100 percent of parity, Congress added a new standard based on the highest price between January 1 and September 15, 1942, which protected all existing price rises. The "adequate weighting" of the costs of farm labor in determining the parity formula was perhaps only a semantical difference from the original request of the farm groups. Maximum prices could be modified to increase production for war purposes. A floor was placed under farm prices based on 90 percent of the parity price—a provision characterized by Senator Josh Lee (D., Norman, Okla.) as "a little piece of cake for the farmers." [6] Wages and salaries were to

[5] C.R., Sept. 24, 1942, p. 7408.   [6] C.R., Sept. 30, 1942, p. 7630.

be stabilized, but they could be adjusted "to correct gross inequities." The President was authorized to issue before November 1 a general order stabilizing prices, wages, and salaries on the basis of the levels of September 15, 1942. The subsequent order provided that salaries in excess of $5,000 could not be increased without the consent of the Stabilization Director and it prohibited those in excess of $25,000 net. Acting under the authority of the Act, the President created a new agency, the Office of Economic Stabilization, whose function was to formulate a comprehensive price program and to reconcile disagreements between agencies. Mr. Justice James F. Byrnes was persuaded to resign from the Supreme Court to become its director.

The relationship between Congress and the Administration deteriorated rapidly following the enactment of the Stabilization Act, and the Administration was confronted with a number of setbacks, some unassociated with price control. For example, the President requested Congress to enact a third war powers bill, but the bill was shelved by congressional committees and never brought to the floor for a vote. Congress repealed the order limiting salaries to $25,000 net. Nation-wide gasoline rationing became effective only after strong opposition from Congressmen. The farm groups continued their attempts to raise farm prices by changing the parity formula; they also sought to create a food czar independent of the Price Administrator. After the elections and the reverses they held for the Democrats, Senator Brown replaced Leon Henderson as Price Administrator. During the year Brown was in office, Congress harried the OPA with a series of investigations. All of these events were surely not anticipated by the President, or by his feckless advisers, when the "I will act" threat was made.

The refusal of Congress to enact the third war powers bill demonstrates how Congress began to stiffen its attitude toward Administration requests, even those closely associated with the conduct of the war. On November 2, a month following the enactment of the Stabilization Act, the President informed Congress that the war effort was being hampered by legislation which restricted the purchase of non-American articles and limited the free flow to our allies of information, personnel, and materials of war. He asked for temporary authority "to suspend the operation of all or any such laws" and the power to negotiate with other countries to take parallel action. Congress opposed such legislation on constitutional grounds, and there was the added fear that the President would use the power to scale down tariffs on farm products. After hearings were held, the legislation was not reported back, an action which Rep. Roy O. Woodruff (R., Bay City, Mich.) said would "go down in history as the first great step in the restoration of action by constitutional methods and procedures." [7]

Congressional irritability extended also to the introduction of gasoline rationing. In this case there was no question that the OPA had legal authority to act as it did, for it had been given the power to ration commodities in scarce supply. When rubber shortages developed, it was decided that nation-wide rationing of gasoline was a necessary conservation measure, and December 1, 1942, was set as the date for rationing to begin. Many members of Congress assumed an attitude more capricious than constructive in objecting to the plan; they wished to have the best of both worlds by opposing rationing without taking the responsibility for forbidding it by law. Was there not enough gasoline? There was. Then why should not one be permitted to wear out his own tires if he wished? Congressmen said that Director Jeffers had appealed "sentimentally" to the people to support rationing; that Administrator Henderson had accused the opponents of rationing of being "ignorant or intentionally traitorous"; that the war could not be won "if the New Dealers, with their foolish planning," continued in power; and that the war effort suffered because "Leon Henderson and his bunch of draft dodgers are shooting blanks at the American people." Despite this kind of opposition, the Congressmen did not attempt to prevent rationing by law, although

[7] C.R., Dec. 10, 1942, p. A4272.

this was well within their power. Once rationing went into effect, the protests disappeared, and as early as December 11 the Truman Committee found that the program of gasoline rationing was going well and "seems abundantly justified by the development of every passing day."

A more incisive form of congressional displeasure was shown toward the presidential order limiting salaries to $25,000 net. In this case, the opposition expressed itself in action as well as in words, and, as has been said, Congress proceeded to repeal the order. The conflict over limiting salaries pointed up the different opinion held by the President and Congress on the extent and type of financial sacrifice required of an individual as well as on the interpretation of the law. Was it necessary to reduce salaries on the basis of some concept of equality of sacrifice, as the President had suggested, or could the government rely on the high tax rates to balance out inequalities which might otherwise exist? Did the phrase in the Stabilization Act authorizing the President to adjust salaries so as "to correct gross inequities" mean that existing salaries could be reduced?

The President's enthusiasm for reducing large salaries seems to have been identified in his mind with a type of symbolic sacrifice, of setting an example of sacrifice by giving up something, such as the suspension of White House social activities during the war. The order reducing salaries would have produced relatively little revenue for the Treasury. When the idea was first broached in April, the President told Congress that in "this grave national danger, when all excess income should go to win the war," no one should have a net income after paying taxes in excess of $25,000.[8] Congress did not share the President's attitude, and it took no positive action to scale down salaries. When the price bill was before Congress in September, the Chairman of the Banking and Currency Committee was questioned closely on whether the proposed legislation would give the President power to limit salaries to $25,000 net. The Chairman, Representative Steagall, answered

[8] C.R., April 27, 1942, p. 3723.

that it was not so intended, and he did not believe "that the President of the United States would deliberately go against a clearly disclosed opinion of Congress." [9] On the other hand, Rep. Albert Gore (D., Carthage, Tenn.) said that Congress may have given the power to the President, and at the risk of being disrespectful he said that the intent of Congress seemed to be "to get rid of a hot potato by turning it over to the President." [10]

The order limiting salaries was roundly denounced in Congress; it was said to be "born out of class hatred"; it violated "our concepts of fundamental law"; it ignored "the expressed and well-known intent of Congress"; it "stifled American initiative." Congress repealed the order by amending a bill raising the debt limit, which was the type of legislation the President could not prudently veto. The Rules Committee was so anxious to repeal the limitation that it reported a rule whereby the bill and the amendment had to be accepted or rejected together; no provision was made for a separate roll call vote on the amendment. The chairman of the committee, Rep. Adolph J. Sabath (D., Chicago, Ill.), who had been outvoted, made the accusation that some Congressmen who did not want to take a public stand on the salary issue would vote differently were there to be a record vote. After being taken to task for this indiscreet remark, Sabath corrected himself to say that the members "had the courage to vote, and wanted to go on record." [11] But there was no separate vote. The House passed the bill, with the amendment, 268–129 (42 percent of the Democrats; 92 percent of the Republicans).

Time was such an important factor in the Senate that there was little controversy over the legislation. The Treasury wanted the debt limit raised immediately so that it could carry on its scheduled bond sale, an objective which Senator Barkley thought was "more important temporarily" than the controversy over the $25,000 limitation.[12] Senator George made it easier for the Senate to accept the amendment by citing case examples where individuals

---

[9] C.R., March 11, 1943, p. 1866.　　　[10] C.R., March 11, 1943, p. 1868.
[11] C.R., March 11, 1943, p. 1862.　　　[12] C.R., March 23, 1943, p. 2343.

who were committed to the regularized spending of large money outlays would suffer hardship by the salary limitation. The Senate passed the bill, as amended, by a vote of 74–3, and the bill became law without the President's signature.

During the great price control debate in September, no final agreement was reached on the composition of the parity formula, and farm groups continued to suggest modifications which would result in higher prices for the farmers. A bill proposed by Rep. Stephen Pace (D., Americus, Ga.) would have extended the scope of the cost of farm labor to include wages for the farmer's wife and the farmer's children as well as for the hired man. Some additional eight million people would have been classified as farm workers under the Pace formula. The House passed the Pace bill twice (in December, 1942, and in March, 1943); however, the Senate refused to pass the bill, for it was worried about the inflationary effect of the legislation and the precedent which would be created for increasing the wages of industrial workers.

Farm groups were also dissatisfied because the Administration included soil conservation payments in computing parity prices. Under the formula then in use, conservation payments were considered to be part of the farmers' income, the result being that parity ceilings were lower than if conservation payments had been excluded. A bill changing the method of computation had wide approval in Congress, passing the Senate by a vote of 78–2 and the House without a record vote. The President vetoed the bill, and he included in the veto message an extended legislative history of the controversy to show that the law had been followed in computing parity prices. The President also said that the inflationary effects of the bill would be to remove from the government "the power to prevent very substantial increases in food prices." Congress made no attempt to override the veto.

During the general guerilla warfare against OPA in 1943, it was proposed that Congress create a food czar with independent power over all aspects of the supply and distribution of food—farm prices, farm manpower, food rationing, transportation, and the supply of farm equipment. Control over farm prices would have been removed from the OPA and given to an administrator who, presumably, would be more sympathetic with the desires of the farmers. The Fulmer bill, which would have created such a czar, was reported to the House by the Agriculture Committee in June, 1943; it had the support of many Congressmen from farm areas as well as the Republican Food Study Committee, a partisan group appointed by the Republican leader, Rep. Joseph W. Martin. The Food Study Committee based its support in part on principles of administration, arguing that government control should be organized by commodities rather than by functions, but of course the war was too far along to destroy existing organizational patterns and start again from new principles of organization.

The Fulmer bill was looked on by the farm groups as an instrument for compelling the Administration to take a more favorable attitude toward the farmers and, as such, was connected with the crisis then developing in the Department of Agriculture. Mr. Chester C. Davis, who had the title of Food Administrator within the department, did not like the manner in which other agencies were developing policies on food prices and rationing. A delegation of Congressmen visited the President during this crisis, asking that a single administrator, presumably Davis, be given unified power over all aspects of food production. The President, however, was cool to the proposal and gave the delegation little encouragement. Following this conference, the House Committee on Agriculture reported the Fulmer bill, which would have created such a food czar by legislation. The next move belonged to the President: he accepted the resignation of Mr. Davis, who was denied a request for an interview, and appointed Mr. Marvin Jones as Food Administrator. Mr. Jones, a former member of Congress and Chairman of the House Committee on Agriculture, had many supporters in Congress and among the farm groups. Following the Jones appointment, Congress temporarily lost its interest in creating an independent food czar, only for it to revive again in 1945, when there were food shortages, in what was then known as the Hoover Plan.

After the election of 1942 Leon Henderson was replaced as Price Administrator by former Senator Prentiss M. Brown, who had failed to be reelected. This appointment was considered to be a step toward improving the relations between OPA and Congress: Brown would be aware of the issues in which Congress was most sensitive, and he had the additional qualification of being sympathetic with the price control program. A difficult year followed. A letter sent to Brown by David Ginsburg, the General Counsel of the OPA, reveals the tensions existing in the agency at that time and the belief that the OPA was being unjustly treated in a world where selfishness was rife. There was also apprehension that the new administrator would not be completely loyal to the old staff.

"Directly or indirectly, sooner or later," Ginsburg wrote to Brown, "every organized interest and pressure group in the country will bring its power to bear on you—first by what will appear to be appeals to reason, then by threats and if need be by force. Every decision which affects them adversely will come to be challenged before you or the Congress or the public as a threat to the war effort or the public interest perpetrated by a college professor or an inexperienced young lawyer." The various groups, Ginsburg added, "will try to divide you from your staff, and then try to undermine you and your staff separately." Brown was told that if he wished "to preserve the loyalty and support" of his staff it would be his "obligation to defend them as you defend yourself." [13]

Ginsburg continued as General Counsel, although the attitudes expressed in his letter would not seem to be those required for improving the relations with Congress, and he himself soon came under the lash of congressional criticism. All in all, Ginsburg was a vulnerable political target, for he was of draft age, being thirty-

[13] *C.R.*, March 24, 1943, p. A1395.

one years old at the time and with only a wife to support, and critics wanted to know why he was not in the Army. Later, when it appeared that he was to be given a direct commission and a preferred assignment, they wanted to know why he was being given special treatment. On another tack, the Smith Committee subpoened Ginsburg's private files and found that he had made plans for using price control as a method for controlling profits, an odious proposal to most members of Congress. More headlines. Whatever plans may have been underway for giving Ginsburg a direct commission and an attractive assignment were scuttled in the light of the harsh criticism in Congress, and Ginsburg entered the Army as a private.

OPA officials other than Ginsburg were also unpopular with Congress, the general complaint against them being that they lacked experience, wisdom, and moderation. Rep. August H. Andresen (R., Red Wing, Minn.) named some five employees in policy-making positions who, he claimed, "knew nothing about business, production, or distribution." [14] According to Rep. Frank B. Keefe (R., Oshkosh, Wis.), there were a "comparatively large number of dreamers" in the attorneys' section and the economists' section of the agency.[15] In order to meet this type of criticism, Congress added a rider to an appropriation bill which provided that the formulation of price policy should be limited to those "qualified by experience in business, industry, or commerce." A number of replacements were made subsequently as a result of the application of this new standard.

The job of administering a price control program would have been difficult under any conditions, but Senator Brown had the misfortune to take over the job during a period of great political discontent. He discovered that working under such conditions was overly strenuous, and he resigned within nine months, ending his letter of resignation with the laconic statement that he was an "expendable" in the war on the domestic front. He also noted that "the drive against OPA before House committees" had been

[14] C.R., May 6, 1943, p. 4075.   [15] C.R., May 6, 1943, p. 4075.

intense.[16] This was no overstatement, for the OPA was under continuous and extensive investigation, and it was considered open game for anyone having or claiming a grievance against bureaucracy. In the process of controlling prices and rents and rationing scarce commodities, the OPA could not be certain that justice prevailed in each individual case, and when some examples of maladministration were exposed to public scrutiny, the OPA often appeared to be bumbling and maladroit if not intentionally mischievous. On the other hand, it was not always clear whether the investigators wished only to improve OPA procedures by exposing delinquencies or whether they wished also to undermine confidence in the agency so that it might be the more readily scuttled.

The most active committee investigating the OPA was the so-called Smith committee, named after its chairman and sponsor, Rep. Howard W. Smith (D., Alexandria, Va.). Its official name was the "Special Committee to Investigate Acts of Executive Agencies Beyond the Scope of Their Authority," and Representative Smith thought the OPA met the specification of an agency which had exceeded its authority. The creation of the committee following the November elections produced some intemperate partisan bickerings, but the overwhelming majority in favor of creating the committee indicated how generally unpopular the bureaucrats were. The Chairman of the Rules Committee, Rep. Adolph J. Sabath (D., Chicago, Ill.) opposed the creation of the Smith Committee, but he had been outvoted in his own committee and again, as on several other occasions, was placed in the embarrassing position of reporting a rule which he himself disapproved. Sabath told the House that the resolution had been "forced through the Committee on Rules by those Democrats opposed to the President with the aid of Republican Members." Partisanship had entered the deliberations, and he found that the actions of the Republicans belied the assurances they had given their constituencies "that they would cooperate with the President in the winning

[16] *C.R.*, Oct. 25, 1943, p. A4481.

of the war." [17] On the other hand, many Congressmen favored creating the committee. Rep. Clifford R. Hope (R., Garden City, Kan.) said that it was "imperative" that Congress take steps to see that executive agencies follow the law in view of the "arrogant attitude" of some of the agencies and "their misuse of the power granted by Congress." [18] Rep. Charles A. Halleck (R., Rensselaer, Ind.) wanted to create a committee which would "ride herd" on the bureaucracy.[19] Rep. Leon H. Gavin (R., Oil City, Penn.) thought that the American people were entitled to relief from "this cancerous growth of bureaucracy" which was "eating the heart of our American way of life." [20] The resolution creating the Smith committee was adopted, 254–50 (73 percent of the Democrats; 100 percent of the Republicans).

The Smith committee was given wide jurisdiction to "ride herd" on the bureaucrats, for it was empowered to investigate any complaint of illegal administrative action or of the lack of opportunity of the accused to present his defense before a fair and impartial tribunal. The committee found that the OPA had been arbitrary and unfair in controlling rents, having a tendency to disregard the constitutional and legal rights of citizens and considering landlords generally as a "greedy and grasping class." It also found that the OPA had abused its authority in setting up a system of administrative tribunals in which the agency reviewed its own order and that price ceilings "were not generally fair." [21]

Another lively investigation was conducted by the Boren subcommittee of the House Committee on Interstate and Foreign Commerce as a result of which the OPA was compelled to give up grade labeling, a device for fixing prices on the basis of commodity standards. Grade labeling was opposed by manufacturers who did not wish to see their own brand-names replaced by a system of letters and numbers. The commitee also investigated the allocation of newsprint by the WPB, but it found no evidence that allocations had been based on political considerations.

[17] C.R., Feb. 11, 1943, p. 872.   [18] C.R., Feb. 11, 1943, p. 875.
[19] C.R., Feb. 11, 1943, p. 874.   [20] C.R., Feb. 11, 1943, p. 883.
[21] H. Rept. 699, July 27, 1943; H. Rept. 862, Nov. 15, 1943; H. Rept. 898, Nov. 29, 1943.

THE SUBSIDY CONTROVERSY

Prices continued to rise following the passage of the Stabilization Act in September, 1942. In the subsequent six-month period, the cost of living rose more than six percent, food prices thirteen percent, and fresh fruits and vegetables fifty-eight percent. To add to the inflationary alarm, farm and labor groups were asking for increases in their income. The farm groups, as we have seen, attempted to legislate an increase in farm prices by modifying the parity formula. The labor members of the War Labor Board first asked for a "realistic" wage increase and, subsequently, that the Little Steel formula be scrapped. Mine workers demanded a wage increase of two dollars a day in their new contract, and when they couldn't get it they closed the mines with a strike.

The Administration was faced with a crisis, a far more serious one than when the President had issued his challenge to Congress the preceding September. If prices continued to rise, many elements of the population would be forced on a lower standard of living and the economy would be ballooning its way toward inflation. If prices were stabilized, the government would have to exert greater control over prices, and perhaps even subsidize costs, and there was no assurance that Congress would approve a program of subsidizing people's grocery bills. The decision was to make a more vigorous attempt to control prices, and an order was issued on April 8, 1943, which was designed to hold the price line on all fronts. More important, the Administration decided to embark on a program of consumer price subsidies, even though such a program lacked the specific approval of Congress.

It may be argued that there was, in fact, a legal base for the subsidy program, but it cannot be argued that Congress supported the subsidy program initially. Later, it did. Things were topsy-turvy. The President instigated the program; Congress could end it only by overriding a presidential veto, and it failed twice to do this. One does not know how Congress might have reacted had it been given the initial responsibility for developing a program

of subsidies, based on specific legislation with specific funds authorized. As it was, Congress was given the devil's choice of accept-
ing as a fait accompli an unauthorized program whose legality
was questionable or of disapproving a program which, once established, could not readily be discontinued and which was in fact
helping keep prices stable.

In the subsidy program, the government purchased certain
commodities and resold them at less-than-purchase price, and in
some cases it assisted in paying certain costs, such as transportation. Funds for these expenditures were supplied by the Reconstruction Finance Corporation and the Commodity Credit Corporation, each having a large revolving fund which made them
independent of Congress for annual appropriations. The major control by Congress over the subsidy program came in extending the
life of these corporations or in replenishing their supply of capital.
As it happened, the law establishing the Commodity Credit Corporation expired during this period, but not that of the Reconstruction Finance Corporation.

The right to spend CCC and RFC money for consumer subsidies
was based on somewhat dubious interpretations of two Acts, passed
in 1940 and 1941, which authorized the payment of bounty prices
in order to acquire scarce commodities. The first Act authorized
the RFC to produce or acquire "strategic and critical materials,"
which were to be defined by the President; contrary to the standard use of the term, "strategic and critical materials" were later
defined so as to include domestic agricultural products. The second Act authorized the Price Administrator to "make subsidy
payments to domestic producers . . . to obtain the maximum
necessary production"; this was later interpreted to mean that
subsidies could be used to control prices as well as to increase
production.

The Administration's decision to engage in a program of roll-
backs and subsidies has certain elements of mystery about it. It is
not clear why the particular method was adopted which greatly
restricted congressional control over the program. Nor is it clear
why the opposition to the subsidy program on the part of the

responsible administrative officials seems to have been ignored. We are told in *The United States at War* that "Byrnes and Brown both agreed with Davis' opposition to the general subsidy program which the President had announced." James F. Byrnes was the former Director of Economic Stabilization and had recently been made Director of War Mobilization; Prentiss M. Brown was the Price Administrator; Chester C. Davis was the Food Administrator who "through an oversight, was not informed of the decision that had been made and learned of the subsidy program through a radio announcement." [22] That is an impressive group of officials opposed to initiating the subsidy program.

The "oversight" in informing Mr. Davis, if it was an oversight, extended also to Congress, for Congress was neither informed nor consulted on the establishment of the subsidy program. Someone, it seems, was being very highhanded at this point. Inasmuch as funds appropriated to the Commodity Credit Corporation were used to pay consumer subsidies, Congress had its first opportunity to consider the subsidy program in June, 1943, when the legislation creating the CCC was about to expire. The Commodity Credit Corporation was popular with Congress and especially with the farm representatives, for it supplied funds for the crop-support and incentive-payment programs. The friends of the CCC wished to continue the agency but to forbid the payment of consumer subsidies. Although there were larger issues at stake, the debate tended to be simplified into a conflict between country and city, between the rural farmer and the urban worker.

Rep. Clarence Cannon (D., Elsberry, Mo.) argued that the subsidy program was unfair to the farmers and that subsidies were favored by all groups trying to reduce the cost of living at the farmers' expense. All followed the same stereotype, he said, of picturing "the robbing, grabbing, profiteering farmer as rolling in unearned wealth" and attempting to starve the city dweller who, as a matter of fact, was "living in the greatest luxury today ever enjoyed by the average family in the history of the world." [23] In the opinion of Rep. Jesse P. Wolcott (R., Port Huron, Mich.),

[22] Pages 400 and 399. [23] *C.R.*, Nov. 23, 1943, p. 9882.

the subsidy program was a device for passing on to the oncoming generations the cost of the war. "Where is the American with blood so thin, may I say so yellow," he asked, "that he would pass on to posterity . . . the payment of any part of his grocery bill for food which you and I are eating today?" [24]

On the other side, it was argued that subsidies were needed to hold down the cost of living and to reduce the cost of the war. This group also vilified the opposition. Rep. Mary T. Norton (D., Jersey City, N.J.), the chairman of the House Labor Committee, said that the opposition to subsidies was easily understood "when you examine the reactionary lobby behind the opposition—the farm bloc in Congress, the farm lobbies, and the various trade interests, such as meat canners and packers." [25] The farm groups must "shoulder the responsibility if inflation engulfs the nation," said Rep. Thomas F. Ford (D., Los Angeles, Calif.), who thought that the opponents of consumer subsidies suffered from a "hate-Roosevelt phobia." [26]

After a good deal of debate of this nature, Congress adopted an amendment prohibiting the payment of consumer subsidies after June 30. The vote in the Senate was 39–37 (41 percent of the Democrats; 83 percent of the Republicans); there was no roll-call vote in the House, but a teller vote stood 160–106 against consumer subsidies.

The President vetoed the bill, the first of his two veto messages on subsidies. He found that the new legislation placed "new and unwarranted restrictions" on the use of funds and powers hitherto given to the Administration. This was not precisely correct, for with more accuracy it could have been said that the President had placed "new and unwarranted interpretations" on the power delegated to him. He thought the measure promoted inflation, high-cost-of-living, and food shortages. The way to protect the farmer, he said, was not to "oppress the consumer" but to allow the CCC "to pay the farmer what he should get for his products and to

[24] C.R., Nov. 17, 1943, p. 9687.   [25] C.R., Nov. 23, 1943, p. 9851.
[26] C.R., Feb. 17, 1944, p. 1846.

sell those products at a loss if need be to keep the costs of living down." [27] The President failed to get the support of a majority of the House, but the opponents of the subsidy program lacked the two-thirds majority necessary to override the veto. The vote to override was 228–154 (24 percent of the Democrats; 96 percent of the Republicans; 60 percent of the House). Congress then extended the CCC for six months and increased its borrowing power by $350 million. This meant that the Administration had further funds available for carrying on the subsidy program during the remainder of the year.

By December, 1943, the subsidy program was making payments at the rate of more than a billion dollars a year: $519 million for selling farm products at a loss, so that all costs would not be reflected in consumer prices; $51 million for subsidizing the transportation costs of corn, apples, and sugar; and $533 million for rolling back the consumer prices on butter, meat, and peanut butter. With the Commodity Credit Corporation expiring in December, Congress again had to determine the conditions for extending the CCC—with or without restrictions on paying consumer subsidies. The debate was again inconclusive, with a repetition of old arguments from old speeches; neither the composition of Congress nor the views of its members had changed sufficiently since June to make any significant difference in the decision on subsidies.

The bill reported by the House Banking and Currency Committee ended consumer subsidies on December 31, 1943, and the House passed this bill, 278–117 (49 percent of the Democrats; 91 percent of the Republicans). Because of its crowded agenda, the Senate was unable to act immediately on the CCC legislation, so, without prejudice, Congress enacted temporary legislation which extended the life of the CCC until February 17, 1944. Senator Barkley assured Congress that the subsidy program would not be expanded during the extension. In January, the Senate Banking and Currency Committee reported out a bill, the purpose of which, according to Senator Bankhead, was "to abolish what is commonly

[27] C.R., July 2, 1943, p. 7051.

known as consumer subsidies, nothing more and nothing less." [28] Senator Francis Maloney (D., Meriden, Conn.), who represented an industrial State, offered an amendment making $1.5 billion available for consumer subsidies, but his amendment was defeated, 26–49 (56 percent of the Democrats; 6 percent of the Republicans). Then the Senate passed the bill ending consumer subsidies by a vote of 43–28 (50 percent of the Democrats; 86 percent of the Republicans).

There was another veto. If the bill became law, the President said in his veto message, the price of food would increase seven percent, and with this increase the wage line could not be held and all costs, including those of munitions, would rise. The veto was upheld in the House, the vote to override being 226–151 (31 percent of the Democrats; 80 percent of the Republicans; 60 percent of the House). Following this, Congress enacted a bill continuing the CCC until June 30, 1945, which was agreed to in both chambers without a roll call vote. However, Senator Taft indicated that he would have more to say about subsidies later that year when Congress considered legislation extending price control. It would be impossible to veto an extension of the Price Control Act, even if it limited subsidies, Taft said, and he indicated his intention of joining price control and the subsidy program in the same legislation.

The expiration of price legislation in June, 1944, compelled Congress to review again the entire price control program. Legislation was enacted extending price control another year, and through the parliamentary adroitness of Senator Taft, legislation on subsidies was joined with legislation on price control. The OPA was not entirely popular with Congress, and Rep. William Lemke (R., Fargo, N.D.) went to the extreme of calling the OPA an "un-American illegitimate child" which had been "put over by an official clique in Washington that think more of foreign institutions than of our own," [29] but, all things considered, the new legislation was satisfactory to its supporters. Many Congressmen found

[28] C.R., Feb. 9, 1944, p. 1455.   [29] C.R., June 8, 1944, p. 5582.

themselves in an unenviable position in extending price control. If Congress were to satisfy many of the specific demands for price readjustments, the whole stabilization program would be shattered; if it were to ignore many of the demands, the political repercussions would be unwelcome. As it turned out, many amendments were approved by one chamber only and were deleted in conference, a process which might be described as a type of reverse logrolling, or of saying that if you do not scratch my back, I will not scratch yours.

Legislative procedures and tactics were especially important in extending price legislation because of the opportunities created for amending the legislation. The passage of the bill was not one act but a series of acts, in any one of which the scope and content of the bill could be affected. Following a controversy with the Rules Committee, the House adopted a rule for considering the price bill which permitted amendments to be offered freely. Two of the most controversial amendments related to a parity price for petroleum and the cost-plus-profit formula for fixing prices. Once there was agreement on the amendments, the price extension legislation was readily passed.

The controversy with the Rules Committee stemmed from the investigation of the OPA by the Smith Committee. The committee had made a series of legislative recommendations on price control which had been referred to the Banking and Currency Committee. This committee, in turn, had adopted some procedural recommendations but had rejected others on wage control and rent control. Under normal conditions, no more would have been heard of the legislative recommendations of the Smith Committee, but it happened that Representative Smith was also a member of the Rules Committee, where he had friends. A rule reported by this latter committee would have made it in order for any section of the Smith bill to be offered as an amendment to the price bill. In other words, the House was asked to consider a bill which had already been rejected by a legislative committee and had never been reported to the House. This was considered a brash proposal.

To add to the parliamentary confusion, Representative Smith gained the floor on a question of personal privilege immediately before the House was to vote on the rule. The newspaper columnist, Marquis Childs, had written that Smith's attempt to amend the price act had a "stealthy, skulking look," a phrase which, the Speaker said, raised a question of personal privilege. Smith was given an hour to answer the charges. After making some uncomplimentary remarks about "scandal mongers" who "sell their filth by attacking men in public life upon issues that may be before Congress," Smith went on to say that the House should be given an opportunity to vote on the results of the investigation of his committee, which had cost the taxpayers $50,000.[30] He then made a general attack on the OPA and a general defense of the findings of his committee.

This rhetoric failed to convince the House that the Rules Committee was not pushing its power too far. Of the several attacks on the proposed rule, the most compelling was made by the Speaker himself, Rep. Sam Rayburn (D., Bonham, Tex.), who asserted that the Committee on Rules "was never set up to be a legislative committee." If the issue were settled correctly, there would be "an end to the trespassing of one committee in the House upon the rights, prerogatives, and privileges of other committees." [31] The House followed Speaker Rayburn's advice and "settled the issue right"; on a division vote the proviso permitting the Smith bill to be offered as an amendment was defeated, 170–44.

The rule under which the House considered the price-control extension legislation permitted debate to continue for nine hours and made in order the consideration of any germane amendment. This wide-open rule was, indeed, a broadside invitation for all to try their luck in submitting amendments. Votes on amendments are taken quickly, without roll call votes, and the quorum is only a hundred. The tactical implications were that proponents of amendments had to mobilize their forces for a brief period of time only, whereas the defenders of the bill had to keep their forces

[30] *C.R.*, June 7, 1944, pp. 5461ff.   [31] *C.R.*, June 7, 1944, p. 5471.

mobilized continuously. Moreover, those who were handling the bill needed to have an intimate knowledge of the effect on price control of any particular amendment in order that they could argue persuasively. The burden of challenging amendments offered from the floor, and of explaining the economic consequences of their adoption, was assumed by a bipartisan group from the Banking and Currency Committee, including especially Rep. Brent Spence (D., Fort Thomas, Ky.), the new chairman; Rep. A. S. Mike Monroney (D., Oklahoma City, Okla.); Rep. Wright Patman (D., Texarkana, Tex.); and Rep. Jesse P. Wolcott (R., Port Huron, Mich.).

Some sixty amendments were offered from the floor of the House, of which more than two thirds were defeated at the time by a voice vote. An itemization of some of the amendments offered shows the wide range of price modification which was proposed. The amendments included a plan to provide a "reasonable profit" for farmers; a return to selective price control; the exemption of fresh fishery commodities, rice, raw fur, strawberries, peaches, cherries, raspberries, blackberries, currants, grapes, and, as a spoof, the exemption of all farm products of Hartford County, Connecticut; the exemption of sales by auctioneers and by inductees; the restriction of price control to articles in the cost-of-living index; and the assurance of a margin of profit in pricing any commodity.

The petroleum industry had been attempting for some time to secure an increase in the price of crude oil, and now another attempt was made. The previous year, Rep. Wesley E. Disney (D., Tulsa, Okla.) told the House that he was under the "definite impression that the price would be raised without legislation." However, the increase was not forthcoming, and the House thereupon passed the Disney bill creating a petroleum czar and establishing a new base for oil prices. The Senate took no action on the bill. The amendment offered to the price bill in 1944 proposed that the price of petroleum be based on the parity relationship which existed in the so-called 1926 all-commodity index, which provided a standard very favorable to petroleum. If this new standard were applied generally, wages would be found to be 183.6 percent of the 1926 "parity"; lumber, 144.1 percent; raw materials, 113.6 percent, and petroleum, 63.8 percent. Representative Disney said he was willing to hold prices stable once a "just" standard had been established, but he found the present price line was "illegitimate, unfair, and dishonest." [32] Senator Tom Connally (D., Marlin, Tex.) put the case for oil on the basis of its competitive position with coal, where a rise in prices had followed an increase in wages. "In the case of oil," Connally complained, "we are told 'No, we froze you back yonder in 1941, and when frozen you have to stay frozen. We have given you the "birdseye" treatment, and you have to keep it up.' " [33] Senator Elmer Thomas (D., Medicine Park, Okla.) suggested that votes in favor of parity for petroleum would be reciprocated, and he offered to vote for other amendments adjusting prices "to the end that all our people and all the products of their labor shall be treated comparably and equally." [34]

Rep. A. S. Mike Monroney (D., Oklahoma City, Okla.), who also came from an oil state, thought that the new proposal was "startling." If the 1926 all-commodity index were to be the standard for fixing prices, he said, then a number of commodities would also have to be raised, including aluminum, magnesium, rayon fabrics, and electric power. It would cost more than $11 billion to raise some eleven items to the "parity" of 1926, and this price increase would further destroy the price relationship. "When we raise an important commodity up to the general average, which is the line, we then raise the line a little bit higher," and he asked whether Congress was fighting inflation or the OPA.[35] Senator Taft thought that at least a dozen industries had presented to the committee a stronger case for price increases. In the end, both Houses voted against the parity-for-petroleum amendment; the

---

[32] *C.R.*, Dec. 13, 1943, pp. 10608ff.; *C.R.*, June 10, 1944, p. 5701.
[33] *C.R.*, June 9, 1944, p. 5628.   [34] *C.R.*, June 9, 1944, p. 5624.
[35] *C.R.*, June 10, 1944, p. 5708.

vote in the House was 178–204 (34 percent of the Democrats; 58 percent of the Republicans) and in the Senate, 25–42 (40 percent of the Democrats; 33 percent of the Republicans).

Another unsuccessful amendment proposed that cotton textiles be priced so that the textile industry as a whole would secure a reasonable profit. This proposal came from an unusual source— Senator Bankhead, of Alabama, who in the past had vigorously represented the interests of the cotton grower. Bankhead reasoned that the manufacturer would increase his production of cotton goods if he had a guaranteed profit, and this in turn would lead to an increased demand for raw cotton. He did not think that buyers would resist paying higher prices for finished cotton goods because those commodities were generally scarce and money was plentiful. The opponents of the amendment argued that there was no assurance that the cotton grower would be paid more for raw cotton, even if the cotton manufacturer made a larger profit. Moreover, it was said that if the profits for the cotton textile industry as a whole were guaranteed, the low-cost producer would receive excessive profits. The Senate agreed to the amendment, 39–35 (48 percent of the Democrats; 59 percent of the Republicans); the New England delegation, representing an area with large textile interests, was evenly split in its vote. The House did not pass the amendment, and the proposal was dropped in the conference committee.

Senator Taft was especially keen on including a provision which would guarantee reasonable profits in setting prices. His theory, briefly, was that prices should reflect the same profit per commodity which had existed at some prior period. Taft claimed that prices were not "generally fair and equitable," as the law said they should be, if they did not reflect a reasonable profit or if existing inequities were frozen.[36] His theory viewed any general freezing of prices as undesirable; prices should be allowed to rise gradually to compensate for the various inequities which developed.

Senator Taft was also primarily responsible for the provision

[36] C.R., June 9, 1944, p. 5619.

that in the future Congress would have to appropriate funds for the subsidy program. The Administration hoped to avoid another controversy over subsidies, for the legislation authorizing the Commodity Credit Corporation still had more than a year to run. Senator Barkley told the Senate that "in an informal way we had agreed in the committee to avoid a revival of the subject of subsidies." [37] The committee, however, had considered the subject of subsidies on an occasion when Barkley was absent, and it reported the price bill with Senator Taft's amendment. The amendment provided simply that after June 30, 1945, the date when the Commodity Credit Corporation expired, funds for the payment of subsidies would have to be specifically approved by Congress.

In Senator Taft's opinion, sentiment in Congress was increasingly favorable toward subsidies, and he said he would have been happy to have voted for "a reasonable sum" had he been given the opportunity. Senator Francis Maloney (D., Meriden, Conn.) opposed the Taft amendment on the grounds that Congress was not equipped to deal with such an intricate topic as subsidies. "It would be a very serious mistake," Maloney said, "to take away from the Office of Price Administration a subject which it has, through long experience, learned much about, and in effect turn the entire matter back to a Congress which cannot be so well informed as is the Office of Price Administration." [38] This type of objection was a set-up for Taft. "I understand the Senator to say that he is in favor of the Administration spending money whenever Congress refuses to appropriate it," Taft said to Maloney. "The only purpose of this amendment is to return to Congress the power over the purse strings." [39] The Taft amendment was adopted, 50–22 (49 percent of the Democrats; 100 percent of the Republicans), and it appeared in the final bill.

In 1945, price control and subsidies were less contentious issues than in former years, and the legislative controversy was relatively tranquil. The surprising feature of the debate was the cheer-

[37] *C.R.*, June 9, 1944, p. 5619.   [38] *C.R.*, June 9, 1944, p. 5294.
[39] *C. R.*, June 9, 1944, p. 5294.

ful manner in which funds were authorized for the subsidy program. The debate was quite serene; the opposition negligible. This turn-about was due to the fact that farm groups now supported subsidies, and whatever opposition remained to subsidies was without effective representation. An explanation of the change in attitude on subsidies was given the House by Rep. Frank B. Keefe (R., Oshkosh, Wis.), who had formerly opposed subsidies as a national policy. "In view of the position the producers have been placed in through the Administration's adoption of this policy," he said, "we must now support the program and continue payment of subsidies or the whole agricultural economy will collapse." [40] And Senator Bankhead told the Senate that "all the farm organizations are together in support of it." [41] The major opposition came, oddly enough, from Representative Sabath, who had formerly championed subsidies so vigorously. Sabath thought it ridiculous to subsidize the dairy industry "for the various makeshift concoctions of cheese now appearing in the market." [42] The vote in the Senate in favor of subsidies was unanimous; the vote in the House was 358–8 (100 percent of the Democrats; 95 percent of the Republicans). Eight votes only against consumer subsidies!

Similarly, the debate on extending price control in 1945 was relatively tranquil and less contentious than in former years. When the bill was before the House, some members were interested in discussing subjects other than OPA; this was a sure sign that interest in price control was flagging and that the standards under which the program was operating were generally acceptable. The principal debate issue was the procedures followed by OPA, and the belief was widely held in Congress that some of the problems of price control could be resolved by improvements in administrative procedures rather than by changes in the basic law. The House committee recommended no change whatever in existing legislation, although it promised to reappraise the law if "serious administrative shortcomings appear which are not

[40] C.R., March 9, 1945, p. 1964.   [41] C.R., Feb. 5, 1945, p. 794.
[42] C.R., March 12, 1945, p. 2051.

promptly corrected by administrative action." The Senate committee suggested that it meet with the Price Administrator and his staff every three months; the House committee wanted "to keep in close touch with the operations of the Price Administrator and to meet with the Administrator to discuss its problems." [43] Price Administrator Chester Bowles made a favorable impression on Congress, partly because he readily acknowledged mistakes made by OPA and volunteered to correct others which were pointed out to him.

[43] H. Rept. 764, June 19, 1945.

5. Higher Taxes
and Lower Profits

FIGHTING A WAR required money as well as men, and the necessity of supplying money raised several problems which were very complicated indeed. If we had been living in a primitive society where the soldier provided his own food to eat and his own knobkerrie to fight with, we could have fought the war and paid for it at the same time. In our more complicated society, we could not pay for the war with the sacrifices of the soldier or with the booty of the conquered. Material to fight the war was supplied by institutions which the soldier did not own and which continued on into the peacetime world. The materials had to be bought; the men who made the materials, on farm or factory, had to be paid. All of this required money.

The picture of wartime economic policy may be clarified by showing the interrelation of its various parts. A large share of the funds for the war (about 60 percent) were raised by borrowing money, and at the end of the war a national debt was outstanding of approximately $280 billion. It was sometimes said in congressional discussions of the debt that a policy of borrowing meant that "future generations" were being asked to pay for the war. Inasmuch as it was unlikely that any future government would undertake to pay off the great debt, or most of it, through taxation, the effect on future generations would probably be an inflationary rise in prices. In any event, the creation of the very sizable debt greatly expanded the credit available and bequeathed to future politicians some added headaches in determining fiscal policy.

Congress showed little interest in the source of Treasury borrowing, although it provided a legal base for such borrowings. Congress raised the debt limit in 1942 to $125 billion; in 1943 to $210 billion; in 1944 to $260 billion; and in 1945 to $300 billion. When Congress considered this legislation, there was little reflective debate on the long-time effect of borrowing money to pay for the war. An exception, perhaps, was the brief backward glance by Senator Taft, who commented in 1945 that "we may question now whether the policy we have pursued was a wise policy." Not enough taxes had been raised, although he had "always felt that we could have increased the taxes by at least $10 billion a year without serious hardship." However, Congress and the President had not been able to agree on the kind of tax bill to be adopted, and in any event there would have been a tremendous deficit. "Any increase in taxes, applied by a uniform rule," Senator Taft said, "was bound to fall with drastic severity on some, even though a large number of others were perfectly able to stand it." [1]

Although Congress took little interest in the Treasury's borrowing policy, it was very much interested in the sources and rate of taxation and in the rate of profit. In the 1930s, when the Administration advocated a policy of spending, many Congressmen claimed that there was a fiscal limit beyond which government borrowing would lead to debt repudiation. The situations were somewhat reversed in the war, with the Administration advocating greater taxes and less borrowing and its opponents losing some of their concern over a large debt. "Balance the Budget" as a political slogan was an early war casualty.

The fiscal policy followed in the war was determined by a multitude of decisions on taxes, profits, government bond sales, prices, wages, and appropriations. The decisions were made over a period of time, and in each case the various congressional committees

[1] C.R., March 26, 1945, p. 2767.

had some part to play in making the policy. The pattern of power within Congress (and within the Administration, too) was not designed for developing an integrated fiscal policy, and in general the emphasis placed on the different aspects of the great fiscal mosaic was quite uneven. It was easier to spend than to tax, for instance, and decisions on spending were frequently made without considering the effect on the tax rate or the future debt. Those interested in production and the maintenance of industrial peace may have been more concerned with raising wages than with the inflationary effect of a higher wage rate. Those interested in controlling prices were willing to borrow money for maintaining price stability, regardless of the effect a greater debt might have on future price policy. In considering the proper rate on profits, committees were often more interested in equity and motivation than in tax revenue. Tax policy was developed independently, the major interest being the source and the rate of taxation, and those who made tax policy were not in a position to affect the flow of income into the economy.

RATE OF PROFIT

From the early part of the defense period, the fiscal committees of Congress were interested in the rate of profit that should be permitted on war contracts, and this entirely apart from the amount of revenue which would be produced by restricting profits. An attempt was made to distinguish between war profits and normal profits; the former were considered "exorbitant," the latter, permissive, and the permissive rate was usually set at seven or eight percent of the gross. A subsidiary issue was whether Congress should rely on high tax rates to recapture war profits or whether the rate of profit would be set low in the initial contract, as Mr. Bernard Baruch had argued. Later, Congress enacted legislation which permitted contracts producing an extraordinarily high rate of profit to be renegotiated.

Stories of war millionaires and munitions profiteers created in the First World War were part of the political lore of the times, and there was a general resolve in Congress to prevent similar developments in the current war. On the whole, a war millionaire was a conspicuous oddity and more likely to be a cartoonist's stereotype than an actuality. On the other hand, some corporations were making large profits on defense contracts, especially on those where the rate of earnings could not be clearly anticipated when the initial contract was made. In the early months of the war, several congressional committees investigated instances where defense contracts had produced extraordinarily high profits. A sample survey made by the House Naval Affairs Committee showed that more than half of the firms reporting had realized an average net profit in excess of 7 percent. The profit on individual contracts was in many cases more than 50 percent and ranged as high as 247 percent. The committee recommended that Congress enact legislation eliminating profiteering on defense contracts.

The Truman Committee was interested in examining the fees received by contract brokers for their assistance in securing war contracts. It presented one case of a contract broker who was to receive one percent of the gross sales of a corporation, which in 1941 amounted to more than $70 million. The committee concluded that while legitimate services were given in many cases, in other cases "the payments . . . can be treated only as compensation for influence." [2]

In order to meet some of the issues raised by these investigations, Congress enacted legislation more closely regulating contracts and profits. Contracts based on cost-plus-a-percentage-of-cost had been shown to be wasteful and were abolished. Contracts based on cost-plus-a-fixed-fee were limited to a fee of seven percent of the estimated cost of the contract. Contracts over $100,000 could be renegotiated when profits could be determined "with reasonable certainty."

As the war progressed, the verve for stringently regulating profits was replaced by concern that the contractor was not being given his day in court and that the heavy taxation of profits would

[2] S. Rept. 480, Part 5, Jan. 15, 1942, p. 73.

adversely affect postwar employment. There were increasing demands that the minimum-sized contract subject to renegotiation be raised (so as to help small business) and that taxes, rather than contract renegotiation, be used for absorbing excess profits. A statement made in 1943 by Rep. Wesley E. Disney (D., Tulsa, Okla.) illustrates this change in attitude. Paramount to the principle "that no inordinate, undue profit should be made out of any war effort," Disney said, was the principle that "when this war is over men returning from the service may have jobs." This could not be done if profits were cut too deeply. Disney added that the lack of a precise meaning for excessive profits meant that "the American system of free enterprise" was "completely at the mercy of the social views of whoever happens to have the job of determining excessive profits." [3]

The renegotiation law was revised in 1943. The minimum size of the contract subject to renegotiation was increased to $500,000; standards for determining excessive profits were written into the law; a War Contracts Price Adjustment Board, composed of representatives of the six agencies concerned, was created to exercise general control over renegotiation; and contractors were allowed to appeal their cases *de novo* to the Tax Court of the United States. The change in emphasis was reflected in the termination date of December 31, 1944—with the President empowered to extend the law for six months—whereas the initial law continued renegotiation for three years after the war. The repricing of articles was separated from renegotiation procedure. Wherever a department head believed a price to be unreasonable or unfair, he could require the contractor to enter negotiations for fixing a fair price. During the debate on these revisions there was a recurrent theme that renegotiation procedure could be arbitrary, and in the opinion of Senator Bennett Champ Clark (D., University City, Mo.) the procedure was "pure and undefiled" bureaucracy. However, after personally examining some 150 cases, Senator Clark found that there had been "remarkably meritorious performance" so far

[3] C.R., Nov. 24, 1943, p. 9927.

as achievement was concerned, and in the main he found the results "fair to contractors" and in some cases "more than fair." [4]

THE REVENUE ACT OF 1942

Congress enacted three major tax bills during the war—the Revenue Act of 1942, the Current Tax Payment Act of 1943 (the Ruml Plan), and the Revenue Act of 1943; it also enacted the Tax Adjustment Act of 1945, which pertained largely to rebates and reconversion. When the Revenue Act of 1942 was enacted, there was some dissatisfaction because it was believed it didn't go far enough, and many resolves were made to levy heavier taxes in the future. These resolves were somewhat modified by later events.

Congress deliberated tax legislation for a good part of the year 1942. The Ways and Means Committee began its deliberations in early March and continued for more than four months, and the new bill of some 575 pages became law in late October. The bill was described by Chairman Robert L. Doughton (D., Laurel Springs, N.C.) as "the largest single piece of revenue legislation ever undertaken by our government or the government of any nation." [5] It was anticipated that it would raise some $11 billion, making the total annual tax revenue more than $26 billion.

The debate on the tax legislation was extended, tedious, technical, and frequently acrimonious, and the passage of the bill increased political tensions perceptibly. Charges were made that the Administration had been unrealistic and dilatory in making its tax requests and that it had frequently changed its mind during the debate. For instance, the Treasury had opposed compulsory savings in March but supported a spending tax in September. It was also charged that the new legislation struck too heavily at the lower-income groups, that it would ruin small business, and that it did not effectively prevent the massing of great profits by large corporations.

A wide variety of proposals was considered during the deliberations. A sales tax was supported by the National Association of

[4] C.R., Jan. 21, 1944, p. 534.   [5] C.R., Oct. 6, 1942, p. 7793.

Manufacturers and the United States Chamber of Commerce but not by congressional committees. A plan for withholding taxes at the source (later achieved in the Ruml plan) was rejected, but a modified version was adopted in the form of a so-called five percent Victory Tax. No change was made in the subjects of perennial tax controversy—community property taxation, depreciation allowance for oil wells and mines, and the exemption of the income from State and local bonds.

The tax rate on corporate income proved to be a contentious subject, and the ranking minority member of the Ways and Means Committee, Rep. Harold Knutson (R., St. Cloud, Minn.) said that the formula "was arrived at through a series of trades and shameless log-rolling." [6] Before the war it was frequently said in Congress that excess profits should be taxed at a rate of 100 percent, but Congress was told during the current hearings that such a high rate would result in business inefficiency. The final Act provided that excess profits should be taxed at a rate of 90 percent, with a postwar credit allowance of 10 percent and a limitation of all taxes to 80 percent of net income. The combined normal tax and surtax for the highest bracket was placed at 40 percent; the former combined rate for the same bracket was 31 percent.

The rule under which the House considered the bill allowed only the Ways and Means Committee to submit admendments. The rule was opposed by those who wanted a stiffer tax bill, such as Rep. Karl E. Mundt (R., Madison, S.D.), who suggested that the rule be modified so that members could offer amendments to increase the tax rates proposed. Rep. Robert F. Rich (R., Woolrich, Pa.), who ordinarily played the role of professional economizer and tax-cutter, said that pressures on the members of the Ways and Means Committee had prevented the committee from reporting an adequate tax bill. He realized that levying heavier taxes "may mean defeat for some of you men," but he thought it also might save the country.[7]

Although various segments of the legislation were controversial,

[6] H. Rept. 2333, July 14, 1942, p. 187.   [7] C.R., July 16, 1942, p. 6260.

the bill as a whole received wide support. It passed the House, 395–2, and the Senate, 77–0. The 1942 tax bill neither represented Congress' best effort nor was it considered its final effort, and, indeed, Representative Sabath told the House that this was not the end but "just the beginning."

THE RUML PLAN

When Congress met in January, 1943, the recently proposed Ruml plan was the major topic of conversation about taxes. The unique feature of the Ruml plan was its proposal to make everyone current in his tax payments, and on a pay-as-you-go basis, through the simple device of skipping a year's tax payments. Everyone would be current in his tax obligations to the government, and the government would, in turn, collect taxes as income was earned rather than collect it on the previous year's earnings.

The originator of this unorthodox tax scheme was Beardsley Ruml, treasurer of R. H. Macy & Co. and chairman of the Federal Reserve Board of New York. The Ruml plan caught fire, as the saying goes, and it was advanced as a crusade by large sections of the press and other communications media. The plan was also popular with many segments of the new Congress, and especially with the Republicans, and it was adopted by Congress in 1943 against the opposition of the Administration and the Democratic leadership. Although the legislation changed the method of tax collection and the year on which taxes were assessed, it neither altered the tax rate nor produced additional revenue. Congress consumed its energies in the controversy over the Ruml plan without, at the same time, enacting a tax bill which would raise adequate revenue to meet the expenses of the war.

Part of the appeal of the Ruml plan lay in the simple solution it offered for collecting taxes, one far more suitable for a payroll type of economy than the cumbersome method then in use. Previously, taxes were ordinarily paid in four installments on money earned the previous year—that is, taxes on 1942 incomes would be paid in installments in 1943. This leisurely method of paying taxes was not designed for a wartime economy. The 1942 tax bill had created some twenty-five million new taxpayers who were unaccustomed to saving a share of their earnings for paying taxes. New war workers could spend currently their entire 1943 income, and the 1943 taxes would be paid from the earnings of the following year. It was now generally agreed that taxes on wage incomes, at least, should be collected at the source; this would assist in the fight against inflation by absorbing free cash which otherwise might be spent for scarce commodities, and it would also help Treasury collections.

The Ruml plan offered a method for establishing a pay-as-you-go system, the need for which was especially acute just at that time. On the other hand, a pay-as-you-go system could have been established without altering the tax year, but there was no general agreement on any alternative method. Neither the Administration nor the tax leaders in Congress had a single plan which was supported consistently, so that the congressional debate was concerned primarily with efforts to modify the Ruml plan. The Ruml saga suggested that the alternative to skipping a tax year was the collection of two years' taxes in one year, although no one advocated this frightening alternative. As an illustration of the tenacious existence of this idea one may cite the comments of George Gallup, the pollster, that the Ruml plan was merely a "bookkeeping device" which "would avoid the problem of trying to collect two years' taxes—1942 and 1943—in the same year.[8]

Was the plan merely a "bookkeeping device," as Mr. Gallup had called it, which would affect neither the income of the Treasury nor the obligations of the taxpayers? Or was common sense right in supposing that the Treasury would lose and the taxpayers would gain if the taxes on an entire year were forgiven? Mr. Ruml claimed that his plan of making taxpayers current—"free of income-tax debt," as he called it—could be accomplished "without hurting the Treasury and without paying two years' taxes in one." [9] Mr. Ruml *seemed* to be correct, for undoubtedly taxes would continue

[8] *C.R.,* Jan. 26, 1943, p. A323.   [9] *C.R.,* Oct. 15, 1942, p. A3710.

to roll in; indeed, the Treasury would have collected more in 1943 than it would have otherwise, inasmuch as the tax base of the 1943 national income was higher than for 1942.

The answer to this puzzler of loss or gain is that the Treasury would have faced an over-all, long-time, theoretical loss by the adoption of the Ruml plan, and some individuals would have gained an immediate tax benefit, but this loss was difficult to demonstrate without the use of logarithms and longevity tables. All taxpayers who were "forgiven" a year of tax payment would, during their lifetime, have one less year on which to pay taxes. The amount of loss cannot be calculated with any degree of precision, but it would be roughly equivalent to the 1942 yield, spread over the tax-paying lifetime of all who were then paying taxes. However, one could not readily win political debates with this type of argument.

Although it was difficult to show how the Treasury would lose money from the plan, it was easy to show that some individuals would gain financially by skipping a year's taxes. Here is what would happen. The tax windfall was available at once to those who had saved cash in 1942 for the tax payments due in 1943. By canceling the 1942 tax liability, the tax payments for an entire year would be available for consumer spending. If all taxpayers had been foresighted, some $15 billion would have been available immediately, but in practice the savings were unevenly distributed. Those who had failed to save for tax payments would receive their windfall in the year following their last year of earnings. In other words, all current taxpayers would have gained a tax year; taxes for "last year" would always be paid up.

The question was raised during the House debate of whether the Ruml plan would be of more benefit to the wealthy than to those in the lower income brackets. Rep. Daniel A. Reed (R., Dunkirk, N.Y.) answered this by inserting in the *Record* a series of questions and answers, including a somewhat equivocal answer to this particular poser. If the theory of progressive tax rates was sound, Reed said, the theory of progressive tax forgiveness was also sound. All taxpayers would be treated alike "in the sense that the basis for his 1943 tax is his current income rather than his past year's income." [10] Rep. Robert L. Doughton (D., Laurel Springs, N.C.), the Chairman of the Ways and Means Committee and a strong opponent of Rumlism, argued that "the very wealthy would derive a windfall equal to five or six years' income after taxes" and that taxpayers with million-dollar incomes "would each pocket a gift from their government of at least $850,000." [11]

In the debate on the issue, the House proved to be anti-Ruml by a small margin and the Senate pro-Ruml by a considerable margin. In the House, the Ways and Means Committee first reported a bill which we may call Doughton Plan No. 1. Representative Doughton said that his committee had been unable to agree on "the novel proposal originating in the brain of the great self-proclaimed tax expert and prophet, Beardsley Ruml, of the House of Macy, calling for complete forgiveness of at least one year's taxes on incomes which have already been earned and enjoyed by the taxpayer." At the same time, Doughton emphasized that the bill he reported was the handiwork of the committee alone; the Treasury Department had at no time "presented any bill or attempted to usurp the prerogatives of our committee or shown any special favoritism toward any bill." [12]

Doughton Plan No. 1 attempted to establish a pay-as-you-go scheme without forgiving a year's taxes. A tax of twenty percent would be deducted from salaries at the source, with the taxpayer having the option of applying the deduction to the present or the past year's assessment. As an inducement "to become current," —even Doughton had succumbed to the Ruml terminology—the bill provided a sliding-scale of discounts which were to be applicable in paying the previous year's tax bill. The House thought this plan did not go far enough in "abating tax payments"—the accepted euphemism for skipping a tax year—and it voted to recommit the bill to committee. The vote was 248–168 (21 percent

[10] C.R., March 26, 1943, p. 546.   [11] C.R., March 25, 1943, p. 2491.
[12] C.R., March 25, 1943, p. 2491.

of the Democrats; 96 percent of the Republicans). An attempt to substitute the Ruml bill was likewise defeated, 198–215 (92 percent of the Democrats; 13 percent of the Republicans).

The Ways and Means Committee subsequently reported Doughton Plan No. 2, which provided still another method for the taxpayer to become "current." The rates in the Revenue Act of 1942 were not to be applicable until 1943, and pay-as-you-go would be adopted. By this device, the 1942 tax burden would be reduced by some $5 billion, but the 1942 tax would nevertheless have to be paid within a period of three years. Representative Doughton defended this proposal as a compromise between his first plan, which was rejected because it did not go far enough in making taxpayers current, and the Ruml plan, which provided too large an amount of forgiveness. However, the House rejected the second Doughton plan also. A motion to recommit Doughton Plan No. 2 and report the Forand-Robertson bill was carried, 230–180 (21 percent of the Democrats; 92 percent of the Republicans).

The so-called Forand-Robertson bill would have canceled the past tax obligations of the first income tax bracket, and in the future 19 percent of salaries and wages would be collected at the source. This plan would have made 89 percent of the taxpayers current; another 9 percent would become current by paying a balance of less than $100. Taxes in the higher brackets—from the second on—would not be forgiven, and those taxes could continue to be paid in the year following the earnings. The major difference between this and the Ruml plan was not in the amount but in the method of tax forgiveness, and the windfall gains would accrue to a different class of taxpayers. This distinction was defended by Rep. A. Willis Robertson (D., Lexington, Va.), a conservative cosponsor of the bill, who argued that forgiveness in the lower brackets could be offset by higher tax rates on the same income group in later years; forgiveness in the top brackets could not be similarly offset because those rates were already very high. He concluded, therefore, that "forgiveness of large amounts for persons in the higher income brackets thus inevitably means a redistribution of tax burden from higher to lower incomes." [13]

The Forand-Robertson bill had wide support, ranging from conservative Republicans to CIO labor leaders. The Ruml proponents preferred this plan to either of the Doughton plans, and there also was the chance that the Ruml plan would be victorious in the conference committee. Many Ruml opponents preferred this plan to straight Rumlism or to the Doughton plans. The House accepted the Forand-Robertson bill by a vote of 313–95 (60 percent of the Democrats; 94 percent of the Republicans).

The Senate Finance Committee reported a bill which contained the essential features of the Ruml plan. Senator George, who reported the bill, found fault with the Forand-Robertson bill because it discriminated between different groups of taxpayers and illustrated his point by referring to three hypothetical taxpayers. The taxpayer earning $3,200 would have 100 percent of his 1942 tax liability canceled; one earning $25,000 would have less than 50 percent canceled; one earning $1 million, 22 percent. Was this equality? Senator Vandenberg added that the Finance Committee had taken the principle of abatement and applied the principle "to every American taxpayer under the flag. It wiped out the last lingering trace of discrimination." [14] The tide seemed to be running strong for the Ruml plan, among the public as well as Congress, and Senator Barbour said that his own State of New Jersey appeared to favor the Ruml plan by a ratio of ten to one.

There were a few dissenters in the Senate. Senator Connally found himself in what he called "a small minority," one who did not accept the thesis that it was necessary to forgive taxes or make all taxpayers current in order to establish a pay-as-you-go system. If a philologist were to make a microscopic analysis of such terms as "abatement," "forgiveness," "giving away," "discharge," or other similar expressions, Connally maintained, one would find that they all meant that "the Government is going to lose the money, and if it loses the money, somebody is going to

[13] C.R., March 11, 1943, p. A1141.   [14] C.R., May 12, 1943, p. 4272.

get it." [15] However, all substitute plans were voted down, and the Senate passed the Ruml plan, 48–31 (38 percent of the Democrats; 91 percent of the Republicans).

It was now left to the conference committee to develop a compromise between the House and the Senate versions of the tax bill. This was not easy to do, as it turned out, and there was general testimony to the effect that the tax bill was one of the most difficult, controversial, and troublesome bills ever before a tax conference committee. During the long conference negotiations, there was never a unanimous vote, and the only vote commanding a majority was the final one. On this vote, the Senate conferees stood together; Representative Doughton voted with the Republican members, and they in turn voted with the Senate. The controversy continued on the floor, although the conference report was adopted by both Houses.

The compromise was a virtual victory for the principle of the Ruml plan, qualified by limitations on the extent of forgiveness to be granted. The plan called for the cancelation of three-fourths of the 1942 taxes due and of all remaining amounts less than $50. The remaining fourth of the 1942 tax bill had to be paid within two years.

One of the odd features of the controversy over the Ruml bill was that it was so soon forgotten. The issues at stake were so complicated and the nature of the windfall gains so indeterminate that, in subsequent political campaigns, the Ruml plan was not a contested election issue.

THE REVENUE ACT OF 1943

The enactment of the Ruml plan took its toll of congressional emotions and energies, and there was no longer very much verve in Congress for levying heavier taxes. The Ruml plan was not a measure for increasing tax revenue, and after the passage of this controversial bill it was still necessary to raise more money. On October 4, after the Ruml plan was well out of the way, the Treas-

[15] C.R., May 12, 1943, p. 4272.

ury Department requested the harassed Ways and Means Committee to raise $10.5 billion in new taxes. The committee was not sympathetic with the size of the request or the proposed source of tax revenue, and, by a vote of 16–9, it decided to develop its own tax bill without Treasury advice or assistance.

The tax bill subsequently reported by the Ways and Means Committee would raise some $2.1 billion in additional revenue, which was far short of the Treasury request. In the subsequent debate, comparisons were made between the "reasonable" bill reported by the committee and the "unreasonable and unrealistic" proposals of the Treasury Department, and Rep. Hamilton Fish (R., Garrison, N.Y.) congratulated "those sound and wise Democrats" who had joined with the Republicans in "opposing the preposterous and communistic proposal of the Secretary of the Treasury to virtually limit net incomes to $10,000." If the Treasury plan had been approved, Fish said, it "would have put us on a level with the Communists." [16]

In defending the bill, Representative Doughton said that a tax committee was not responsible for controlling inflation. Once money had been paid out in wages or prices, "taxation simply cannot completely rectify the damage," and to him the "inflationary gap" seemed "a statistical abstraction" which was not capable of any reasonable ascertainment.[17] Doughton reminded the House that tax rates had been increased 700 percent within the past four years, contrasted with an increase of only 100 percent in the national income.

On the Senate side, Senator George defended the bill by saying that further taxes would adversely affect postwar employment. "If the status of the great middle-class is to be preserved and the function of investing savings carried by those who can save," George said, "then there should be no confiscatory taxation. Otherwise, we will make it very difficult to provide employment for our returning soldiers after the war." [18] It was unwise to tax all un-

---

[16] C.R., Nov. 24, 1943, p. 9907.   [17] C.R., Nov. 24, 1943, p. 9910.
[18] C.R., Jan. 12, 1944, p. 89.

spent income, for without savings the soldier would have no post-war job. This dispiriting advice on the part of the chairmen of the tax committees was not designed to inspire Congress to pass a stiff tax bill. It didn't.

The House debate on the new tax bill was extraordinarily tepid, in part because the rule did not permit any contentious point to be decided. No amendments other than those sponsored by the Ways and Means Committee could be offered, so that the House had no choice but to reject the bill or to accept it as written. It accepted the bill, without a roll-call vote. The tax bill reported by the Senate Finance Committee differed only in detail from the House bill—there were variations in the excess profits tax, in some excise taxes, and in postal rates—but the amount it was expected to raise was comparable.

The President chose to comment on the tax bill, then before the Senate, in the State of the Union Message which he delivered on January 11, 1944. The bill, he said, failed to meet the test of "a realistic tax law" which would "tax all unreasonable profits, both individual and corporate" and which would reduce "the ultimate cost of the war to our sons and daughters." [19] It is unusual indeed for the President to comment publicly on legislation which Congress is still considering, but whatever the merits of the comment, or the advisability in making the comment, Congress made no changes in the legislation as a result. Rather, Congress seemed to agree with the estimate of the tax situation made by Senator George the following day, that "other sources to which we can turn for additional revenue, such as the general sales tax, a compulsory savings tax, or a tax on increased individual incomes due to the war . . . have been frowned upon by the Treasury." The Finance Committee was therefore of the opinion "that we have about reached the bottom of the barrel so far as existing taxes are concerned." [20] A number of complicated, technical amendments were offered to the bill in the Senate, but there was little debate on total tax requirements, and there was no major effort to in-

[19] *C.R.*, Jan. 11, 1944, pp. 55ff.   [20] *C.R.*, Jan. 12, 1944, p. 93.

crease tax revenues. As in the House, the bill was passed without a record vote.

The President refused to sign the bill and returned it to Congress with an ill-tempered veto message. The veto resulted in an immediate political crisis, for Senator Barkley, the faithful leader of the Senate majority, denounced the veto from the floor and resigned his position as party leader. Events followed quickly. The cleavage in the party was lacquered over when the Senate, with the blessings of the President, reelected Barkley Majority Leader, and Congress then proceeded to override the veto. One effect of the political schism was that Congress levied no more taxes during the war.

The events leading up to the Roosevelt-Barkley break show that there was some misunderstanding over the veto, enough to have touched off the explosion, but the major causes of the break included many grievances long held but little expressed by the Majority Leader. As for the veto itself, we know that the President consulted Barkley on its content and changed some passages at Barkley's suggestion. Barkley claimed that he objected to the veto itself; his suggestion that certain passages be modified did not mean that he approved of the veto. Not at all. When he learned that the President "had definitely decided to veto the measure notwithstanding any arguments" which he could make, he felt "that there was no further occasion for discussion." [21] Barkley did not tell the President in so many words that he would denounce the message from the floor, but he apparently would have, had he known the message "would be couched in the language which it contained." The veto was not unexpected; indeed, the contemporary press and other sources of information assumed that there would be a veto. As for Barkley, the unexpected was the President's strongly worded message; as for the President, Congress, and the nation, the unexpected was Barkley's volatile reaction.

The message reflected the Administration's cumulative concern with Congress's failure to raise more taxes. Few responsible

[21] *C.R.*, Feb. 25, 1944, pp. 1964ff.; the veto is found in *C.R.*, Feb. 22, p. 1958.

administrators could have advised the President to sign the bill and many, surely, were piqued at the way they had been treated by Congress. Congress had humiliated the Treasury and brusquely disregarded its proposals; it had ignored the attitude of the So-cial Security Agency on social security taxes, and it had denied the Court of Claims jurisdiction over matters within its primary field of competence. The bill was not an effective brake on in-flation. The new revenue came mostly from excise taxes, and the amount produced was less than had been requested and less than what was required. In addition, the bill contained a number of amendments to adjust the tax position of special economic groups.

The message of the President and the response of Senator Barkley to the message illustrate how two different personalities approached the political problem of raising taxes. The Chief Executive was disappointed with the tax bill and wanted Con-gress to pass a better one; the Majority Leader was also disap-pointed with the tax bill—and none had been more critical of the bill than he—but Barkley was willing to accept what Congress had done. In referring to the amendments in the bill adjusting tax inequities (and creating new inequities), the President said that "in this respect" the bill was "not a tax bill but a tax relief bill pro-viding relief not for the needy but for the greedy." Barkley thought that this statement was "a calculated and deliberate assault upon the legislative integrity of every member of Congress." For the first time in his long congressional career, he said, he had been accused "of voting for a bill that constituted a relief measure impoverishing the needy and enriching the greedy." Other mem-bers could do as they pleased, but he did "not propose to take this unjustifiable assault lying down."

The President said he had requested Congress to enact a tax bill which would raise ten billion dollars: this request was said to be too low by "persons prominent in our national life." This was a reference to Mr. Wendell L. Willkie, Roosevelt's opponent in 1940. Barkley did not like this reference, and he belittled Willkie as "the up-to-date Halley's comet darting across the firmament hither and yon to illuminate the heavens with an array of fantastic figures which neither it nor anybody can comprehend." The President said that freezing of social security taxes at one percent would cancel out "automatic increases in the social security tax which would yield $1,100,000,000." Barkley answered that the President had no right to say that if the pay-roll tax were "left in the pockets of employers and employees, instead of being collected from them, it would reduce the annual income of the Treasury by that amount or any other amount. It simply is not an accurate statement of the facts, and everyone knows it." The President found the bill to be "replete with provisions which afford not only indefensible special privileges to favored groups but set dangerous precedents for the future." The probable loss to the Treasury was estimated at $150 million. Barkley answered that the President had "gone forth with a searchlight and magnifying glass to find inconsequential faults"; regardless of the merits of the amendments, an insignificant amount of taxation was involved.

Barkley then went on to review his record as Majority Leader of the Senate for the previous seven years. He had "carried the flag" of the Administration with pride, he said, because he felt that in the period of domestic and international crisis President Roosevelt was a dynamic leader "for whom the people yearn." Things had not always been easy, and during that period he had "carried that flag over rougher territory than was ever traversed by any previous majority leader," sometimes "with little help here on the Senate floor, and more frequently with little help from the other end of Pennsylvania Avenue." He concluded with the dictum that if Congress had "any self-respect yet left," it would "override the veto of the President and enact this tax bill into law, his objections notwithstanding." The *Congressional Record* indicates that after this peroration, there was "prolonged applause on the Senate floor, Senators rising."

The President immediately wrote Barkley a conciliatory letter —he was out of the city and could not talk with Barkley personally —expressing the hope that he would not resign as Majority Leader and that, if he did, his colleagues would unanimously reelect him. He regretted that Barkley believed that the veto message "attacked the integrity of yourself and other Members of Congress," for "such you must know was not my intention." The fact that there were differences on important questions "does not mean we question one another's good faith." The President ended the letter by telling Barkley that "your differing with me does not affect my confidence in your leadership nor in any degree lessen my respect and affection for you personally." [22]

Barkley resigned, but the Democratic caucus reelected him unanimously, and he responded to the President's "gracious letter," as he termed it, in a tone considerably more conciliatory than that used in his Senate speech. The President had his "utmost confidence and affection." He hoped that "the personal and official relations which have been a source of infinite pride" might be continued. The events surrounding the writing of the veto message were reviewed. He went on to suggest a broader basis of understanding between Congress and the White House be established with the hope "that this incident may be instrumental in bringing the executive and legislative departments closer together in fullest cooperation."

After this bewildering display of disaffection and affection, the actual vote to override the veto was anticlimactic and the results predictable. In both Houses, the leadership was somewhat petulant about hastening the procedure, wanting to vote at once, to get the matter on record, to proceed with dispatch in defending Congress, endorsing Barkley's stand, and humiliating the President. There was no need to debate another issue when the pride of Congress was at stake. In the House, Chairman Doughton called for a vote immediately. The rules permitted an hour of debate, but Doughton neither wished to use the hour himself nor to have it used. Under the guise of a parliamentary inquiry, Rep. Martin J. Kennedy (D., New York, N.Y.) asked if there was any parliamentary method by which those who supported the veto "would

[22] C.R., Feb. 25, 1944, p. 2051.

have an opportunity to be heard in support of the President and his courageous stand on the pending tax bill." [23] The Speaker ruled that this was not a parliamentary question. The regular order was demanded, and the clerk droned out the names of the members, 299 voting to override, 95 to sustain (53 percent of the Democrats, 97 percent of the Republicans).

When the veto came before the Senate, the cries of "vote" almost prevented Senator Claude Pepper (D., Tallahassee, Fla.) from being recognized. Senator Pepper was worried about the effect on party fortunes of such a humiliating conflict in the party leadership. He resurrected from some forgotten archive a letter which he had written to Governor-elect Roosevelt on December 28, 1928, when Pepper had just been elected to the Florida Legislature. Pepper brought the letter to light, he said, to show that he had had a historic interest in the fortunes of the party and of Mr. Roosevelt. He would have voted to override were the issue only that of enacting the tax bill, but he believed the real issue was "the permanent course and character of our party." [24] Senator Scott W. Lucas (D., Havana, Ill.) was unmoved by sentiment or party fortunes, and he somewhat defensively announced that his vote would be cast "on pending tax legislation, and that alone." He was impatient with the criticism made by those "who are unfamiliar with this complicated tax procedure" and who "sometimes fail to understand the real difficulty legally to reach and tax the new money which has been made through the war effort, without doing real violence to the taxpayers who have not profited through the war effort." [25] With these brief speeches out of the way, the Senate voted to override the veto, 72–14 (75 percent of the Democrats; 97 percent of the Republicans).

Congress made no further efforts to raise taxes during the war. One more tax bill was enacted—the Tax Adjustment Act of 1945 —the major concern of which was in rebating taxes to assist postwar recovery.

[23] *C.R.*, Feb. 24, 1944, p. 2013. [24] *C.R.*, Feb. 25, 1944, p. 2049.
[25] *C.R.*, Feb. 25, 1944, p. 2050.

6. Military Strategy and Alliances

MILITARY POLICY is an exception to the ordinary method by which Congress formulates and controls policy, and especially so in time of war. On such a subject, the opinion of the layman might be of little value, and decisions are not made by the usual political method of striking a compromise between competing economic and regional claimants. Speed and secrecy may be required in making decisions. Moreover, the Armed Services are functionally disciplined organizations where the political standards for the behavior of civilian bureaucrats are not ordinarily applicable. Yet, in a larger measure, military policy cannot be excluded from the area of serious congressional concern. Congress has to supply funds and create the basic law, and it cannot wash its hands of responsibility when decisions on military policy affect our foreign and domestic interests. During the war Congress attempted to exercise a kind of control which would protect the interest of the Armed Services in getting about their job and the interest of the public in seeing that the job was done properly. The Armed Services did not have to compete politically in order to survive; this freedom enabled the military leaders to devote their energies to their profession, and it gave the war effort a national rather than a partisan aspect.

The difficult problem of establishing a satisfactory relationship between Congress and the conduct of the war was raised on the first day of the war. There was considerable alarm in Congress and not a little curiosity concerning the damage to the fleet. The chairmen of the two naval affairs committees visited the Navy Departments to find out what had happened at Pearl Harbor, but they learned nothing. Senator David I. Walsh (D., Clinton, Mass.) told the Senate that "the Navy was not in a position to give us any information" other than that which had already been made public, and Admiral Stark had suggested "that we defer requesting any further information until after the President on the radio tonight presents such information as he thinks it wise and proper to give to the American people." [1] Senator Charles W. Tobey (R., Temple, N.H.) was not satisfied with this answer, and he claimed that if the Japanese knew that a large part of the Pacific fleet had been wiped out, "the American people and their representatives in Congress ought to know it." [2] Other members were not so confident that war news should be broadcast to the winds. Rep. A. L. Bulwinkle (D., Gastonia, N.C.) told the House that in a time like this it was necessary for every American, and especially every Congressman, to be guarded in his words so as not to give aid and comfort to the enemy.[3] Less elegantly, Rep. Charles A. Plumley (R., Northfield, Vt.) told the House that unless the members were individually prepared to take over responsibility for running the war, "you had better shut up." [4]

No method was worked out by which Congress as a whole was informed on the developments of the war, and, in the aggregate, members of Congress had no more intimate knowledge of how the war was going than the average reader of a metropolitan newspaper. The Senate held a so-called secret session in 1943 to hear the report of five Senators who had just returned from an inspection of the battlefronts, but a badly garbled version of the session soon reached the press, and Senator Richard B. Russell (D., Winder, Ga.), who had been on the trip and reported to the Senate, found it necessary to scold his colleagues for their loose tongues.

[1] C.R., Dec. 9, 1941, p. 9542.   [2] C.R., Dec. 9, 1941, p. 9542.
[3] C.R., Dec. 9, 1941, p. 9562.   [4] C.R., Dec. 9, 1941, p. A5506.

Rumors of what had been said reached the ear of Prime Minister Churchill, who made an oblique reference to a country "where the soldiers are fighting abroad and the politicians are fighting at home with equal vigor and ferocity." [5] Senator Russell correctly predicted that it would "probably be a long time before another executive session is held," [6] and no more secret sessions were held during the war.

The point can be raised, of course, that Congressmen have no need for secret military information other than to satisfy their curiosities. The core of the problem, however, is not whether Congress should be given information on such transient military events as troop movements or the location of submarines; here the case for secrecy is obvious, and reliance is placed on disciplined military leaders and well-developed military procedures. The core of the problem, rather, lies in establishing confidence and trust between the military and political leaders so that military decisions having political overtones will be recognized as such at the time and not be revealed later, to the general embarrassment of all.

A procedure was developed for relating the responsibilities of the Armed Services for prosecuting the war to the legitimate interests of Congress. Committees were used. A cooperative and sympathetic relationship developed between the Army and Navy and the respective House and Senate committees; the Armed Services confided in these committees and relied on them for political support. Each of these committees was given regular reports on the progress of the war, and in addition each committee conducted investigations on such questions as procurement and production. Reports were made to the committees, not to Congress as a whole, and even a report containing such general interest as Secretary Knox's resumé of the Pearl Harbor attack was made to a House committee only.

Congress played a very small role, either as critic or as participant, in the several military and military-political conferences in

[5] *C.R.*, Oct. 14, 1943, p. 8329.   [6] *C.R.*, Oct. 28, 1943, p. 8859.

which the United States participated during the war, although
it was given some general information on the decisions made at
these conferences. The President discussed the results of the
Casablanca Conference (1943), where the policy of unconditional
surrender was developed, in an off-the-record conversation with
some eleven leaders from Congress and with representatives of
the State, War, and Navy Departments. On the Quebec Conference (1943), the President sent a report to Congress in which
he defended the policy of keeping some matters secret. It was
difficult to remain silent, he said, "when unjustified attack and
criticism come from those who are not in a position to have all
the facts," and he asked for faith that decisions were being made
on better evidence than critics had implied.[7] Secretary Hull spoke
before a joint session of Congress following the Moscow Conference (1943). President Roosevelt also addressed Congress—as it
happened, for the last time—on the results of the Yalta Conference (1945).

Congress did not participate in these military and military-
political conferences. It was not invited, and it did not ask to be
invited; Congress seemed to consider that the prerogative of
making commitments at such conferences belonged to the President as Commander-in-Chief of the Army and Navy. One can
nevertheless raise the question of the advisability of giving representation to Congress at such conferences, much as Congress
was given representation at various international conferences
which were held during and after the war. It is probably true
that the representation of Congress at military and military-political conferences would have established a greater feeling of confidence on the part of Congress in the wisdom of the commitments
which were being made. However, in all frankness, this question
could not have been answered on abstract principles alone; it
would also be necessary to consider what the representation would
consist of, or, more particularly, what members of Congress would
expect to be invited from the status of their positions. As one

[7] C.R., Sept. 17, 1943, pp. 7585ff.

example, the strict rule of seniority had made Senator Robert R. Reynolds (D., Asheville, N.C.) the Chairman of the Military Affairs Committee; Reynolds's record in the Senate was not one to inspire confidence in his judgment, and his several irresponsible speeches during the war were surely enough to have his name deleted from any list of prospective delegates. But could one invite other members of Congress to a military or military-political conference and exclude the Chairman of the Senate Committee on Military Affairs?

On the whole, there was little debate in Congress on the results of the conferences; there was no criticism at the time of the policy of unconditional surrender, and little of the Yalta Conference, although the proposed Polish settlement was vigorously attacked by some members. The silence of Congress, or the lack of contemporary criticism, did not mean that the policy made by the President was therefore agreeable with Congress. The President and his party were believed responsible for these commitments, and they could be held accountable later as necessity determined. In other words, Congress felt no obligation to defend the commitments, having had no part in making them or in approving them, and later some members even attacked their legitimacy.

Similarly, Congress did not make the great decisions on the strategy of the war; there was a marked difference of opinion on whether the Atlantic or Pacific war should be fought first, but Congress made no major criticism of the conduct of the war (the wisdom of the Rapido River crossing in the Italian campaign was debated in after years). There was also a minor controversy which developed shortly after Pearl Harbor on the disposition of troops and ships.

After war had been declared, Congress had to repeal a law, enacted in the days of neutrality, which prohibited sending reserve components outside the Western Hemisphere or our territorial and insular possessions. The Armed Services asked that the restriction be repealed at once because, in effect, it made it illegal to seek out the enemy in his homeland. However, when a unanimous consent request was made to repeal the restriction, Senator Hiram Johnson (R., San Francisco, Calif.) objected. By December 11, however, two more wars having been declared against the United States, Senator Johnson capitulated, and the repeal measure passed both Houses without a dissent.

When Senator Hiram Johnson finally consented, he was a frightened man indeed, and he told the Senate in alarm that "we do not have the necessary protection on the West Coast." It was necessary that Senators understand "the absolute transcendent importance of some care and some thought being given to Washington, Oregon, and California." [8] Senator Johnson's regional counterpart was Senator Walsh of Massachusetts, who wanted to strengthen the defenses of the East Coast. As Chairman of the Naval Affairs Committee, Walsh was at least partly responsible for securing adequate Navy installations, but he called the attention of his colleagues to "a dramatic exposé" in the Sunday press which showed "the complete lack of necessary defenses for the City of Boston and the Massachusetts coast." The report had "stirred up the people in my section of the country," but he could only give them the cold comfort of knowing that their plight was different "only in degrees" from that of other coastal cities. Walsh ended his speech with the ominous prediction that "the day may come when we shall have to bring back from the four corners of the world our depleted Navy to be a source of defense for our own shores." [9]

For most Congressmen, the great schism on military strategy did not relate to the fortifications of San Francisco, the home of Senator Hiram Johnson, or of Boston, near the home of Senator Walsh, but to the relative emphasis to be placed on the Atlantic or the Pacific phase of the war—on defeating Germany first or Japan first. The most vocal advocate of fighting the Pacific war first was probably Senator Albert B. Chandler (D., Versailles, Ky.), a member of the Military Affairs Committee and later Commissioner of Baseball. In the first of two speeches on this subject delivered in April and May, 1943, Senator Chandler expressed his

[8] *C.R.*, Feb. 17, 1942, p. 1332.   [9] *C.R.*, Feb. 17, 1942, p. 1332.

concern for the safety of the Aleutians and Alaska; the Japanese had previously bombed Dutch Harbor and occupied the islands of Attu, Agattu, and Kiska. Chandler contended that the high command of the Army and Navy did not appreciate the dangers of Japanese penetration into Alaska and the Pacific Coast and that it had not given proper support to commanders in the field. Chandler's concern with the defense of Alaska developed from an inspection trip made by him and three other members of the Military Affairs Committee in August, 1942; a secret report on the trip had been transmitted to the Joint Chiefs of Staff and to the President. Senator Barkley, who also came from Kentucky, thought that his Senate colleague was poorly equipped to play the role of military strategist, and he told the Senators that they were "bound to assume that our military and naval authorities are fully apprised of the situation, and are not asleep with respect to it." [10] They appear to have been fully apprised, and, as it developed, Attu and Agattu were retaken by American forces in June of that year and Kiska by American and Canadian forces in August.

Chandler's second speech was a formidable exposition of the beat-Japan-first school of thought, but it lost some of its effectiveness because it was saturated with anti-Allied sentiment and because it failed to develop some of the strategic reasons which might have been advanced. The immediate purpose of the speech was to influence the decisions on Pacific strategy then being made at a British-American conference in Washington. With the end of the North African campaign, Chandler said, the United States could make an independent decision on the conduct of the war. The objective of preventing Great Britain and the Soviet Union from being knocked out had now been achieved, and the war in Europe had reached a point where the United States could direct its major effort against Japan. The war in the Pacific must not be neglected, he said, and it was Chandler's opinion that we should attack Japan first. Chandler's proposal was largely based on po-

[10] C.R., April 16, 1943, p. 3451.

litical reasons, and he in effect argued that the Japanese war was the more important because the European settlement was the more important. "If we do not press the war against Japan," Chandler said, "and if we push in and finish the war with Germany very quickly, I hate to think how little influence the President of the United States will have when Russia and Great Britain begin to develop their spheres of influence on the continent of Europe." [11]

Another tenet of the beat-Japan-first school of thought was that the British were not doing all they could in the Pacific war. Some two million British troops in India were "being held off from Burma by about 60,000 Japanese," and Chandler implied that the British were not moving their troops because they feared a revolt in India. Chandler then tauntingly suggested that two million men "ought to be able to quell an uprising in India and ought to be able to drive the Japs out of Burma. Two million of our boys could do it." On hearing these figures, Senator Henrik Shipstead (R., Carlos, Minn.) did not see "how Great Britain could render a greater aid to Japan than what she is doing now." [12]

Two days later, Mr. Churchill answered some of Chandler's criticisms when addressing a joint session of Congress. Churchill remarked with some asperity that "if all that was necessary was for an order to be given to the great army standing ready in India to march toward the Rising Sun and open the Burma Road, that order would be given this afternoon." The problem was "very strictly governed by what your American military men call the science of logistics." He repudiated "the slightest suspicion that we should hold anything back that can be usefully employed." The British, he said, had as great an interest as the United States in waging an "unflinching and relentless" war against Japan. "I am here to tell you," he concluded, "that we will wage that war side by side with you in accordance with the best strategic employment of our forces while there is a breath in our bodies and while blood flows in our veins." [13]

[11] C.R., May 17, 1943, pp. 4503ff.   [12] C.R., May 17, 1943, p. 4507.
[13] C.R., May 19, 1943, pp. 4619ff.

Chandler also believed that the Russians could be of more assistance in the Pacific war. "If Stalin would let us use air bases in Siberia for bombing Japan the defeat of the Japs would come quickly," he said. The issue of the desirability of using Russian bases for bombing Japan was persistently raised in Congress until the end of the war.

An indeterminate number of Senators supported the Chandler thesis of beat-Japan-first, but of course the issue was not posed in such a fashion that there was an actual vote in Congress on the question. From their comments and questions, it is apparent that Senator Wheeler and Senator Shipstead enjoyed Chandler's speech. Senator Vandenberg said that he did not know whether Chandler's analysis was right or wrong; if he had an opinion, "it would be that he is wholly right," and he added that he would "be very proud to be making that speech" which Chandler was making.[14] Senator Tydings was also unwilling to endorse Chandler's conclusions, but he had "a sort of feeling" which he could not substantiate "that the military leaders are more inclined to take a larger interest in the Pacific than has been taken up to now." [15]

Several Senators criticized Chandler. Senator Homer T. Bone (D., Tacoma, Wash.) raised the question of how far the Senate was entitled to go "in telling the Commander-in-Chief and the War and Navy Departments what they should do in the disposition of troops and planes." [16] As a member of the Naval Affairs Committee, Senator Scott W. Lucas (D., Havana, Ill.) said he had as much knowledge of the military situation as most Senators, yet he felt he would be hurting the war effort if he attempted to lay down the strategy of the war. Chandler took this criticism with poor grace. "I have a right to put my oar in," he said. While he made no claim to being a military strategist, he would not permit any one "to accuse me of trying to run the war by politics or by armchair strategy because I happen to assert what seems to me to be of prime and vital interest to the people of the United States." [17]

[14] C.R., May 17, 1943, p. 4511.   [15] C.R., May 17, 1943, p. 4513.
[16] C.R., May 17, 1943, p. 4518.   [17] C.R., May 17, 1943, p. 4518.

On the lighter side, the following bit of doggerel, inserted in the *Record* by Rep. Joe Starnes (D., Guntersville, Ala.), argued against the theory that Japan should be defeated first:

Our high expert advisors think that Japan's defeat
Would not force Germany to fall, nor drop back in retreat
But the defeat of Germany, by whatsoever plan,
Would prove to be, undoubtedly, the downfall of Japan.[18]

There was little congressional criticism of the conduct of the war in the West. On the issue of the second front, Senator Wheeler said that while "everyone would like to see a second front opened," he believed "the whole matter should be left up to the General Staff rather than to Mr. Willkie or columnists or other persons who are trying to tell the Army General Staff how to carry on the war."[19] Some members counseled caution or delay in the proposed invasion of the European mainland. Rep. Jessie Sumner (R., Milford, Ill.) thought the invasion plans were "anachronistic,"[20] and she introduced two resolutions to postpone the European invasion and to concentrate on the Pacific war. Senator Sheridan Downey (D., Claremont, Calif.) thought that air power would make a land invasion of Europe unnecessary. Certain military officers had supported his theory in confidential conversations, he said, but no names were identified with opinions, and it was not clear within the Armed Services. On the issue of invading Europe, Downey said that "the issue is . . . between the high command and me"; so stated, the Senate had little difficulty in deciding whom to support, and Downey's resolution was referred to the Military Affairs Committee, where it remained.[21]

MILITARY LEADERSHIP

Congress was particularly interested in the military leadership of the Armed Services, for these leaders had the primary responsibility for the conduct of the war and for the care and safety of the troops. The Senate had special power in this regard, for its consent was required for all appointments or promotions of gen-

[18] *C.R.*, May 5, 1943, p. A2598.
[19] *C.R.*, Oct. 2, 1942, p. 7707.
[20] *C.R.*, March 14, 1944, p. 2608.
[21] *C.R.*, Sept. 29, 1943, p. 7913.

eral officers or officers of equivalent rank. It was difficult for the
Senate to develop standards of judgment in this area, for the
Senate would not necessarily know who would make a competent
general or admiral, nor could the Senate know whether the advice
of military experts was being followed in the conduct of the war.
There was no agreement, either, on the extent to which civilian
leaders should be held responsible for following what turned out
to be bad military advice.

For the most part, the military and naval appointments were
noncontentious, but some half-dozen controversies over military
personnel developed in which Congress became interested. The
Army Chief of Staff, General George C. Marshall, was widely respected in Congress, but his status was debated when a rumor
developed that he would be named commander of the allied
troops in Europe. The rumor appeared first in the *Army and Navy
Journal;* it was neither confirmed nor denied, but it was generally
believed that General Marshall had been selected at the Quebec
Conference to lead the invasion forces. In Congress, Rep. Jessie
Sumner thought the plan was nothing but a British plot to kick
General Marshall upstairs "because he stands up for our American
rights." The British technique was subtle, Miss Sumner said, for
"whenever they find an officer who stands up for American rights
they get some American officer they can handle to ask that the
officer they cannot handle be put somewhere that looks like a
promotion, or sent to South America, or given a vacation. I re-
iterate—they are going too far." [22]

At the time of the Marshall rumor, it happened, that Lt. Gen.
Brehon B. Somervell, the Commanding General of the Services
of Supply, was formulating plans to reorganize the procurement
procedures of the War Department. Distortions of this plan were
combined with the Marshall transfer to become a diabolic military-
political plot of malevolent proportions. Rep. Paul W. Shafer (R.,
Battle Creek, Mich.) said that the plan proposed "to convert that
great department into a New Deal political association," and in

[22] C.R., Sept. 20, 1943, p. 7682.

his opinion the activities of the men behind the plan "are nothing less than treasonous." [23] He went on to suggest that Marshall was being moved to a figurehead command, that the procurement program was to be used for an election slush-fund, and that General Somervell might be the vice-presidential candidate on the Democratic ticket to offset the nomination of General Douglas MacArthur by the Republicans.

General Marshall was vastly annoyed at such stories, and he personally asked several congressional leaders to deny that political standards were used in selecting military personnel. This they did. In addition, Representative McCormack, the Democratic Floor Leader, was authorized to say for Secretary of War Stimson that the President had "absolutely refrained from interfering in any way" with the choice of Army generals and their assignments. The President had followed the advice of his military advisers in the consideration of all questions of strategy, and as for his intrusion in any political or personal way, it had been nonexistent.[24]

The rumors concerning Generals Marshall, Somervell, and Eisenhower eventually ran their course, but we may now ask whether they had any basis in fact. After the war, Mr. Stimson wrote that the claim that General Marshall's proposed new assignment was a British plot was "an outrageous libel," but he added that "it was not so easy to quiet those who sincerely felt that Marshall was indispensable as Chief of Staff." Stimson assumed that the choice of Marshall for commander "was settled as, in fact, it had been agreed on in Quebec," but the President reopened the subject following the Teheran conference and discussed the subject with General Marshall at a luncheon conference in Cairo. The President decided that "he would be more comfortable if he kept Marshall at his elbow in Washington and turned over OVERLORD to Eisenhower." By the middle of 1944, Stimson says, he was happy to acknowledge to his diary "that the two men were in the right place after all." As for the proposed reorganization of

[23] *C.R.*, Sept. 22, 1943, p. A3987, and Sept. 27, p. A4001.
[24] *C.R.*, Sept. 28, 1943, p. 7884.

procurement, Stimson said that he believed with Somervell that the proposed changes would increase the efficiency of the Service Forces, although there were also certain disadvantages in the creation of bad feeling. Following a conference with Assistant Secretary of War McCloy, who opposed the project, Stimson "had the matter out in a conference with the soldiers, and the proposal was killed." [25]

General Douglas MacArthur became identified in congressional debate with certain members of Congress and with certain political attitudes, although it is not entirely clear why this should have been so. Indeed, the entire Pacific campaign became strangely intertwined with political alignments preceding Pearl Harbor, with the curious result that General MacArthur became, as it were, the military hero of the former isolationists. As one small instance of this relationship, Senator Robert M. La Follette, Jr. (Prog., Madison, Wis.), one of this group, sponsored a resolution designating June 13, 1942, as Douglas MacArthur Day, the day being "the forty-third anniversary of the appointment of General MacArthur to the Military Academy at West Point, which marked the beginning of his brilliant career." [26] It does seem that this resolution, passed by Congress, was straining at a gnat to find a suitable occasion for honoring a hero.

There is more evidence than this. On the murky edge of politics, where innuendo is substituted for fact, an attempt was made to promote or expose a feud between the Administration and General MacArthur. Rep. Hamilton Fish (R., Garrison, New York) once told the House that "the wolf pack of communistic smearers and radical New Deal and fellow traveler stooges" (in Fish's vocabulary, the Administration) were "gunning" for MacArthur. MacArthur was our greatest fighting general, Fish said, and, with little to fight with, he had been winning victories over

[25] Henry L. Stimson and McGeorge Bundy, *On Active Service in Peace and War* (New York: Harper, 1948), pp. 440ff.
[26] 56 Stat 358, June 11, 1942, S. J. Res. 144.

the Japanese "while our invasion troops have been bogged down in Italy for six months." [27]

The War Department, wishing not to be pulled into the vortex of the coming political campaign, issued an order on February 25, 1943, stating that "no member of the military forces on active duty will hereafter become a candidate for or seek or accept election to any public office not held by him when he entered upon active duty." Some members of Congress said that the purpose of the order was to prevent General MacArthur from becoming a candidate for President. Senator Vandenberg was "shocked" by the order, and he denied that the War Department had a right "thus indirectly to control American elections." He could understand the necessity for discouraging "ordinary" political activities, but this order denied "the rights of our whole people to turn to the military establishment for high authority if civilian judgment wants to turn in that direction." [28] Senator Barkley responded that the policy was not new; the order recodified existing policy, including the prohibition on political activities which had been in effect since 1925. He said that Senator Vandenberg had overlooked the final paragraph, which allowed a member of the military service to be honorably discharged "for the convenience of the government upon his request in a proper case." [29] Vandenberg was not entirely mollified, however, and remained suspicious of the purpose of the order. Officials in the War Department seemed "very anxious to be sure the order is out," he said, but no such order "would ever foreclose the American people from choosing a great General of the Army as President of the United States."

The persistent rumors that the Republicans might nominate General MacArthur received a shot in the arm when Rep. A. L. Miller (R., Kimball, Neb.) released for publication an exchange of letters between himself and the General. General MacArthur's

[27] C.R., March 14, 1944, p. 2594.   [28] C.R., April 8, 1943, p. 3102.
[29] C.R., April 8, 1943, p. 3125.

sympathetic comments on Miller's anti-Administration views were so extravagantly phrased that one did not know whether the General was only being courteous to a friendly Congressman or whether he was trying to win delegates to a political convention. Representative Miller was convinced that General MacArthur had "the qualifications and experience to make a great President, and that the Republican Party should present his name to the people as its nominee." [30]

The National Guard had been called up in 1940 and made a part of the Army of the United States for the duration of the emergency. The blending of the Regular Army and the National Guard was not entirely harmonious, but without going into the details of the controversy one can say that the National Guard Officers felt that they had not been given equal treatment. The National Guard, moreover, had strong political ties in many States, so that it was natural enough that politicians should know of the resentment and to some extent share the grudge. The resentment of the National Guard was expressed in the Senate debate on the promotion of General Ben Lear to the permanent rank of lieutenant general. Senator Bennet Champ Clark (D., University City, Mo.), one of the founders of the American Legion and a strong supporter of the National Guard, led the opposition to Lear's nomination.

In attacking Lear, Senator Clark revived the story of the "yoo-hoo episode," which had occurred two years previously. The episode concerned the behavior of soldiers from the Thirty-Fifth Division who were being transported overland to their camp in Louisiana after a bivouac in Tennessee. As they passed a golf course near Memphis, some of the soldiers made some loud and, apparently, lewd remarks to some women golfers, and the cry of Yoo-hoo! seems to have been one of the most quotable and innocuous of the comments. These boisterous troops came under the command of the Second Army, the head of which was General Lear, and the general happened to be on the Memphis golf course

[30] C.R., April 18, 1944, p. 3549.

and personally heard the offensive remarks. The general immediately asserted his authority: as a disciplinary measure he ordered certain units of the division to make a forced march—and the weather was very hot. The affair was further complicated because the division was under the command of Major General Ralph T. Truman, a Missouri National Guardsman whose cousin, Harry, was in the Senate. Senator Clark said that inasmuch as the Articles of War prevented training devices from being used for disciplinary purposes, General Lear had violated the Article by punishing the troops with a forced march.

Senator Clark also claimed that the Army had discriminated against General Truman in the 1941 maneuvers. The Regular Army officers had planned to have General Truman's division wiped out in the mock campaign, but the division had won a surprising victory over an armored unit. Subsequently Truman was removed from command and persuaded to resign. Senate debate on the Lear nomination was inconclusive, for no relationship was established between General Lear and the attitude of the War Department toward National Guard officers. At best, it provided an opportunity to publicize the grievances of the National Guard, and this may have had some effect. After the long debate, during which Senator Truman remained silent, the Senate consented to promoting General Lear to the permanent rank of lieutenant general.

Another disciplinary action in which Congress became interested was the episode in which Lieutenant General George S. Patton, Jr., slapped the faces of two unwounded soldiers suffering from "battle anxiety." The story, revealed to the public by the radio commentator, Drew Pearson, immediately created somewhat of a stir, both in and out of Congress. Rep. Jed. Johnson (D., Anadarko, Okla.) was so incensed that he wrote to General Marshall suggesting that "General Patton be relieved of his command immediately." [31] Rep. Charles E. Hoeven (R., Alton, Iowa) drew attention to the anxiety of parents that "their boys" were "being

[31] C.R., Nov. 24, 1943, p. 9965.

abused by hard-boiled officers." Hoeven intimated that the Army did not believe in fair play, for "if the soldier had struck the general, we would have had a different story." [32]

On request, the Senate Committee on Military Affairs was given a report of the incident from General Eisenhower, who was responsible for all disciplinary matters within his theater of command. The report said that General Patton had upbraided the two soldiers "in an unseemly and indefensible manner"; on learning of the incidents, General Eisenhower had expressed his "extreme displeasure" to General Patton, and a round of apologies followed.[33] This frank report would no doubt have satisfied congressional interest had not an earlier communiqué said that General Patton had never been "reprimanded at any time by General Eisenhower or by anyone else in this theater." [34] Why was this misleading information released, the committee now wished to know. Secretary of War Stimson replied that the reason was "a military one." It was considered necessary to deny that there would be a change in the command of the Seventh Army or that its morale had been impaired. "This may have been an error in judgment from a public-relations viewpoint," he said, "but it was eminently sound from a military standpoint." [35] So ended the Patton episode.

THE ALLIES

Congress was faced with the recurring problem of the attitude it should adopt toward other members of the United Nations alliance. The military difficulties of waging war with an alliance are ordinarily recognized; similarly, an alliance creates difficulties, though of a lesser magnitude, for the civilian politicians. The issue, perhaps, was the extent to which Congress should restrain its natural propensity to debate the policy of other countries: should it be on permanent good behavior and act as if the war was an extended diplomatic soirée where differences and diffi-

[32] C.R., Nov. 24, 1943, p. 9906.   [33] C.R., Nov. 26, 1943, p. 10008.
[34] C.R., Nov. 24, 1943, p. 9965.   [35] C. R., Dec. 13, 1943, p. 10567.

culties were glossed over and not mentioned? Or should it behave
less decorously but more naturally and discuss critically the policies of our allies? Even in peacetime there is no easy solution to
the question of how far Congress can safely extend its sphere of
praise or invective. The problem was compounded by the war,
where anything said about an ally could be magnified and made
to seem more important than it was; and it could also be distorted
and made to seem something different from what was meant.
Foreign officials who believed that the President only could speak
for the United States might be puzzled over the correct interpretation to be made of statements made by Congressmen.

Congress could not keep entirely silent, for it had to deliberate
on issues where the United States and other countries had an interlocking interest. On the other hand, it was easily possible to say
too much and to say it maladroitly. In general, Congress was no
more successful in determining what could be said discreetly in
public about the Allies than individuals are in determining how
far they should go in talking about their friends and neighbors or
politicians are in talking about their opponents. In the area of dealing with the Allies, the watchwords were caution and discretion,
but not all Congressmen were cautious or discreet, and some of
the debate was boorish and impolite.

The unity of the war softened, but it did not totally dispel, the
anti-British sentiment existing in some quarters before the war,
which tended to characterize America's position as the cat's paw
of the British Empire. Some Congressmen believed that the political responsibility for India extended beyond the British and that
they were free to suggest their own solution. Motives were important, for the independence of India could be advanced as a
desirable end in itself or as a method for disrupting relations
with Great Britain. In August, 1942, a strong speech in favor of
the independence of India was made by Senator Reynolds, the
Chairman of the Military Affairs Committee, who tended to be a
British-baiter and who had never expressed any particular interest
in India before. He asked, however, for American assistance in

"extending freedom—unqualified, unlimited freedom—to the people of India and thereby making those people a part of the great program and crusade for freedom and independence now being engaged in throughout the world." [36]

What was the meaning of Senator Reynold's remarks? As Chairman of the Military Affairs Committee, he might conceivably have been floating a trial balloon for the Administration. As a pre-Pearl-Harbor isolationist with pronounced views on foreign policy, he might only have been giving another twist to the lion's tail. Senator Barkley felt obliged to admonish his colleague. He also had great sympathy for a free and independent India, he said, but such questions were "delicate matters," and we were living in "delicate times." Because the tide of war might turn "upon some delicate expression of opinion from an authoritative source," he believed that silence was "more golden at times like these than otherwise it would be." [37]

Palestine was another subject within the orbit of British policy making where congressional critics were vocal. In advocating further use of Jewish manpower, Senator Guy M. Gillette (Cherokee, Iowa) claimed that Palestine had, unused, the equivalent of eight or ten divisions. Some groups pressed for a separate Jewish army, others for a Jewish military force "as an integral part of the British and allied components." [38] Congress took no specific action, and the issue lapsed after August, 1942, when the British authorized the formation of Jewish units.

Palestine again became an issue in 1944, when it was proposed that the United States use its good offices to restore free immigration into Palestine. Resolutions on this subject had bipartisan sponsorship, which increased the possibility of their passage, but as it happened their consideration in committee was suspended by an unusual request of Secretary of War Henry Stimson. He wrote that, without reference to the merits of the resolutions, it was the "considered judgment of the War Department" that

[36] C.R., Aug. 20, 1942, pp. 6887ff.   [37] C.R., Aug. 20, 1942, p. 6892.
[38] C.R., May 7, 1942, p. A1661.

"further action on them at this time would be prejudicial to the successful prosecution of the war." In the summer of 1944, however, the conventions of both political parties advocated unrestricted Jewish immigration into Palestine as well as the eventual establishment there of a Jewish Commonwealth. In view of the official action of the two parties, Senator Taft, a cosponsor of the resolution favoring unrestricted immigration into Palestine, asked the War Department if there were *still* objections to the resolution being considered. Secretary Stimson yielded to the superiority of prevailing political opinion. Many officers of the War Department, he said, had a "strong feeling" that "the passage of such a resolution would interfere with our military effort." However, in Stimson's judgment, "political considerations now outweigh the military, and the issue should be determined upon the political rather than the military basis." [39] The House Committee reported a resolution on November 30, 1944, but no further action was taken by either House.

Anti-British sentiment in Congress continued spasmodically during the war. Rumors of British intentions had reached such proportions by December, 1943, that Speaker Rayburn felt compelled to make one of his infrequent admonitory speeches. "Every day or every week," he said, "somebody, somewhere asks: 'What are we going to do with England after the war is over? Is England in diplomacy going to outdo us after the war is over?' . . . Then somebody says to me: 'What are we going to do with Russia after the war is over?' . . . Another thing, especially since the Patton affair, which was tragically unfortunate, the Army has not escaped whispering. . . . Unity in this war effort we must have." [40]

Our military alliance with the Soviet Union presented a puzzling and somewhat different type of political question for Congress to consider. There was a feeling, indeed, that now we were walking with the Devil himself, whereas our experience hitherto had conditioned us only to walking with the British Empire. This Strange Alliance, as Major General John R. Deane later called it, was

[39] H. Rept. 1997, Nov. 30, 1944.   [40] *C.R.*, Dec. 9, 1943, p. 10535.

defended by a variety of explanations, justifications, and rational-
izations; but there was no debate on the supplementary question
of the position of the Soviet Union in the postwar world, or the relation of Soviet strength to our own policy of demobilization.

There was implicit and continuous political support of our policy toward China; the long debate over the proper policy to take,
or to have been taken, did not develop until after the war. An
instance of the faith of Congress in China, and in our policy toward
China, was the congressional authorization of a grant to China of
$500 million in 1942. The Administration made the request sud-
denly, and the congressional leaders were scarcely told in advance that such a request would be made; in defending the request, the Administration gave Congress no clear knowledge of
how the money was to be spent or the purposes which were to be
accomplished. Despite the paucity of information about the purposes for which the money would be spent, Congress passed the
authorization unanimously.

During the war, Congress abolished American extraterritorial
rights in China and repealed the Chinese Exclusion Act. The treaty
abolishing extraterritoriality, Senator Connally said, was "nothing
more than a real act of justice," [41] and Senator Vandenberg said
that it was "an act of faith in the dependability and the destiny of
the new China." [42] Senator Thomas, of Utah, who had advocated
such a policy for a long time, was even more refulgent in his comments, and he said that the action of the Senate would "outlive in
the memory of men many of the spectacular deeds whose echoes
reverberate and almost deafen our ears from day to day." [43]

The President told Congress that the repeal of the Chinese Exclusion Act would "correct a historic mistake and silence the distorted Japanese propaganda." [44] The "historic mistake" was that in
1882 Congress enacted legislation prohibiting Chinese from becoming naturalized citizens. In reporting a bill giving the Chinese
an immigration quota, the House Committee on Immigration and

---

[41] C.R., Feb. 11, 1943, p. 839.   [42] C.R., Feb. 11, 1943, p. 839.
[43] C.R., Feb. 11, 1943, p. 839.   [44] C.R., Oct. 11, 1943, pp. 8199ff.

Naturalization said that the motivation for passing the Exclusion Act was entirely economic and not ill will toward the Chinese people. The proposed legislation, it said, expressed the opinion of the American people that "freedom depends upon respect for the integrity of others and that their own freedom and security demand that they accord to others the respect that they ask for themselves." [45]

A minority in Congress opposed repealing the Act. It did not wish to change the immigration laws during the war, nor did it think it possible to legislate "enemy propaganda out of existence." Among those who objected to repealing the Act was Senator Reynolds, who had advocated the independence of India the year before. Reynolds said that the repeal of the Exclusion Act would mean "the opening wedge"—"the sticking of the big toe in the door which many radical internationalists want to open up." [46] The bill, which passed both Houses without a record vote, provided for a quota of one hundred Chinese immigrants a year, with a preference up to seventy-five percent being given to Chinese born and resident in China.

A minor constitutional crisis developed in the Philippine Government in Exile, which had its wartime headquarters in Washington, and inasmuch as the Philippines were not yet fully independent, Congress was asked to solve it. The crisis related to the position of President Manuel Quezon after the expiration of his term of office. The Philippine Government wanted him to remain in office, arguing that it was not possible to hold general elections while the Philippines were occupied. Vice President Osmeña was eligible to succeed Quezon, but he would have assumed this office solely because elections could not otherwise be held. The Senate was sympathetic to the proposal, and it quickly passed a resolution which provided that the Philippine Government should continue in office "until the enemy is driven from the land he has seized" and until a new government had been "duly elected and qualified in accordance with the constitution and laws of the Philippines."

[45] H. Rept. 732, Oct. 7, 1943.   [46] C.R., Nov. 26, 1943, p. 10016.

There was more discussion in the House, with dissent expressed. Some members doubted the advisability of suspending constitutional procedures when it seemed to be unnecessary, for, in fact, the Constitution permitted Osmeña to become president on the expiration of Quezon's term of office. Señor Osmeña, however, supported the proposal, and he told the Filipino people in a broadcast that if the leadership were changed the enemy would say that "President Quezon has withdrawn from the fight and that he was no longer interested in the war." [47] The issue of domestic politics was also interjected into the debate by Rep. W. Sterling Cole (R., Bath, N.Y.), which surely accounted for some of the votes against the proposal. Representative Cole wanted to know whether the resolution "retaining in office indefinitely the two Filipino officials" could be taken as "any criterion or precedent which the American people might follow in 1944." [48] The House passed the legislation, 181–107 (97 percent of the Democrats; 29 percent of the Republicans).

Congress was on its best behavior in the protocol which permitted it to be addressed by various political leaders of the United Nations alliance. The long parade of dignitaries which appeared before Congress during the war was led, appropriately enough, by the singularly successful parliamentarian, Mr. Winston Churchill. In the first of his two speeches before Congress, Mr. Churchill spoke as a parliamentarian with whom Congressmen could identify themselves, and being also a politician, he would have it so. "I cannot help reflecting," Mr. Churchill said, to the delight of Congressmen, "that if my father had been American and my mother British, instead of the other way round, I might have got here on my own." [49] When Mme Chiang Kai-shek addressed Congress, there was a long ovation, and Senator C. Wayland Brooks (R., Chicago, Ill.) later commented that the Generalissimo's "delightful wife" had "thrilled this body as I have never seen it thrilled." [50]

The list of speakers included President Manuel Prado of Peru;

---

[47] *C.R.*, Nov. 18, 1943, p. 9655.   [48] *C.R.*, Nov. 10, 1943, p. 9377.
[49] *C.R.*, Dec. 26, 1941, p. 10117.   [50] *C.R.*, May 17, 1943, p. 4511.

President Manuel L. Quezon of the Philippines; King George II of Greece; King Peter II of Yugoslavia; Queen Wilhelmina of the Netherlands; President Carlos Alberto Arroyo del Rio of Equador; Major General Fulgencio Batista, President of Cuba; General Enrique Penaranda, President of Bolivia; President Eduard Benes of Czechoslovakia; President Edwin Barclay of Liberia; General Higinio Morínigo, President of Paraguay; General Isaias Medina, President of Venezuela; Dr. H. H. Kung, Vice President of the Executive Yan of China; and President Sveinn Bjornsson of Iceland. The hospitality of the House of Representatives extended also to General Julius F. Howell, the acting Commander-in-Chief of the United Confederate Veterans, who spoke to the House on June 3, 1944.

7. A New Foreign Policy

WHILE THE ISSUE of whether we should go to war was determined by the attack on Pearl Harbor, the broader issues of our foreign policy, which had been debated so long as offering the alternatives of isolation or intervention, remained unresolved. A new foreign policy was created during the war which vastly altered the nature of our commitments and interests. The foreign policy which developed during the war was largely based on assumptions widely held in the 1920s and 1930s but which had not received general support. The broad goals of the policy were enunciated by the President in the form of the Atlantic Charter (developed jointly with Prime Minister Churchill) and the Four Freedoms (contained in a Message to Congress), and a complex United Nations organization was established with American participation. In developing foreign policy in Congress, bipartisanship and bicameralism were increasingly utilized so that policy tended to be the product of both Houses and of both parties.

PARTISAN RESPONSIBILITIES

The sharp partisan debate on foreign policy which was going on when war broke out was not suddenly forgotten once the shooting began. The issues were too grave and the emotions too intense for this to happen, and, besides, neither politicians nor other people adjusted their positions or change their minds so quickly. Prewar alignments on foreign policy were often recognizable throughout the war, although the issues were no longer associated with neutrality but with the newer topics of the Atlantic Charter, the Four

Freedoms, the political responsibility for the attack on Pearl Harbor, the administration of Lend Lease, the creation of UNRRA, and other such subjects. Positions on foreign policy assumed before Pearl Harbor were rarely disavowed, either by the electorate or by its representatives, but over a period of time new positions were taken, so that there was substantial agreement on foreign policy by the end of the war.

After war had been declared, a number of partisans were still anxious to get at each others' throats on the old issues of isolationism and interventionism—words which were gradually discarded during the war as inappropriate partisan brands. During the week after Pearl Harbor, Rep. Emanuel Celler (D., Brooklyn, N.Y.) taunted the isolationists for their prewar stand. They should "apologize to President Roosevelt," he said.[1] They always claimed that he was violating his campaign pledges; what would they say now that America had been attacked? No apology was forthcoming, and the isolationists believed none was due. On the contrary, if anyone wished to discuss our prewar policy, they would charge that interventionist policy had led to war and that continued references to isolationism was a threat to national unity. For instance, Senator Robert La Follette (Prog., Madison, Wis.) criticized "former enthusiastic interventionist publicists" who, he said, were now looking for a scapegoat when they learned that Japan was not the pushover they expected it to be. La Follette claimed that these men were "deftly sniping at those who opposed the administration's foreign policy before war was declared" and were "trying to peddle the falsehood that the United States is ill-prepared for war because of the isolationists."[2] Senator C. Wayland Brooks (R., Chicago, Ill.) said during his primary campaign in the spring of 1942 that isolationism was dead, "it was sunk at Pearl Harbor."[3] However, everyone did not seem to think it was dead, and Senator Brooks himself attacked the "purge and smear" campaign which he said was directed against "loyal citizens whose

[1] C.R., Dec. 9, 1941, p. 9563.   [2] C.R., Feb. 9, 1942, p. A441.
[3] C.R., April 21, 1942, p. A1465.

heroic patriotism can never be challenged, merely because they did not agree before Pearl Harbor." [4] The Administration refrained from making an issue of isolationism in the elections of 1942 and 1944, tempting though this policy was to some, and they seemed to agree with Senator Truman that such recriminations would be "unwise and unjust," [5] as he put it, and would threaten the unity of the war effort.

Throughout the war Congress maintained its interest in the military and political responsibility for the attack on Pearl Harbor, but it did not create an investigating committee to dig into the matter until the war was over, when the full facts would presumably be available. During this period of "watchful waiting," partisans kept the issue alive by developing new hypotheses and making new charges on where the blame should properly fall. Shortly after the attack on Pearl Harbor, Senator David I. Walsh, the Chairman of the Naval Affairs Committee, advanced the theory that the Executive Branch was wholly responsible for Pearl Harbor, thus exculpating Congress and, inferentially, himself from blame. It was not fair to say "that there has been any failure on the part of Congress to act in any manner that would have prevented what happened at Pearl Harbor," he said. "The operations at Pearl Harbor were an executive function, and responsibility for them was lodged in the departments." [6]

The issue was also discussed during the legislative controversy surrounding the proposed courts martial of Admiral Husband E. Kimmel and General Walter C. Short, the highest ranking Navy and Army officers at Pearl Harbor. Some believed that Kimmel and Short should be tried immediately in order to establish the extent of their guilt, but no court-martial proceedings were initiated, and the two officers were retired on a pension. Rep. Stephen M. Young (D., Cleveland, O.), who wanted court-martial proceedings instituted at once, was incensed that the two officers would be permitted "to feed at the public trough the balance of

[4] C.R., Aug. 10, 1942, p. 6787.   [5] C.R., Feb. 3, 1942, p. 950.
[6] C.R., Feb. 3, 1942, p. 952.

their lives" even though "guilty of gross failure and gross dereliction of duty." [7]

The statute of limitation for such cases ran two years, and as
the expiration date drew near some Congressmen felt that the
time limit should be extended. As it happened, there was no necessity for extending the statute of limitations by law, so far as Admiral Kimmel and General Short were concerned, for each had
voluntarily waived the statute of limitations as a defense in the
event of trial. This was not generally known at the time, and in
any event the belief was growing that a court martial would show
that civilians rather than military officials were responsible for the
debacle.

A resolution extending the statute of limitations was quickly
passed by the House on Dec. 6, 1943. The leader of this legislative
coup was Rep. Dewey Short (R., Galena, Mo.), who was a so-
called pre-Pearl Harbor isolationist. The long, rambling preamble
of the resolution made it clear that Short hoped to catch other
than military officers in his net. There was good reason for believing that civilians "may also share in any dereliction of duty," the
preamble said, and these civilians should not be allowed "to escape
their full share of the responsibility and any just punishment." [8]
The resolution proposed that the deadline for prosecutions be
extended until a year after the signing of the peace treaty with
Japan, which would give ample time for rounding up all guilty
civilians. In the Senate, however, Senator Bennett Clark (D.,
University City, Mo.) took the view that certain individuals were
"conniving" to postpone the trial of Kimmel and Short "so that the
delay may be availed of for the purpose of protecting others." [9]
As a result of Clark's objection, a compromise was reached limiting the new extension legislation to six months.

Six months later was June, 1944, and it thus became possible
for partisan legislators, without the necessary facts at hand, to
debate the responsibility for Pearl Harbor during a presidential

[7] C.R., Feb. 16, 1942, p. A526.   [8] C.R., Dec. 6, 1943, p. 10321.
[9] C.R., Dec. 7, 1943, p. 10347.

campaign year. Representative Short now wanted action at once; his new resolution extended the statute of limitations for three months only and directed the Secretaries of War and of the Navy to institute court-martial proceedings against all persons involved. The rhetorical questions raised by Rep. Hamilton Fish (R., Garrison, N.Y.) were indicative of the attitude of many Congressmen. "What is the Administration trying to cover up? Who is the Administration trying to cover up? And why?" [10] The House agreed to Short's resolution, 305–35 (79 percent of the Democrats; 99 percent of the Republicans).

The Senate was not in such a hurry. It amended the resolution by extending the time a year—the conference reduced the time to six months—and by directing the Secretaries of War and of the Navy to proceed with an investigation of the facts—not, as the House had it, to start proceedings. These charges meant that any possible court-martial proceedings would not be held until after the elections. Representative Short was furious. He thought the proposed revision made the resolution "impotent and innocuous." If the "stalling" continued, he proposed to introduce a resolution "whereby the Congress itself will investigate this great catastrophe and dismal disaster." [11] The demand for a brief extension amused Rep. Hatton W. Sumners (D., Dallas, Tex.), who, deadpan, as if he did not know an election was in the wind, said: "This is one of the strangest things I have ever seen done in my life. The very people who are professing interest in this prosecution want the smallest length of time in which the prosecution can be initiated by anybody or any agency of the Government." [12] The conference report, extending the deadline for six months—after the election—was agreed to, 213–141 (100 percent of the Democrats; 24 percent of the Republicans).

During the subsequent political campaign, some Congressmen made further allegations about the events at Pearl Harbor without waiting for the War and Navy Departments to report their

[10] C.R., June 5, 1944, p. 5342.   [11] C.R., June 7, 1944, p. 5475.
[12] C.R., June 7, 1944, p. 5475.

findings, as they were directed to do by the new legislation. Rep. Forest A. Harness (R., Kokomo, Ind.), who wanted to keep the Pearl Harbor issue alive, alleged that the Australian government had notified the American government that a Japanese task force was headed for Pearl Harbor some seventy-two hours, forty-eight hours, and twenty-four hours before the attack. Harness said that he had no "personal knowledge" of the facts he presented, but they came from a source which he believed to be thoroughly reliable and trustworthy. Harness proposed that an investigating committee report its findings within thirty days—which would have been immediately before the election. If the President were innocent, Harness said, he "should be cleared promptly," but if the President had been "culpable in directing our military activities in Hawaii, the American people should have the true facts before they are called upon to pass judgment on his fitness for re-election to a fourth term as President." [13]

The Australian rumor was too pat to be authentic, for one could ask how the Australian government would know in advance that precise time which later would be exactly seventy-two, forty-eight, and twenty-four hours before the Pearl Harbor attack. The House Majority Leader, Rep. John W. McCormack, later presented to the House statements from the State, War, and Navy Departments and from the Government of Australia which said the charges were false. "The rumor upon which the gentleman from Indiana bases his statement was a lie—and the rumor is a malicious lie," McCormack told the House, and it was all the more malicious "because it comes at a time when our country is engaged in a war of preservation, and at a time when the heat of political contest exists." [14] Rep. Ralph E. Church (R., Evanston, Ill.) called attention to the fact that while three departments were referred to, McCormack had "not yet quoted nor has he yet inquired . . . of the White House." [15] "I think that is contemptible," McCormack answered. "That shows the gentleman's state

[13] C.R., Sept. 11, 1944, p. 7649, and Sept. 18, pp. 7866–67.
[14] C.R., Sept. 21, 1944, p. 8111.   [15] C.R., Sept. 21, 1944, p. 8111.

of mind . . . If the gentleman's votes were the votes of the majority of the Members of this Congress, when Pearl Harbor happened we would have been defenseless." [16]

After the election was at last over, the statute of limitations was again extended in December, but at that time there was little discussion and less interest; there were no threats from Representative Short and no rumors from Representative Harness, and the legislation was not sufficiently controversial for a record vote to be taken in either chamber.

PERSONALITIES AND PROCEDURES

The uneasiness which Congress often feels in foreign affairs was reflected in many of the debates. The subject matter of foreign affairs is less familiar to some Congressmen than domestic topics; it is also more elusive and less definable and cannot so readily be encompassed in the form of law. But there are additional reasons for congressional disquietude. Issues of foreign policy aggravate the old dispute between the President and Congress inherent in the separation of powers. The extensive powers which the President normally has in foreign affairs are augmented by the powers he exercises as Commander-in-Chief of the Army and Navy. Congress is never quite certain of the role it is supposed to play in foreign affairs, and to a considerable degree the President may be able to state the conditions under which Congress participates in forming foreign policy. The development of an effective foreign policy requires a good deal of trust on the part of Congress in the men who are carrying out this policy. Attempts were made during the war to establish greater confidence between the President and Congress through consultative procedures with bipartisan representation, but these devices were not so well developed that Congress could rely on them with confidence, and in many cases they were not used at all.

The President's enunciation of the war aims expressed in the Atlantic Charter and the Four Freedoms were not submitted to

[16] *C.R.*, Sept. 21, 1944, p. 8111.

Congress, and there seems to have been no consultation with congressional leaders on the content of these aims. In general, it can be said that Congress did not consider that it was necessarily bound by these statements, and yet somehow the nation had been committed. The opposition was able to take both sides of the issue, opposing the goals when they seemed unrealistic and defending them when the Administration seemed to be wavering on them. Senator Taft expressed the attitude of many members of the opposition when he said that he did not believe "that we went to war to establish the 'four freedoms' or any other freedom throughout the world," nor did he believe that "we went to war for the purposes set forth in the Atlantic Charter." [17] On the other hand, the Atlantic Charter and the Four Freedoms were used as a gauge to measure the limitations of the Administration's foreign policy, and it was charged that the Administration had broken faith with the people by violating the Atlantic Charter or compromising the Four Freedoms.

During the early years of the war, the relations between Congress and the State Department were especially good. The Secretary of State, Cordell Hull, was a former Senator who was widely trusted and respected in Congress. The Under-Secretary of State, Sumner Welles, also commanded the confidence of Congress. During the period of the Hull-Welles regime, a liaison with Congress was established which later permitted development into a procedure whereby Congressmen could take part in international conferences and in postwar planning. This liaison helped develop support for the UNRRA agreement, the Dumbarton Oaks Conference, and finally the United Nations Conference at San Francisco in 1945.

Edward R. Stettinius followed Mr. Hull as Secretary of State in 1944. The Senate confirmed the nomination by a vote of 68–1 (Senator Langer, of North Dakota, voted in the negative), but, compared to Hull, Stettinius was a newcomer to Congress, and he had had limited experience in foreign affairs. A few days later,

[17] C.R., Nov. 4, 1943, p. 9095.

the President nominated Mr. Stettinius's "team," as he called it, consisting of new appointments for the post of Under-Secretary of State and five Assistant Secretaries of State. These nominations created a feeling of uneasiness in the Senate inasmuch as foreign policy would now be directed by a new and partially unknown group. The nominations proved to be more controversial than the President or Mr. Stettinius thought they would be, and the episode momentarily threw a shadow across the political support given to foreign policy.

Four days after Mr. Stettinius was confirmed, the President nominated the career diplomat and former Ambassador to Japan, Joseph G. Grew, to be Under-Secretary of State, and Nelson Rockefeller, W. L. Clayton, and Archibald MacLeish to be Assistant Secretaries. Subsequently the President also nominated Brig. Gen. Julius C. Holmes and James C. Dunn to be Assistant Secretaries of State. When the Foreign Relations Committee considered the nominations at its next meeting, there was some objection raised to the Clayton and MacLeish nominations, but inasmuch as no proposal was made for holding hearings, the nominations were reported to the Senate. The Foreign Relations Committee met an unexpected defeat when the nominations were subsequently considered, for the Senate peremptorily returned all nominations to it. Senator Bennett Champ Clark (D., University City, Mo.), a member of the committee, proposed that MacLeish's nomination be recommitted for hearings lest his acquiescence in reporting the nomination "be considered to amount to my approval," [18] and Senator Burton K. Wheeler (D., Butte, Mont.) in an attempt at humor interjected that he understood "a poet was wanted in the State Department." [19]

Trouble developed from another source when Senator Joseph F. Guffey (D., Pittsburgh, Pa.), ordinarily a party-line Democrat, indicated that he was dissatisfied with all the nominations, and he quoted from a newspaper editorial which stated that "a good many liberals" believed that the new appointments "add up to a

[18] *C.R.*, Dec. 5, 1944, p. 8822.   [19] *C.R.*, Dec. 5, 1944, p. 8823.

national calamity." [20] More trouble developed when Senator Chandler joined in, saying that people "all around the world" were asking embarrassing questions about the Atlantic Charter and its relation to British policy; [21] he wanted hearings. So did Senators O'Mahoney and Murray, both Democrats. Chairman Tom Connally, who was getting no help at all from members of his committee, asked the Senate not to return the nominations, which he regarded "as a very unusual proceeding." [22] But Connally lost, and the Senate voted 37–24 to return all nominations to the committee (56 percent of the Democrats; 61 percent of the Republicans).

Hearings were subsequently held in the Senate caucus room before crowds and klieg lights, and the testimony was headline news. The poetry of Mr. Archibald MacLeish was again mentioned. At length, on December 14, the committee once more approved the nominations. Mr. MacLeish barely made it; he was approved at a midnight vote, long after the others, and after several hours of unfavorable or tie votes.

Again the Senate debated, and by this time a New Deal coterie, composed of Senator Pepper, Senator Murray, Senator Guffey, and Senator La Follette proposed that the consideration of all nominations be deferred until the next session of Congress. As a counterirritant, Senator Clark, a charter member of the original defectionist movement, believed that the effort made in the Foreign Relations Committee "to defeat such very excellent appointees as Mr. Grew, Mr. Clayton, and General Holmes" was "entirely unjustifiable," and he intended therefore "not only to vote, but, if necessary, to speak for the confirmation of Mr. MacLeish and the other nominees." [23] Clark said that Pepper had been attacking Stettinius, and asked him whether he had opposed his confirmation. Pepper answered that if he had been present he would have voted for Stettinius's confirmation, "but I did not expect every man in the Department to be a Stettinius." [24]

[20] C.R., Dec. 6, 1944, p. 8900.   [21] C.R., Dec. 6, 1944, p. 8902.
[22] C.R., Dec. 6, 1944, p. 8906.   [23] C.R., Dec. 16, 1944, p. 9598.
[24] C.R., Dec. 18, 1944, p. 9653.

The New Deal opposition soon dissolved. Senator Pepper and his three coobjectors presented their case to the President, who told them he would nominate the same men if the Senate postponed action until the following session. The only consolation the group received was the President's assurance that he would remove any nominee who failed to discharge his duties properly. Senator Pepper, after reporting these conversations to the Senate, said that he was now ready to vote because "we feel that nothing is to be gained by our prolonging the discussion of the nominations further." [25]

In the subsequent votes, Mr. Grew was confirmed, 66–7 (93 percent of the Democrats; 88 percent of the Republicans); Mr. Rockefeller, 62–10 (87 percent of the Democrats; 88 percent of the Republicans); General Holmes, 61–9 (84 percent of the Democrats; 90 percent of the Republicans); Mr. Clayton, 52–19 (73 percent of the Democrats; 79 percent of the Republicans); Mr. Dunn, 62–10 (88 percent of the Democrats; 84 percent of the Republicans), and Mr. MacLeish, 43–25 (97 percent of the Democrats; 20 percent of the Republicans). One of the ironies of the voting was that Senator Clark, who had brought on the episode by proposing that MacLeish's nomination be recommitted, and Senator O'Mahoney, who had made the motion to recommit, supported all six nominations.

WAR AND POSTWAR COMMITMENTS

Congress was continually apprehensive that the Administration would make permanent postwar commitments without congressional authorization or consultation, and the Senate, especially, feared that an attempt would be made to by-pass its treaty-making power. The Senate tried to defend itself against this prospective peril by raising a loud voice of warning whenever it felt its rights might be threatened and by inserting amendments from time to time designed to protect its rights. This attitude of suspicion, always latent, was expressed early in the war on the so-called

[25] *C.R.*, Dec. 19, 1944, p. 9682.

Panamanian resolution, which was thought at the time to be a dress rehearsal for some nebulous and half-dreaded treaty showdown which would occur after the war. It was also expressed in legislation affecting lend-lease and UNRRA.

The Panamanian resolution was a catch-all instrument. It attempted to settle several long-standing issues between Panama and the United States and, on America's part, to express appreciation for Panama's generosity in making available some hundred military sites to the United States without cost. There was no attempt to balance reciprocities or to strike a balance but rather to promote harmonious relations between the two countries. The total cost to the United States was to be some $10 million. The Senate debate was concerned less with the subject matter of the resolution than with the proposal to make foreign commitments by joint resolution. Senator Vandenberg, who initially opposed the resolution, wanted to know the extent to which "the State Department can commit the United States by agreement, instead of by treaty, respecting the ultimate treaty of peace, which will conclude the pending war." [26] Senator Connally, the Chairman of the Foreign Relations Committee, answered that he himself favored a treaty for terminating the war, and he recalled that the Republicans had terminated World War I by a joint resolution after the Treaty of Versailles had been defeated. The Senate at length passed the resolution, 40–29 (84 percent of the Democrats; 8 percent of the Republicans). The House, however, did not act.

The failure of the House to consider the Panama resolution in 1942 made it necessary to consider the legislation *de novo* at the new session in 1943. This time, the House acted first: there was little opposition in the House either to the content or to the procedure, and the resolution passed by a voice vote. In the meantime, some Senators had shifted their position, and among them were Senator Vandenberg and Senator Clark, of Missouri, who now supported the resolution. Under "normal circumstances,"

[26] *C.R.*, Dec. 3, 1942, p. 9267.

Vandenberg said, he would vote against it, but these were not normal times. Since "obviously it has to be done," it were better to act promptly and graciously "and get what we can out of a bad bargain." [27] Senator Clark, however, was no longer convinced that the proposal was a bad bargain, and he went on to praise the Good Neighbor policy and to indicate the importance of Panama in the defense of the United States. In April, the Senate passed a resolution identical with that passed in December, but the favorable vote now was 37–19 rather than 40–29 (100 percent of the Democrats; 30 percent of the Republicans). Slowly, then, a new bipartisan policy was developing.

The extension of lend-lease legislation in 1943, 1944, and 1945 gave Congress further opportunities for examining the basis for a postwar policy. The question of whether lend-lease should be extended was hardly the issue, for, as Senator Vandenberg described it, "lend-lease was the king-pin in the chain of international cooperation for victory." [28] The votes in favor of the extensions show how widely the basic principles of lend-lease were supported, for the three extensions were approved in the House by votes of 407–6, 334–21, and 354–28, and in the Senate by votes of 82–0, 63–1, and unanimously by voice vote. These overwhelming majorities, however, do not reveal the disquietude which existed in Congress over some phases of the lend-lease program.

The most controversial aspects of lend-lease extension related to the possibility that postwar agreements would be made by the Administration over which Congress would have no control. A section of the initial Act stated that, in settling accounts, payments might include any "direct or indirect benefit which the President deems satisfactory." This was a very broad standard indeed. During the various debates on extension, Congress attempted to clarify the standard by providing specifically that Congress should control the final postwar settlement. In the master agreements for settling lend-lease accounts, the Administration had included a proviso that the final settlement should not "bur-

[27] C.R., April 26, 1943, p. 3752.   [28] C.R., March 11, 1943, p. 1846.

den commerce" and that, eventually, a multilateral agreement should be negotiated, directed toward the elimination of discriminatory treatment and the reduction of tariffs in international trade.

This provision gave rise to new fears in Congress. Some members believed that the President might consider that he had the power to change tariff schedules and to make agreements on commercial aviation and on air and naval bases, all without the further consent of Congress. The supporters of the Administration argued that there was nothing in the lend-lease legislation which would give the President such power, and that no purpose was gained by enumerating specifically everything that the Act did not permit. This type of argument did not satisfy the opposition. Rep. John M. Vorys (R., Columbus, O.) attempted to protect the powers of Congress by providing specifically that Congress must approve "any final determination of benefits." [29] This proposal seemed reasonable enough, but it was pointed out that in some instances a treaty would be required, and in other instances an immediate decision on the spot. Could one tell General Eisenhower, it was asked, that he could make no final agreement with any regime in North Africa because Congress would have to approve? The Vorys amendment was defeated (there was no roll-call vote), and the lend-lease extension in 1943 contained no new provisions for the final settlement of accounts.

The question of how to control postwar commitments was again raised in 1944, when Congress adopted an amendment stating that the President could not commit the United States to any postwar policy "except in accordance with established constitutional procedure." Unlike the Vorys amendment of 1943, this amendment was limited to postwar policy, and the provision that "constitutional procedure" be followed was more flexible than one demanding congressional approval of all commitments. The House Foreign Affairs Committee, which initiated the proviso, claimed that Congress could now be assured that it could not be committed to any postwar policies "which properly lie within its

[29] *C.R.*, March 10, 1943, p. 1804.

province to determine." [30] The Senate Committee on Foreign Relations remained critical of this type of negative legislation, and it repeated its belief that the Act did not authorize the government to make any general postwar commitments. The proviso was not deleted, however, and it became part of the new legislation.

The controversy over postwar policy came up again in 1945, with a slightly shifted emphasis. Congress no longer believed it desirable to approve all lend-lease settlements, but it did believe that lend-lease should not be used for postwar relief, rehabilitation, and reconstruction. The House Foreign Affairs Committee initially reported the bill without amendments, although proposing that lend-lease be quickly liquidated after the war. However, five Republican members of the Foreign Affairs committee filed a minority report which criticized the bill because there were "no limitations on the use of lend-lease as a postwar mechanism." In order to meet this criticism, the committee consulted further with the government agencies involved and agreed to add an amendment stating that the President was not authorized to enter into agreements for postwar relief, rehabilitation, or reconstruction.

But could one always separate equipment for war and equipment for reconstruction? Indeed, the United States had recently reached an agreement to supply France with locomotives, which could be used for prosecuting the war as well as for postwar reconstruction. The House approved this type of agreement, which, as Senator Vandenberg told the Senate, "discloses the right way in which Congress wants all lend-lease handled in this respect." [31] Senator Taft thought otherwise, and he offered an amendment deleting congressional approval of agreements such as the one made with France. He was willing to support a loan to France, he said, but he did not think it should be made under lend-lease. Senator George made a vigorous speech denouncing the Taft amendment, which he said "would destroy the liquidating provision in the

[30] H. Rept. 259, March 6, 1945.   [31] *C.R.*, April 9, 1945, p. 3198.

original Lend-Lease Act." [32] The Taft amendment was defeated by the tie vote of 39–39 (100 percent of the Democrats; 5 percent of the Republicans).

The theory of reverse lend-lease, whereby our Allies supplied goods and equipment to the United States, was naturally popular with Congress, but it also led to odious comparisons and some ill will. The keeping of accounts on reverse lend-lease was involved and often inaccurate; the dollar equivalent of many items could not readily be ascertained, and in some cases it appeared that the Allies were charging a stiff price for services rendered. In any balancing of accounts, the manifestly greater contribution of the United States led some members to doubt that other nations were carrying their share of the load. Rep. Hamilton Fish made a different type of criticism—that the British were selling lend-lease goods directly to the British people and "were taking the money they received . . . and putting it into their own exchequer." [33]

It was also charged that the administration of the Act had been wasteful, resulting in shortages in the American economy, and Rep. Philip Philbin (D., Clinton, Mass.) told the House that he understood that "good American shoes had been sent to North Africa where most of the natives, never having worn shoes, are reported to utilize them by slinging them around their necks and using them for pockets." [34]

Senator Vandenberg went to the defense of reverse lend-lease. The proper test should not be in terms of dollars, he said—and the Committee on Foreign Relations had not been able to establish reciprocal values in cash terms—but rather "whether our allies are cooperating with us to the total extent of their capacities." The answer to that question was Yes. [35]

The Lend-Lease Administrator, Edward Stettinius, received an unusual number of encomiums from Congress, and his appearance before the committees was most successful. In 1943, Rep. John M. Vorys (R., Columbus, O.) said of Mr. Stettinius: "His

[32] C.R., April 10, 1945, p. 3246. [33] C.R., March 7, 1943, p. 1641.
[34] C.R., March 10, 1943, p. 1814. [35] C.R., March 11, 1943, p. 1846.

willingness to spend time with a congressional committee, his willingness to hear complaints and investigate them were so different from the typical Washington bureaucrat, and so refreshing, that I feel it my duty to make special mention of him." [36]

The creation of UNRRA (United Nations Relief and Rehabilitation Administration) in 1943 offered Congress another chance to debate the question of procedures in making international agreements. When the UNRRA agreement was initially negotiated by the Administration, it was planned to restrict the part played by Congress to appropriating funds. Senator Vandenberg was not satisfied with this procedure, and he asked Secretary of State Hull whether the State Department planned to submit the UNRRA draft agreement to the Senate for ratification. Secretary Hull answered "No," that after consulting with the leaders of the majority and minority in both Houses "it had been decided that United States participation in the establishment of this United Nations administration should be through an Executive Agreement." [37] Vandenberg commented that whereas Congress paid the bill, it had "nothing to say about what the bills shall be," and he asked the Foreign Relations Committee to report "whether in its judgment this draft agreement partakes of the nature of a treaty, and should be submitted to the Senate for ratification." [38]

This set the wheels rolling. A subcommittee was appointed which discussed the Vandenberg resolution with Secretary Hull and Assistant Secretary Acheson, and a new procedure was developed for considering the UNRRA Agreement by Congress. Some seven months later, Senator Vandenberg told the Senate that the State Department had agreed immediately that there should be "total congressional consultation"; from that point on, he said, "the State Department worked in closest and most sympathetic co-operation with the sub-committee of the Foreign Relations Committee in re-writing the entire agreement. . . . The net result is that we have an instrument here submitted to the

[36] *C.R.*, March 8, 1943, p. 1652. [37] *C.R.*, July 8, 1943, p. 7436.
[38] *C.R.*, July 8, 1943, pp. 7433ff.

Senate which I can stand and defend and recommend to my colleagues." [39]

The procedure followed was that of incorporating the text of the rewritten Agreement in the resolution authorizing the expenditure of funds, so that Congress indirectly endorsed the Agreement itself. The resolution also included reservations on the extent to which the Agreement committed the United States. Some of the reservations seem to have extended beyond the legal power of Congress, such as the prohibition on UNRRA incurring obligations, but they did reflect congressional policy, and Congress was in a favorable position to secure the policy it wanted by the fact that it was supplying the funds. The State Department assured Congress that its control over funds would be maintained, and, in particular, Mr. Acheson said that "Congress would have complete power at any time to stop its contributions or to lay down the conditions as to their uses." [40]

There was considerable support for the UNRRA resolution in Congress, although there was opposition both to the procedure followed and to the content of the Agreement, and some members voted for UNRRA grudgingly. The argument that the Agreement should have been in the form of a treaty was now quite hopeless, but it was raised in the House by Rep. Bertrand W. Gearhart (R., Fresno, Calif.), who asked whether Congress was "giving encouragement to this Administration to go on and on and on, until finally they get sufficient courage to negotiate a peace treaty under the guise and in the form of an Executive Agreement?" [41] Senator Taft, also concerned about precedent, said he would vote for the proposal, albeit "with a good many reservations and doubts." He argued that if an Executive Agreement could be used to create an international food relief organization, "then exactly the same thing could be done in the case of a League of Nations . . . and at once we would lose entirely the power to carry out the treaty-making process provided in the Constitution." He did

[39] C.R., Feb. 16, 1944, p. 1739.   [40] C.R., Feb. 16, 1944, p. 1740.
[41] C.R., Jan. 20, 1944, p. 471.

not believe that "this Executive Agreement can be validated simply because it is subject to congressional approval." [42]

Senator Guy M. Gillette (D., Cherokee, Iowa), a cosponsor of the Hoover plan for feeding the children in occupied Europe, opposed UNRRA, being unwilling to appropriate money for "an organization which we did not create, an organization in which we would have but only one vote, an organization for the machinery of which we would give approval, an organization which is a policy-making organization with power to determine and change in the future its policies under which the money is to be expended and over which we would have no control except the negative control over appropriations when it asks us for additional money." [43] Rep. Jessie Sumner (R., Milford, Ill.) thought the proposal was unconstitutional. She believed that "the safe, sane, constitutional, and Christian way to relieve the victims of Nazi barbarism" was to organize "a tremendous drive for voluntary contributions" to be distributed by the Red Cross, the Quakers, and other nonpolitical organizations.[44] Rep. Edith Nourse Rogers (R., Lowell, Mass.) wanted relief handled by military rather than civilian authorities.

An amendment, supported by the farm groups, was adopted which earmarked $50 million for the purchase of American farm products, and in this case for raw wool and cotton. A good deal of controversy was aroused by the propaganda amendment, proposed by Senator Raymond E. Willis (R., Angola, Ind.), which provided that no funds be expended "in the promotion of any educational, religious, or political program in any country in which rehabilitation is carried on." [45] The stated purpose of the amendment was to prevent UNRRA from being used to spread communist propaganda. The Senate accepted the amendment, 45–18 (55 percent of the Democrats; 98 percent of the Republicans) and then went on to adopt the UNRRA resolution, 47–14 (81 percent of the Democrats; 71 percent of the Republicans). After voting

[42] C.R., Feb. 17, 1944, p. 1815.   [43] C.R., Feb. 16, 1944, p. 1753.
[44] C.R., Jan. 20, 1944, p. 472.   [45] C.R., Feb. 17, 1944, p. 1827.

for his amendment, Senator Willis voted against the UNRRA Agreement.

The conferees rejected the Willis amendment. In explaining this action, Senator Connally said that the House conferees had taken the attitude that "there was nothing in the joint resolution which would authorize the acts which the Senator's amendment denounced," and they wouldn't agree to keeping the amendment in the bill.[46] Rep. James W. Wadsworth (R., Geneseo, N.Y.), who was also on the conference committee, assured the House that UNRRA had not the slightest intention of controlling education, much less religion. The conference had deleted the amendment, he said, because "it might have been construed as forbidding UNRRA to repair glass windows in a half-wrecked school, on the ground that that was interfering with educational institutions." [47]

Here was a new issue for debate which replaced such questions as whether the Agreement should be in the form of a treaty. Senator Willis was disappointed that the conferees had deleted his amendment without asking the House to vote on it, and he branded their action as "an example of democracy in reverse." [48] Willis's proposal to send the resolution back to conference was defeated, 22–36 (0 percent of the Democrats; 76 percent of the Republicans). The Senate then adopted the conference report, 47–9 (97 percent of the Democrats; 69 percent of the Republicans); the House adopted it by a vote of 287–57 (93 percent of the Democrats; 75 percent of the Republicans). Bipartisanship in making foreign policy was slowly developing.

BIPARTISAN CONSULTATION AND BICAMERALISM

During the war, members of Congress were increasingly invited to participate in international negotiations, either at the preparatory stage or at the conference level. For the most part, invitations were given to members of both Houses and of both parties, so that a type of bipartisan and bicameral consultation

[46] C.R., March 21, 1944, p. 2803.   [47] C.R., March 22, 1944, p. 2938.
[48] C.R., March 21, 1944, p. 2804.

resulted. An unsuccessful attempt was made to amend the Constitution so as to give the House an equal share in the treaty-making power.

Although there is much to recommend the practice of consulting members of Congress in the formulation of foreign policy, it had not been used in the past with any regularity. Indeed, the practice has been frowned on by some administrators, who disliked to trouble themselves with politicians at the consultative stage of negotiations, and by some Congressmen, who did not wish to forfeit their freedom to criticize or reject a proposal by having participated in earlier negotiations. Nevertheless, consultation does provide a method for keeping Congress informed; at the minimum it should prevent the spreading of unfounded rumors, and under ordinary circumstances it should provide members with additional facts on which to base their decisions.

The use of congressional representatives at international conferences was on the whole successful, but the practice got off to a halting start. Plans were made for a conference on refugees to meet in Bermuda in April, 1943, and for a conference on food and agriculture to meet in Hot Springs, Va., in May, 1943. When it was announced that both meetings would be closed, with neither Congressmen nor reporters present, many Congressmen feared the worst. It was widely suspected that commitments would be made by American delegates without the knowledge or approval of Congress. Rep. A. Leonard Allen (D., Winnfield, La.) insisted that the meetings should be given publicity and that members of Congress should attend, after which they would report to Congress. A similar proposal was made by two members from the Michigan delegation. Although no member of Congress was invited to attend the conference on food and agriculture at Hot Springs, two members nevertheless showed up unannounced, without credentials. Mr. Marvin Jones, the head of the American delegation, announced to the press that "two of my former colleagues have visited us." They had been extended every possible courtesy, with full opportunity for meeting and talking with the delegates, but the uninvited guests did not attend the executive sessions of the committees. Mr. Jones defended the need for secrecy at such sessions by comparing the practice with the executive sessions of congressional committees. "Every practical legislator," Mr. Jones said, "knows that frequently in drafting the details on legislation it is necessary to have executive sessions of the committee in order to get the work done without interruption. As soon as a measure is reported to the House for approval or disapproval it is known to everyone. This is especially true in a conference of many nations. If visitors are admitted to the working sessions from one nation, they must be admitted from all and work would become totally impossible." [49] A few days later, Mr. Jones attempted to allay continuing fears by stating that "no commitment of any kind will or can be made at this conference" [50] and by describing the conference as a fact-finding body which had nothing to do with relief.

Attacks on the procedure of the conference were made in Congress. Rep. Frederick C. Smith (R., Marion, O.), one of the unbidden guests, told the House that "the American farmers will be intensely interested to learn that they are to be the first group to be liquidated under the grandiose scheme that is being concocted by the so-called food conference at Hot Springs to make our nation over into a totalitarian state and to put it under the heel of a world dictatorship." After the conference was over, Mr. Jones reported to the House Committee on Agriculture at a public meeting, but Representative Smith remained unsatisfied. Mr. Jones "told the committee practically nothing of the real work that was done at the Hot Springs meeting," he said, and his statement before the committee "was representative of the tactics he pursued all through the conference to shield in secrecy its activities." Smith said that "the dominating thought of the delegates collected together at Hot Springs was to form an international body to which

[49] C.R., May 25, 1943, p. A2594.   [50] C.R., May 25, 1943, p. A2602.

it would give functions so great as to constitute what would amount to an authoritarian super-state." [51] The records in his possession showed that Jones "failed utterly in telling the Committee on Agriculture what really took place at Hot Springs."

Some members of Congress were also critical of the procedures and the results of the Bermuda Conference on Refugees. Proposals were made in this case also that Congress send its own delegation to the conference, but they were not adopted. However, the Administration decided to include two members of Congress in the American delegation, selecting for this purpose Rep. Sol Bloom, (D., New York, N.Y.), the Chairman of the House Committee on Foreign Affairs, and Senator Scott W. Lucas (D., Havana, Ill.). The results of the Bermuda Conference were not published at the time—it was learned after the war that secrecy was invoked because the conference discussed methods of rescuing refugees from Nazi-occupied Europe—and this secrecy caused some apprehension on the part of critics.

Congressional representation did not completely allay these fears, and the members of Congress who attended the conference were handicapped in not being able to tell their colleagues what agreements had been reached or why secrecy was necessary. Rumors developed at once suggesting that there had been no proper discussion of Palestine immigration or of American immigration quotas. Rep. Emanuel Celler believed that the Bermuda Conference "has dismally failed," [52] and Rep. Samuel Dickstein added the conference had ended "the hopes of millions of people." [53]

On returning to Washington, Senator Lucas found himself in an embarrassing position. A six-column political advertisement appeared in the New York *Times* which called the Bermuda Conference a "cruel mockery." The statement was signed by Lucas's colleague, Senator Edwin C. Johnson (D., Craig, Colo.), in his capacity as national chairman of the Committee for a Jewish Army of Stateless and Palestinian Jews, and it was endorsed by some

---

[51] *C.R.*, June 1, 1943, p. 5168, and June 2, p. A3168.
[52] *C.R.*, May 3, 1943, p. A2155.   [53] *C.R.*, May 12, 1943, p. A2329.

thirty-nine Senators. On inquiry, Lucas learned that several Senators were surprised to learn that their names had appeared in the advertisement. Senator Johnson was impelled to write to the committee that he and members of his committee "must come to an understanding at once, that greater caution be exercised in publishing the names of Senators who favor our cause." Having exposed the synthetic nature of the pressure group's propaganda, Lucas proceeded to defend the conference in general terms. However, he could not reveal the recommendations of the conference because he was "pledged to secrecy until the report is officially released." He had no intention of "violating that trust by revealing on the floor of the Senate, or elsewhere, any confidential information concerning the conference." [54]

The House of Representatives, it will be seen, wished to participate in making international commitments, but it was unable to persuade the Senate that it should be given equal power over treaties. In 1945, the House voted on a proposal to amend the Constitution so that treaties would be submitted to both Houses of Congress. The House passed the resolution by a vote of 288–88 (98 percent of the Democrats; 52 percent of the Republicans), but the Senate was in no mood to share its power, and it took no action. The proposal may have been made too late to have attracted very much public or political support, and there seemed to be no general demand for changing the treaty-making process at that time. When the Senate ratified the United Nations Charter the following month by a vote of 89–2, the argument for changing the method of considering treaties lost much of its appeal.

THE UNITED NATIONS

During the period of the war, Congress considered it essential to develop a foreign policy which would outlast the military coalition of the war itself. Initially, Congress was reluctant to look beyond the clouds of war, but in 1943 it took a firmer stand in the matter as opinion began to crystallize around the creation of a

[54] *C.R.*, May 6, 1943, p. 4045.

new international agency which hopefully would keep the peace. Public opinion developed before Congress took any concrete action. In March, 1943, the so-called B_2H_2 resolution (for the sponsors, Ball-Burton-Hill-Hatch) was introduced in the Senate, recommending that the United States take the initiative in creating a United Nations organization. The resolution stimulated public interest and public debate and, in a singular fashion, caught the imagination of the public. The four Senate sponsors of the resolution had not hitherto played an active role in foreign affairs; they were not members of the Committee on Foreign Relations and did not represent congressional leadership in foreign policy. They were Senators Joseph H. Ball (R., St. Paul, Minn.), Harold H. Burton (R., Cleveland, O.), Lister Hill (D., Montgomery, Ala.), and Carl A. Hatch (D., Clovis, N.M.).

The generally favorable attitude of the public toward creating an international agency was reflected in the public-opinion polls, and many legislators were now persuaded that nothing was to be gained by deferring action on a statement outlining postwar policy aims. The Senate Foreign Relations Committee proceeded to consider a postwar resolution introduced by its Chairman, Senator Connally. At length, the Senate adopted a resolution which stated that it recognized "the necessity of there being established at the earliest practicable date a general international organization . . . for the maintenance of international peace and security." With typical caution, the Senate included a paragraph which stated that any treaty made in pursuance of the resolution would and could be made only by and with the consent of the Senate. The Senate adopted the resolution by a vote of 85–5; negative votes were cast by Senators Hiram Johnson of California, William Langer of North Dakota, Robert R. Reynolds of North Carolina, Henrik Shipstead of Minnesota, and Burton K. Wheeler of Montana.

The House took action on a similar resolution, sponsored by Rep. J. William Fulbright (D., Fayetteville, Ark.). There was scant opposition in the House, although Rep. Clare E. Hoffman (R., Allegan, Mich.) did say that the adoption of the proposal

would mean "that we repeal the Declaration of Independence." [55]
The House adopted the resolution by a vote of 360–29 (98 percent of the Democrats; 87 percent of the Republicans). While
the Connally and Fulbright resolutions did not legally bind the
Administration to any specific policy, they were significant revela-
tions of the attitude of Congress, and some believed that they
placed the Administration under a moral obligation to proceed
in developing an international organization to keep the peace.

The Administration proceeded to develop plans for such an
organization, and in August, 1944, these plans were discussed at
an international conference held at Dumbarton Oaks, in Washington, D.C. A great deal of preparatory work had preceded the
conference, during which period members of Congress had been
freely and extensively consulted. Shortly before the Dumbarton
Oaks Conference, Senator Connally told the Senate that a group
from Congress had talked over the plans with the Secretary of
State "almost weekly during a period of nearly a year." The Senate had been and would be kept advised, he said, and no one need
fear "that there will be any sort of ignoring of the Committee on
Foreign Relations." [56]

Senator Vandenberg, who was developing as the Republican
leader of a bipartisan foreign policy, told the Senate that Secretary of State Hull had personally placed at his disposal "any information I may seek at any time regarding any phase of the
Dumbarton Oaks Conference." Vandenberg was in "cordial agreement" with Senator Connally in his "dedication to an unpartisan
approach to this tremendously vital achievement." He was less
certain than Connally about international commitments which
had already been made and was mildly critical of the "lack of
information, particularly regarding postwar understandings, at
Casablanca, Quebec, Cairo, and Teheran." [57]

Not all members of the Senate were as dedicated to the bipartisan approach as were Senators Connally and Vandenberg, nor

[55] C.R., Sept. 20, 1943, p. 7649.   [56] C.R., Aug. 22, 1944, pp. 7174ff.
[57] C.R., Aug. 22, 1944, p. 7175ff.

did the assurances of these leaders prevent the rise of rumors. Senator Harlan J. Bushfield (R., Miller, S.D.) told the Senate that "leaks" from the conference showed that "we Americans are to be called upon to surrender our sovereignty and our liberty to the caprice of one man." Under the plan proposed, the "President will have the power to declare war without the consent, the knowledge, or the approval of Congress." Bushfield then asked rhetorically of President Roosevelt whether that was the platform "upon which you are running for the fourth term as President of the United States." [58] Connally responded that the question raised by Bushfield could properly be discussed later, inasmuch as the current conference was at the technical level only. Connally had no intention, he said, to "fall into the trap so skillfully set" of discussing the question from a partisan angle.[59]

In 1945, there was an unusually high degree of cooperation between Congress and the Administration, and broad commitments were made in foreign policy. Four members of Congress acted as advisers to Secretary of State Stettinius at the Inter-American Conference which met at Mexico City in February, 1945. The Act of Chapultepec was developed at the conference, the essence of which was that a treaty should be negotiated providing for collective security in the Western Hemisphere. In reporting the results of the conference to the Senate, Senator Connally said he construed the participation of members of Congress at Mexico City and at the coming San Francisco Conference as "an evidence of a better spirit between the executive department and the Congress." [60] The constitutional provision that treaties be made by and with the advice and consent of the Senate was being recognized, Connally said, and the Senate was "being consulted before the actual drafting and submission of the treaties, and, of course, will be called upon later to act upon, and to ratify or reject."

The careful, detailed preparations for creating a postwar organization and the foresight in bringing in congressional advisers at

[58] C.R., Sept. 5, 1944, p. 7522.   [59] C.R., Sept. 5, 1944, p. 7523.
[60] C.R., March 12, 1945, p. 2020.

an early stage of the planning were abundantly evident when the Senate considered the ratifications of the United Nations Charter. Senators Connally and Vandenberg, from the Senate Foreign Relations Committee, and Representatives Bloom and Eaton, from the House Foreign Affairs Committee, attended the San Francisco Conference as American delegates. They approved the results and urged the Senate to ratify the treaty. Senator Connally told the Senate that there had been "splendid unity and harmony within the United States delegation" at San Francisco.[61] The delegation had voted as a unit on all matters, and minor differences had been adjusted within the delegation. Senator Vandenberg was equally laudatory in his report of the conference, and he particularly praised the ability of his colleagues and the nonpartisan nature of the discussions. During the conference, he said, there had not been "the faintest hint of partisanship at any time." [62] The Senate paid Connally and Vandenberg the unusual compliment of rising and applauding at the end of their speeches.

The subsequent proceedings on the United Nations Charter were largely routine and the results fully anticipated. President Truman addressed the Senate on July 2, urging ratification. Hearings were held for some three weeks, during which time a large number of groups indicated their approval of the Charter. The debate began in the Senate on July 23, with Senator Connally describing the nonpartisan approach with which the subcommittee of eight had assisted in developing the plans for the Charter. Speech followed speech, most of them being lengthy, documented, and profound, clearly written for posterity and for the constituents who wanted their Senators to be statesmen. Senator Walter F. George (D., Vienna, Ga.) made an impressive speech; it was reflective and philosophical, rather than factual and incisive, as George's speeches usually are, and it dwelt on the possibility that in time the General Assembly would develop into a type of parliament which could keep the peace of the world. The effectiveness of the speech was enhanced by the general knowledge that Senator George had lost

[61] C.R., June 28, 1945, pp. 6874ff.   [62] C.R., June 28, 1945, pp. 6981ff.

a son in combat. When the speech was over, Senator Charles W. Tobey (R., Temple, N.H.) remarked that those fortunate enough to have heard "the truly wonderful address" had been "moved to our very souls," [63] and the Senate then stood in silence as a token of the esteem they held for their colleague, Senator George.

The vote for ratification was 89–2, the negative votes being cast by Senator Langer, of North Dakota, and Senator Henrik Shipstead, of Minnesota. If present, Senator Hiram Johnson, of California, would also have voted nay.

[63] *C.R.*, July 27, 1945, p. 8111.

8. Reconversion to Peace

ONCE the economy had been converted to war, Congress began to consider how it could be reconverted to peace, and it evolved several major pieces of reconversion legislation while the war was still on. It was thought desirable to plan reconversion policy somewhat in advance of actual need in order that the production of civilian goods could be quickly resumed when the war was over. Some of the issues surrounding reconversion were quite controversial inasmuch as the various economic groups had different interests at stake. An attempt had been made during the war to preserve the economic relationships which existed before the war, but many of these relationships had been vastly distorted. For instance, industry which could convert to war production was in a superior economic position to one which could not convert. Now, in planning reconversion, it was obvious that some industries could profit by a quick reconversion and that others would be at a considerable disadvantage.

But, one asks, was it necessary to make plans for reconversion? Could not industry return to the manufacture of civilian goods without government assistance? Could not the whole economy be unfrozen at once, and, at some certain date, government controls over individuals and over business be terminated? The goal, certainly, was the quick return to a civilian economy, but if this were to be achieved, some decisions would have to be made in advance. Should government contracts be terminated quickly when military demands slackened, even at the cost of a rise in unemployment? If surplus government property were made available to the public at cheap prices, how would this affect the legitimate commercial market? If reconversion resulted in considerable unemployment, should the federal government or the States develop public works projects? What type of tax rebates would assist business to reconvert? Should an industry be allowed to reconvert when it no longer had war contracts, or should all of industry begin reconversation at the same time under equal conditions? What provisions should be made for absorbing the veteran in the economy? In addition, one could ask specific questions about the effect of reconversion on specific groups, such as small business, large business, farmers, former war workers, veterans, and, of course, Republicans and Democrats.

In 1943 the Senate and the House each created special reconversion committees, commonly called the George and the Colmer committees, after the names of their chairmen, Senator Walter F. George (D., Vienna, Ga.) and Rep. William M. Colmer (D., Pascagoula, Miss). It was anticipated that these committees would develop an integrated reconversion plan, but this did not occur. The reason in part lay in the complicated committee structure of Congress and in the jurisdiction which the regular standing committees had over various parts of the reconversion plan. The George and the Colmer committees could not report legislation; this could only be done by the regular standing committees. Everything had to be done at least twice in each chamber, and sometimes three, four, and five times. In considering reconversion legislation, Congress had to operate within a committee mosaic of distressing complexity, and the recital of various steps followed may very probably exasperate the average reader. A rather detailed recital of procedures is given, however, in order to make complete the picture of congressional diligence in a confusing system of decentralized committees.

In advancing its reconversion plans in 1944, Congress created the Office of War Mobilization and Reconversion as the agency primarily responsible for planning and carrying out reconversion policy. This agency, initially created by Executive Order, was now reorganized and renamed and directed by law to act as the supreme coordinator for war and for peace. The Director was instructed to make plans and issue orders on problems "arising out of the transition from war to peace," and he was to have general supervision over the administration of the Contract Settlement and the Surplus Property Acts, both of which were also enacted. Legislation for the so-called G.I. Bill of Rights and for mustering-out pay was also enacted. By the end of 1944 most of the reconversion legislation had been enacted.

CONTRACT SETTLEMENT

The first of the series of reconversion measures developed a fixed policy on the settlement of contracts. The subject of contract settlement commanded, in its day, the interest of a good many informed persons, although it was by nature scarcely the type of subject to hold the interest of the public. Certainly there can have been few subjects in the past on which more committees spent more time, for contract settlement policy was considered by the George and Colmer committees; the Senate and House Military Affairs Committee; the Senate Small Business Committee, and the House Judiciary Committee. In the Senate, policy was to some extent coordinated by the interlocking committee membership of Senator James E. Murray (D., Butte, Mont.), who was a member of the three interested Senate Committees and, with Senator George, was cosponsor of the legislation. Senator George said that the bill "really was produced" by Senator Murray, who had "performed what I believe to be a magnificent service to the country in advancing our reconversion program thus far." [1]

The Administration was also interested in contract settlement. The so-called Baruch-Hancock Report on war and postwar adjustment policies, which was prepared for the Office of War Mobilization, proposed that the government adopt at once a uniform policy of quickly terminating unnecessary contracts. Such a policy was imperative, the report said, in order that business interests

[1] *C.R.,* May 3, 1944, p. 3905.

would "know where they stood" and in order that contracts would not be continued merely to provide employment. The need for establishing some specific policy was emphasized by the magnitude of existing cancellation. As of March 31, 1944, the Army had canceled some 21,000 contracts and the Navy some 4,000, and with any sudden termination of the war the number would rise perceptibly.

Within Congress there was full and widespread support for the principles enunciated in the Baruch-Hancock Report, and the controversial phases of the contract termination debate were centered on the peripheral issues. One issue related to the scope of the legislation; another to provisions for auditing contracts. Senator Harley M. Kilgore (D., Beckley, W. Va.) wanted a single-package reconversion bill which established policy on contract cancellation, demobilization, unemployment benefits, and the disposal of war plants and surplus property. Kilgore had the support of most of the influential labor leaders, who thought the "piecemeal" approach failed to consider "the human side of demobilization." These leaders believed that labor, unlike war contractors, was not strong enough to weather any period of reconversion, and they therefore proposed that the legislation include unemployment compensation benefits. Senator Murray, who was certainly not unfriendly to labor, responded that he had been in touch with representatives of labor "in an effort to work out a provision for unemployment compensation, to be inserted in the pending bill," [2] but that they had been unable to prepare such legislation. Assurances were given that the "human side of reconversion" would not be overlooked in the future. An added reason for considering one subject at a time was the difficulty of considering an omnibus bill in the House, where there would surely be jurisdictional disputes in the jealous committee hierarchy. With these assurances and explanations, the Senate passed the bill without a record vote.

[2] C.R., May 3, 1944, p. 3901.

The contentious issue in the House debate was the authority to be given the General Accounting Office in settling accounts, an issue further complicated by the contest between the Military Affairs Committee and the Judiciary Committee for control of the legislation. The Committee on Military Affairs, which wanted to increase the power of the General Accounting Office, lost out on both issues. Bickerings between members of the two committees continued throughout the debate. The Chairman of the Military Affairs Committee, Rep. Andrew J. May (D., Prestonsburg, Ky.), for instance, told the House that inasmuch as his committee had been "the war policy committee" for more than a hundred years "it would have been better from the beginning to have allowed that committee, that handles all war legislation, to consider the subject instead of scattering it around over Congress." [3] He was answered by Rep. Estes Kefauver (D., Chattanooga, Tenn.), a member of the Judiciary Committee, who said that if legislation involving "intricate legal questions," such as the bill on contract termination, were not referred to the Judiciary Committee, "then I do not know what function the Committee on the Judiciary has to perform." [4]

It was argued that an independent audit of contract settlement by the General Accounting Office would help prevent fraud. Some members recalled that war frauds had been exposed by the so-called Graham Committee after the First World War and that these exposures led to the creation of the General Accounting Office. Under ordinary circumstances, members of Congress would have demanded that this "arm of Congress" be empowered to protect the public interest against possible arbitrary decisions made by the bureaucrats. However, the theme of contract cancellation was "hurry, hurry, hurry," as Mr. Baruch put it; settle the contracts quickly and made the settlement final and binding. In this case, the bureaucrats were to be trusted, at least those in charge of settling contracts. The amendment to increase the power of

[3] *C.R.*, June 16, 1944, p. 6082.   [4] *C.R.*, June 16, 1944, p. 6082.

the General Accounting Office was defeated without a roll-call
vote. The House then passed the bill, 326–21 (90 percent of the
Democrats; 96 percent of the Republicans).

SURPLUS PROPERTY

The second reconversion measure developed a policy for disposing of the surplus war property, which had an estimated value
ranging from $50 billion to more than $100 billion. The disposal
of surplus property was not a new problem for the armed services
or the government, but a special situation had been created because of the amount of surplus property to be disposed of and the
impact the disposal would have on the civilian economy. In a nation where all civilian goods were in short supply, the prospects of
the sale of surplus war goods stimulated the imagination of the
people, with high school students dreaming of cheap jeeps and
Republicans hoping that the receipts from surplus sales would
help pay off the national debt.

The Surplus Property bill was also the composite product of an
amazing number of committees, and these committees failed to
reach agreement on the content of the legislation. During the deliberations on the floor, controversies developed over the structure of the agency, the control which Congress should assert over
the sale of surplus plants, and the use of income from sales for retiring the national debt.

The structure of the agency was directly related to the objectives
the program was supposed to achieve, and on this question the Senate and House had different opinions. The objectives listed in the
final Act were an amazing compilation of platitudinous prescrip-
tions which formed no clear guide for the administrators in formulating policy. The Act was to give maximum aid in reestablishing
free independent private enterprise, stimulate full employment,
discourage monopolistic practices, develop independent operat-
ors, foster family-type farming, protect veterans, promote postwar
employment, discourage sale to speculators, develop foreign mar-

kets while avoiding dislocations in the domestic economy, and foster broad and equitable distribution of surplus property at fair prices which were to be established with due regard for the protection of free markets and competitive prices. Normal channels of trade were to be utilized, and new independent enterprise was to be fostered. Unusual and excessive profits were to be prevented insofar as possible; and the government was to obtain the fair value of the property.

So many different purposes had to be achieved, so many interests to be weighed and considered, that the Senate was reluctant to create a single-headed agency, with one person responsible for administering the entire program. It decided to create an eight-man board which, in miniature, represented the same interests as Congress. The Senate provided that the board would be selected with due consideration given "to the various geographical areas and economic interests of the nation." In its deliberations, the board was directed to "take into account the interests of all economic groups, such as consumers, industry, agriculture, and labor."

The House followed a different theory—that the sale of surplus property was a business operation, not a device for sharing the wealth, and that the agency should be directed by a single administrator who would be responsible for carrying out the program. The House was largely influenced by the opinions of W. L. Clayton, a businessman from Houston, Texas, and later Under-Secretary of State, who at the time was in charge of the surplus property program then being carried on by the government. Throughout the House debate it was assumed that Mr. Clayton would administer the new Act, and the House passed a bill creating an agency with a single administrator in charge.

The diverse positions of the Senate and the House were resolved in a conference which lasted some three weeks. Each group of conferees was reluctant to change its views. During the conference Mr. Clayton made the unusual gesture of removing himself from the controversy. He wrote to his superior, Mr. Byrnes, the head of the Office of War Mobilization, that he could not accept an appointment as administrator of the surplus property program, if offered it, because of his growing conviction "that the surplus property disposal program is no longer to be conducted in a business-like manner." [5] The conference later adopted the compromise position of creating a board of three men to administer the program.

The Senate and the House also disagreed on the disposition of war plants, in which the government had invested some $15 billion. The House advocated quick disposal; the Senate, a wait-and-see attitude. The House Committee on Expenditures in the Executive Department urged that the plants be disposed of promptly "so that they can be put to productive peace-time use and reemploy workers at the earliest possible moment." It was necessary to "weigh the social value" of restrictions "against the delay in re-employment which will result if no buyers can be found," and in totaling up the weights, the balance tilted in favor of no restrictions.[6] There was an exception: because of "an overwhelming national interest" in the disposal of rubber and aluminum plants, special procedures were recommended. The agency was to present to Congress plans for the disposal of all such plants costing more than $5 million; if Congress took no adverse action within six months, the agency could proceed with its plan. (The agency was allowed to make leases for five years without further consideration by Congress.) On other types of plants, the disposal was to be widespread and monopoly prevented.

The Senate wanted Congress to maintain greater control over the sale of surplus war plants and, indeed, over the entire program of surplus property disposal. Senator Allen J. Ellender (D., Houma, La.) wanted to create a committee which would "make a full and complete study and investigation with respect to the sale and other disposition of surplus Government-owned property." [7] Senator

[5] C.R., Sept. 18, 1944, p. 7857.   [6] H. Rept. 1757, Aug. 10, 1944.
[7] C.R., Aug. 23, 1944, p. 7237.

Joseph C. O'Mahoney (D., Cheyenne, Wyo.) argued that Congress should establish continuous liaison with the agency and thus make future investigations unnecessary. He wanted Congress to know "what is going on at the time it is going on," instead of "being compelled, as we now are, to wait until after the fact" to find out what has been done.[8] On the question of controls over the sale of surplus war plants, the Senate proposed that Congress retain general supervisory power over the disposition of a wide category of items, including magnesium plants, chemical plants, aviation plants, iron and steel plants, pipe lines, and patents, processes, techniques, and inventions. Government plans for the disposal of property within these categories would be submitted to Congress, with thirty days allowed in which the plans could be disapproved. In the conference the Senate's plans for establishing a continuous liaison with the agency were dropped, but the Senate's plans for controlling the sale of surplus property were, on the whole, adopted.

The controversy over the use of the income from the sales of surplus property developed only after the bill reached the conference stage. Earlier, each House had adopted an amendment which provided that receipts from sales should be deposited with the Treasury "to the credit of a special fund which shall be used exclusively for the reduction of the public debt." This proposal had been suggested in the Baruch-Hancock Report as a method of "dramatizing" the relation between the sale of surplus war property and the reduction of the debt.

The conference committee seemed less interested in dramatizing the reduction in the debt than in avoiding extra bookkeeping, and the amendment applying the receipts from the sale of surplus property to the reduction of the debt was deleted from the bill. The conferees argued that this provision would not reduce the debt by a penny and, in fact, would increase the costs of administering the program. The Treasury Department upheld this point of view, saying that the requirement would be "wholly

[8] *C.R.*, Aug. 23, 1944, p. 7237.

ineffective" in reducing the debt. "During the present period of deficit financing," the Treasury said, the requirement "would have to be fulfilled by the futile mechanical measures of applying the special fund to retire a given amount of outstanding public debt while simultaneously offering additional public-debt obligations to recoup the same funds to meet Government expenditures required by congressional appropriations not covered by the proceeds of revenue measures enacted by Congress." [9] In other words, the rate of spending was determined by congressional appropriations. If Congress spent more money than the revenue available, the debt would go up; if Congress spent less money than the revenue available, the debt would go down.

The legal power of the conference to delete the amendment was subject to challenge, for the rules of each chamber provide that a bill is subject to a point of order if the conferees delete material agreed to by both Houses. However, the matter was further complicated by the fact that the amendments were located in different sections of the bill, so that, technically, it could be claimed that the conferees had not deleted material which had been agreed to by both Houses. No point of order was actually raised.

The action of the conference in deleting the debt-retiring amendment was sharply attacked in both chambers. An attempt was made in the House to send the bill back to the conference committee, but a motion to do this was defeated, 150–169 (15 percent of the Democrats; 79 percent of the Republicans). Senator Kenneth S. Wherry (R., Pawnee City, Neb.) said that he would refrain from making a point of order inasmuch as "the hour is getting late, and the Senators are restless to get away." [10] To win their point the Republicans did not need to prolong their deliberations by raising a point of order or sending the bill back to the conference committee. It was enough to charge that the Democrats were planning to use the revenue from the sale of surplus property for paying current expenditures rather than for retiring the debt.

[9] *C.R.*, Sept. 19, 1944, p. 7941.   [10] *C.R.*, Sept. 19, 1944, p. 7939.

THE "HUMAN SIDE OF RECONVERSION"

The third of the reconversion measures created the Office of War Mobilization and Reconversion, which was given general supervisory powers in the transition of the economy from war to peace. All things considered, the legislation disappointed its sponsors in that Congress did not go as far as they wished in providing for "the human side of reconversion." The bill was most contentious; tempers were often high as Congress proceeded to debate political questions of great sensitivity in the teeth of a presidential election. There was an air of unreality about the debate, for there was no demonstrable need for the legislation at that particular time. No one knew whether a depression would follow the war, and the legislation was variously interpreted as a prudent method of preventing a depression and as a foolhardy attempt to reestablish a New Deal works program. The debate was conditioned by a vaguely remembered experience of the Wilson-Harding era (when there was a recession), by the shiboleths, slogans, and political alignments of the prewar years, and by the approaching presidential election.

The phrase "human side of reconversion" was broadly used to mean provisions for unemployment, employment, and reemployment. Promises had been made earlier in the year that legislation on the "human side" would eventually be considered—as when the Senate was considering the bill on contract termination. The postponement of the issue, however, proved to be a handicap to the proponents of the legislation, for the issue now had to be decided during the election, when many Congressmen felt obliged to make a legislative record on this type of legislation. It also had to be decided as a separate issue rather than as part of an integrated reconversion plan.

The relative unity which Congress had displayed, say, in passing the contract-termination bill had now disappeared completely. There were strenuous contests in both the Senate and the House over the content of the legislation and later between the Senate and the House over their respective versions of the legislation. In the Senate, the relatively modest George plan won over the more liberal Murray-Kilgore plan, but in the House the George plan was defeated because it was thought to be too generous.

The George bill, developed by the postwar policy committee (it was actually reported by the Finance Committee), proposed to extend the benefits of unemployment insurance to some 3,500,-000 federal workers who, shortly, would be out of a job. The federal government was to pay the costs of the program, with the States having the responsibility for administering the program and determining the rates of payment. The Murray-Kilgore bill was reported by the Military Affairs Committee, but it actually represented the position of labor leaders and of some officials of the Administration. The plan called for an unemployment insurance program with national standards to continue for two years after the war. It also contained provisions for retraining veterans and nonveterans, the continuation of the United States Unemployment Service under federal jurisdiction, and the payment of transportation costs of workers to locations where new job opportunities existed.

The Senate deliberations were extraordinarily complicated because the baffling procedure was followed of considering at the same time two bills reported from two different committees. At one point in the deliberations, Senator Francis Maloney (D., Meriden, Conn.) became so alarmed at "the existing excitement and confusion," as he termed it, that he suggested the Murray-Kilgore bill be returned to the committee. The Senate was attempting to write a bill of tremendous magnitude on the floor, he said. A large number of amendments had been presented to the Senate, with "vigorous attempts at compromise" being made in the lobbies.[11]

The George plan, which gave the States greater control over unemployment benefits, was preferred by the Senate, and it was adopted by a vote of 49–25 (51 percent of the Democrats; 90 percent of the Republicans). The Senate also approved the plan for

[11] *C.R.*, Aug. 11, 1944, p. 6895.

paying the transportation costs of workers. After disposing of other contentious amendments, the Senate at length passed the bill, 55–19 (60 percent of the Democrats; 97 percent of the Republicans). Senators Murray and Kilgore were disappointed in the final bill and voted against it, and Senator Barkley expressed the hope that the House of Representatives would amend the bill "so as to make it satisfactory." [12] This was a fruitless hope indeed, for the trend against legislation of this kind was running so strong in the House that even the George bill was defeated.

The bill developed by the House postwar committee (it was actually reported by the Ways and Means Committee) contained no provisions for retraining civilians, for paying transportation costs to new labor markets, or for granting unemployed benefits to federal workers. Even without these provisions in the legislation, ten Republican members of the Ways and Means Committee thought that the proposals went too far. They supported what they called a "well-rounded security program," but they did not believe that "federalized unemployment compensation" should replace "productive employment by private enterprise." On the other hand, four members of the Ways and Means Committee thought that the unemployment benefits provided in the legislation were insufficient, and they also thought that provisions should be made for "public works of a necessary and permanent character." While industry had "been taken care of," they said, "not one single provision" had been included "to take care of the men and women who will become unemployed after having been patriotically engaged in making our war-production program such a great success." [13]

An attempt was made on the House floor to offer a substitute bill, similar to the Murray-Kilgore proposal, which had been prepared by representatives of the American Federation of Labor and certain members of Congress. However, the proponents seemed unsure of the provisions of the measure and Rep. Jerry Voorhis (D., San Dimas, Calif.) began his advocacy by admitting that the

[12] C.R., Aug. 11, 1944, p. 6916.   [13] H. Rept. 1798, Aug. 24, 1944.

substitute "could be improved" and that it contained material "which I think would have to be worked out." [14] The substitute measure fell, as did also proposed amendments on retraining, transportation, and federal unemployment benefits.

The attitude of the House during the debate seemed to be extraordinarily belligerent. The impending election was a factor, according to Rep. John E. Fogarty (D., Harmony, R.I.), who observed that the oratory he had heard was "apparently more concerned with the defeat of Roosevelt than with the prevention of another depression." [15] Another factor was the attitude many members held toward war workers. "These workers have been drawing the highest wages and salaries in history," [16] Rep. Robert L. Doughton (D., Laurel Springs, N.C.) said. They knew what their compensation would be when they accepted employment, and there was no need now for the federal government to give them what would amount to a bonus. Rep. Frank Carlson (R., Concordia, Kan.) did not believe that the war worker and the veteran should be given the same unemployment compensation benefits. He would not support legislation "that will place the veterans of this Nation on the same basis as the folks who have stayed home and drawn higher wages than they ever made before." War workers were not entitled "to the same consideration as our boys who have gone through torture and faced death." [17]

The conferees were initially unable to reach an agreement on the Senate amendments on transportation costs and unemployment insurance for federal workers. When Representative Doughton asked for further instructions, the House reaffirmed its previous stand. The vote against paying transportation costs was 241–91 (58 percent of the Democrats; 87 percent of the Republicans); the vote against unemployment insurance for federal workers was 174–157 (40 percent of the Democrats; 66 percent of the Republicans). Senator Barkley told the Senate that these votes "fortified the adamant position of the House conferees," [18] compelling the

[14] C.R., Aug. 31, 1944, p. 7433.   [15] C.R., Aug. 31, 1944, p. 7436.
[16] C.R., Sept. 18, 1944, p. 7823.   [17] C.R., Sept. 18, 1944, p. 7838.
[18] C.R., Sept. 18, 1944, p. 7901.

Senate to recede from its position. The Senate conferees—Senators George, Barkley, Walsh, Vandenberg, and Taft—then issued a statement in which they expressed their regret that it had not been possible "to care for these two highly desirable steps in the program for human demobilization." They called attention to the fact "that the way is still open to enact these two provisions by separate legislation." [19] No more legislation of this nature was enacted, although unsuccessful attempts were made in 1945. However, the so-called Full Employment bill, which was concerned with general economic stability, was enacted in December of the following year.

SPOT AUTHORIZATION

While Congress was considering reconversion legislation, several administrative agencies were engaged in a vigorous dispute over the so-called Spot Authorization plan to permit increased civilian production in areas where manpower and materials were available as a result of contract readjustments. The dispute began in the latter part of 1943 and continued intermittently for the remainder of the war; it split the War Production Board into pro-Nelson and anti-Nelson factions and created a feud between the WPB and the War Department. Congress seemed to favor the plan, and certainly the Truman Committee did, but no attempt was made to decide the question independently by legislative action.

The War Department was initially in favor of increasing civilian production if manpower and materials were available. However, it adopted a more cautious attitude as the European invasion drew nearer, and after the Battle of the Bulge it opposed the expansion of civilian production. It argued that a number of unfortunate events would follow any shift in production to civilian goods. Existing controls were not sufficient to prevent interference with the production of essential items, it was said, and labor markets would become even tighter. If there was no resumption of the production of civilian goods, surplus labor could be absorbed by the draft or transplanted to areas where labor was scarce. Moreover,

[19] *C.R.*, Sept. 18, 1944, p. 7900.

it was argued that the manufacturers of competitive products would wish to begin the production of civilian goods at the same time; otherwise the producers of war goods would be at an unfair disadvantage in reentering the civilian market. The Truman Committee noted that the opposition to the plan did not say that labor and materials were unavailable; they said, in effect, that surpluses "would make it easier for the procurement agencies to achieve their programs." [20] The committee questioned whether labor migration could be stimulated by creating pools of unemployment. Women and older men, especially, would be unwilling to move, and workers were now leaving tight labor areas because of the shortages of civilian goods.

The Truman Committee also argued that the supply of civilian goods should be increased in order to keep inflation in check and to preserve business firms which did not have war contracts. It saw no injustice in permitting firms without war contracts to make civilian goods. Although most business concerns claimed that "nothing but patriotism" had induced them to take government contracts, the committee was aware that their principal officers spent most of their energy in securing the greatest possible amount of war contracts. Because profits were "liberal and almost certain" and risks were "negligible," the committee did not think there would be "any great desire to avoid taking such contracts and to hand them over to competitors." [21]

The controversy over increasing the supply of civilian goods was never resolved during the war. The Spot Authorization plan was eventually abandoned, but there was no perceptible increase in civilian goods until the war was over.

Reconversion tax legislation was also enacted in 1945, the purpose being, in the words of the House committee, to improve "the cash position of business enterprise" and to relieve smaller business "from some of the burdens of the excess-profits tax." [22] The bill, modest in scope, was thought to be but part of a comprehensive plan of tax revision, developed by the so-called Joint Com-

[20] S. Rept. 10, Part 16, March 3, 1944.   [21] S. Rept. 10, Part 16, March 3, 1944.
[22] H. Rept. 849, July 2, 1945.

mittee on Postwar Taxation. The complete plan was not revealed at this time. The bill advanced the date on which postwar tax credits would be available and increased the exemption on excess profits from $10,000 to $25,000. The main controversy in each chamber centered around the proposals to make the excess-profits exemption apply to the income of 1945 rather than of 1946, but these amendments were defeated.

THE VETERAN

The veteran presented a different kind of reconversion subject —and one, certainly, with obvious political ramifications. The first piece of legislation for veterans authorized mustering-out payments ranging from $100 (for those in service less than 60 days) to $300 (for those serving outside the continental United States or Alaska). The President had advocated such legislation under the theory that the members of the armed forces had "been compelled to make greater economic sacrifice and every other kind of sacrifice than the rest of us." [23] Congress agreed with this theory, and both Houses passed the mustering-out payment bill without a dissenting vote.

The second piece of legislation for veterans was the so-called G.I. Bill of Rights, which provided various types of benefits for the returning servicemen. The origins of this legislation extended back to the controversy over drafting eighteen-year olds into the services. When the President signed the Act, he also appointed a committee to develop plans so that soldiers whose school training had been interrupted by the draft could later resume their education. The committee submitted its report the following year, and legislation to implement the report was introduced in both Houses and referred to the education committees. The American Legion also became interested in postwar benefits for veterans and, joined by the Veterans of Foreign Wars, sponsored the "G.I. Bill of Rights." The core of the Legion bill, like that of the report of the President's committee, was the free-education feature, but

[23] *The Papers and Addresses of Franklin D. Roosevelt* (New York: Random House, 1938–50), 1942, No. 122, p. 470.

the Legion bill gave more centralized authority over education to the Veterans Administration. The Legion bill was also more comprehensive and included items on loans, unemployment and re-employment, and hospital facilities for veterans.

The political sensitivity of the G.I. Bill was revealed in the Senate by its multi-member sponsorship and by the members' eagerness to get "on the record." The bill was introduced by Senator Bennett Champ Clark (D., University City, Mo.), himself a founder of the American Legion, and Clark was joined by some seventy-nine listed cosponsors. Some slight opposition developed to this mass sponsorship of legislation, Senator Wallace H. White (R., Auburn, Me.), for instance, believing that it was "poor, unsound legislative practice to undertake to sign up a large number of Senators as sponsors for a bill." [24] Senator John A. Danaher (R., Portland, Conn.) pointed out that, "in the form in which it came before us," there were many sections "which no eighty Senators, no eight Senators, should have approved." [25]

The Senate considered the bill at the end of a busy day in which the exhausting subjects of the diversion of water of the Colorado River and TVA appropriations had been considered. There was little energy left to debate the G.I. Bill adequately, and there was scarcely anything controversial to debate, since the bill, with its eighty sponsors, had been reported unanimously by the Finance Committee. However, Senator David I. Walsh (D., Clinton, Mass.), the chairman of the Naval Affairs Committee, raised an objection which had been passed on to him by Admiral Randall Jacobs, the head of the Bureau of Personnel of the Navy. The bill provided that benefits be extended to those who were discharged "under conditions other than dishonorable"; and Admiral Jacobs, anticipating that such a catch-all phrase would include those with "bad-conduct discharges" and "undesirable discharges," believed that "this might have a detrimental effect on morale by removing the incentive to maintain a good service record." [26]

Senator Clark answered the objection definitively and vigor-

[24] *C.R.*, March 24, 1944, p. 3080.   [25] *C.R.*, March 24, 1944, p. 3080.
[26] *C.R.*, March 24, 1944, p. 3076.

ously, and he seemed inspired by the fact that the objection had originated with the Navy. The points raised by Admiral Jacobs, Clark said, were "some of the most stupid, short-sighted objections which could possibly be raised." The committee had purposely used the phrase, "under conditions other than dishonorable," Clark explained, so as not to penalize "boys who lied about their age in order to enlist or who did something of that sort." The proviso did not say that all who had not received a dishonorable discharge would be eligible; rather, the proviso was flexible so that the Veterans Administration would have some discretion. Indeed, the committee was "more interested than any one else could possibly be in keeping the gold-brickers, the coffee-coolers, the skulkers, and the criminals, the bad soldiers and bad sailors and bad marines, off the benefit rolls." As a parting dig at the Navy, Clark said that it was probable that the higher authorities had not "consulted their representatives who were present at the committee meeting, in order to find out exactly what the language means." [27]

The question before the Senate was not whether the bill would pass but whether a roll-call vote might cause future embarrassment for members not present. The hour was late, Senator Barkley explained, and many Senators were absent who would have attempted to be there had they been advised that a yea-and-nay vote would be taken. Senator Francis Maloney (D., Meriden, Conn.) said that it didn't make any difference to him whether there was a vote "after telling the Majority Leader that I intended to vote for the bill." [28] Others, however, wanted to go on record with their vote, so the roll call was ordered. Senator Clark was ready. He had a tally sheet in his hand, he said, and would "take care of the sponsors of the bill who are not present." He read into the *Record* the names of those absent Senators, "all sponsors and co-introducers of the bill [who] are unavoidably detained, but if present would vote 'yea.' " [29] Senator Kenneth S. Wherry (R., Pawnee City, Neb.), in order that there might be "no mistake in

[27] *C.R.*, March 24, 1944, p. 3076.   [28] *C.R.*, March 24, 1944, p. 3080.
[29] *C.R.*, March 24, 1944, p. 3081.

the Record regarding the absence of Republican Senators who are necessarily absent . . . and if present would vote 'yea,' " read the names of the absent Republicans.[30] With one exception, the names of Senator Wherry's list were also on Senator Clark's list, the new name dredged up by this double-checking device being that of Senator Taft. The vote was 50–0.

The deliberations in the House were of a different order. The House debated the bill for six days, compared to forty minutes for the Senate, and it considered some of the important issues raised by the legislation. There was, in effect, a contest between two House committees and two different bills. The G.I. Bill was reported by the Committee on World War Veterans' Legislation; the so-called Barden bill, by the Committee on Labor. The Barden bill implemented the report of the President's committee on veterans' education—the so-called Armed Forces Committee on Postwar Educational Opportunities for Service Personnel. The Legion bill was more extensive than the Barden bill; the Barden bill was more generous in assisting participating schools and provided for more control by the States. Indeed, the Labor Committee said, with some asperity, that the average veteran was "more interested in the 'little red schoolhouse' than in a more powerful Veterans Administration." Decisions on veterans' education, it said, should "be left with the educational agencies experienced in planning such programs, namely the local education institutions." [31]

Each committee asked for a rule for its bill. The Rules Committee, in an attempt to remain neutral, reported out a rule for considering the G.I. Bill, thus making it possible for the House to substitute the Barden bill for Title II, the educational section of the G.I. Bill. In the meantime, an active lobby of college administrators and State officials was organized to support the Barden bill. This new lobby was very active, as the following excerpt from what it called its "call to arms" reveals: "Please use your telephones, your telegraph blanks, or better still, follow what the

[30] C.R., March 24, 1944, p. 3081.   [31] H. Rept. 1417, May 4, 1944.

American Legion has done, and, if possible, have your members come to Washington and talk with your Representatives in the House and your Senators about this legislation." [32]

The Legion lobby was also active, and for one thing it presented to the House a petition purportedly signed by a million people, asking that the G.I. Bill be enacted without amendment. A letter sent by the Legion to all members of Congress said that amendments would delay the adoption of the bill. "Conceivably, the bill might be improved in some slight degree" by amendments, the Legion admitted, but it thought that "the value of any changes would be doubtful as compared with the present carefully considered and prepared measure." Rep. John M. Rankin (D., Tupelo, Miss.), who was leading the fight for the G.I. Bill, was annoyed by these pressure tactics, and he told the House that "we refuse to be stampeded, excited, or dominated by any outside influences that undertook to tell the Congress what to do." [33] Not one man out of a thousand who signed the telegrams to Congress had ever seen a copy of the bill, Rankin said, and he asked whether that was an intelligent way to legislate.

As it developed, there was no vote on the Barden proposal itself. The sponsors of the G.I. Bill were not completely satisfied with the educational features. The sponsors of the Barden bill were willing to submit amendments, rather than substitute the entire bill. A compromise was reached when Representative Rankin offered an amendment on school expenses which had been taken from the Barden bill. When an agreement of this order had been reached between competitive committees and competitive leaders, the friction vanished all down the line. The Rankin-Barden amendment was accepted without a record vote, and the bill was passed, 388–0.

[32] *C.R.,* May 15, 1944, p. 4505.   [33] *C.R.,* May 11, 1944, p. 4337.

9. Conclusions

WARS place a severe strain on political institutions, with the high stakes being nothing less than the survival of the government itself. While abroad an enemy is attempting to destroy authority by force of arms, at home the backwash of war is creating new tensions, with the further possibility that political authority will disintegrate or prove inadequate to win the war. The political function of adjusting competitive wants is made more difficult because of material shortages and the necessity for restricting freedom of action. Victory will depend on wise political decisions as well as on the willingness of individuals and groups to accept galling restrictions on their behavior. During a total war, where the mass armies of the belligerents are sustained by the industrial might of the nations concerned, there is an interlocking relationship between foreign and domestic policy, with the needs of the external war governing the actions of the internal economy. The government must readjust the organization of society, mobilize the energies of all who can contribute to victory, allocate the burdens of war, and ration goods in scarce supply.

An attempt will be made in this chapter to evaluate the behavior of Congress during the crisis of the last war and to assess the adequacy of its procedures for periods of crisis. Was Congress largely ineffective, as wartime legislatures are often held to be, with the bureaucrats having enough delegated power to run the war on their own? Or was Congress stubborn and obstructive, hesitant in enacting needed legislation and in appropriating required funds? Were its internal structures and procedures satisfactory? Did the war alter the power relationships between Congress and other political institutions?

The role of Congress during the war period might be placed under the threefold classification of authorizing action in the form of law, of adjusting conflicts of interests, and of exercising oversight over the execution of policy. In the American political ideology, the actions of government not authorized by law are illegal and as such are unenforceable in courts. During the war, there was a propensity to delegate power to the President in somewhat sweeping terms, so that, whatever else might happen, the government would have a plenitude of legal authority for carrying on the war. Extraordinary power is required to fight a war, as President Lincoln discovered in the early days of the Civil War. Finding the laws on the statute books insufficient for the emergency action required, Lincoln was forced to raise troops, money, and supplies without specific legal authority. Congress subsequently legalized the action. In the emergency period preceding the last two great wars, Congress delegated wide powers to the President, often supplementing this legislation at a later date with more precise authorizations.

For the purpose of simplicity, one may distinguish two categories of legislative grants of power which, while not always distinct, at least indicate the ambivalence of Congress in enacting war legislation. In the first category one may place those broad, almost boundless grants of authority which allowed the President to mobilize the resources of the country and to reorganize, and perhaps create, government agencies. In the second category one may place those specific grants of authority relating to a particular policy, such as price control, where specific standards were set. In addition, Congress had opportunities for periodically reviewing policy through extending the legislation or providing funds for its administration. Although many grants of authority in this category were also very broad, they followed the customary legislative pattern.

Because the extent of power delegated to the President was not always clear, segments of Congress sometimes claimed that executive action went beyond the scope of the law. The most vexatious controversy in this area related to consumer subsidies, which were inaugurated by the President on the basis of some rather shaky legal authority. There was also controversy over the legitimacy of the President's order placing a limitation on salaries. In some areas of policy, such as the allocation of civilian manpower and the adjustment of labor disputes, an attempt was made to base policy on voluntary compliance, with only a shadow of legal sanction.

The list of war powers delegated to the President is imposing, but one should not conclude that these powers were absolute or that they were delegated to the President for his use only. The term "delegation" is, in fact, somewhat of a misnomer. Perhaps it would be more accurate to say that new powers were created which were not exercised before, that once created they affected Congress as well as the President, and that, having been created, they became enmeshed in the whole scheme of politics. As the war progressed, the creation of these powers provided additional work for Congress, and in many areas the role of Congress was increased rather than diminished.

Although great powers were delegated to the President, Congress still had to make many decisions on organizing the energies of the nation and allocating men, money, and material among competitive claimants. Political competition resulted from alternative choices, with partisans justifying their proposals with different standards of judgment. All agreed on the basic premises that everyone should do his part and that no one should use the war to exploit his fellow countrymen, but an assortment of permissible behavior could be encompassed within these broad limits. One of the standards persistently advanced in the early phase of the war was that of equality of sacrifice. The standard was obviously attractive, combining as it did the truism that sacrifice was required and the belief that everyone should do his part, but it revealed serious shortcomings when applied to specific problems. It did not provide very much guidance, say, in determining whether farm workers should be drafted or left on the farm, whether the parity price was adequate, and whether a withholding tax should be enacted. Equality of treatment might have placed the farm worker in the Army, but a series of new inequalities would have developed if this policy had resulted in food shortages.

The standard of equality of sacrifice could be advocated in such a manner that it placed a distorted interpretation on the degree or the nature of the sacrifice required. If a man claimed, for instance, that he should not be asked to sacrifice more than his neighbor, the standard supported the argument for preserving the economic relationship which existed before Pearl Harbor. On the other hand, if a man claimed that all profits should be taxed away (for soldiers made no profits) or that civilians and soldiers should be treated equally by placing both under military discipline, the standard became an end in itself. The President's proposal for a flat limitation on salaries, which was never defended as a method of raising revenue, reflected such a belief in sacrifice for its own sake. Sacrifice was required, but no law could guarantee that all sacrifice would be equal. From the nature of war, some—but not all—were required to sacrifice their lives. In making decisions on allocating men, money, and materials, Congress also had to consider other, more measurable, factors, such as the probable effect of a policy on winning the war, or, as in the latter months of the war, of the effect on postwar employment.

The universal draft, which is based on the premise that all men have an equal obligation to fight, was again used in the war and proved its effectiveness in recruiting large land armies. The decision of Congress to garnish military service with such welcome perquisites as dependency allowances, cheap insurance, free mail, a substantial pay scale, mustering-out pay, and G.I. benefits limited possible defections from the rigors of military discipline. In all, the general acceptance of the draft by the public greatly increased the military power of the nation. The war ended before the principle of the draft could be applied to civilian manpower, but Congress seemed willing to enact the so-called work-or-fight

legislation once it was convinced that this stern measure was required to win the war. In any future military crisis where there is
no backlog of unemployed one may expect controls over employment to be imposed more quickly, and perhaps more rigorously,
than in the last war.

The government made a commendable record in maintaining
price stability during the war, although price policy was always
contentious politically. Special groups beseeched Congress to enact amendments which would improve their competitive price
position, and price officials often antagonized legislators. Although
the Administration assumed the initiative in advocating price
control, the legislation was supported in Congress by many
courageous members who often jeopardized their political careers
by speaking and voting for a national price policy. Congress did
not give its consent initially to the program of consumer subsidies,
which were instigated by the President on his own responsibility.
Even if one accepts the argument that the President had legal
authority to do what he did, it is nevertheless regrettable that Congress was not given an honest choice of alternatives in making a
decision on the issue of consumer subsidies. Congress had either
to accept what many members believed to be an illegal program
or to reject a program which, once started, could not readily be
stopped.

The war taxes doubtless seemed high enough to the average
taxpayer, although from the point of view of a prudent fiscal policy insufficient funds were raised by taxation, and a situation was
created which led to a period of postwar inflation. In assaying the
responsibility for this costly failure, one should not overlook the
part played by the sponsors of the Ruml Plan. The tax needs of
the nation were to raise more revenue, and up to this point Congress had expressed its willingness to do so. The fiscal requirements
were not for everyone to "become current," as the Ruml slogan
put it, but to raise more money, and the Ruml plan did not add a
penny to the revenue. After this unbecoming controversy over the
distribution of windfall tax gains, Congress was too dispirited to

enact an adequate tax bill, and by then, too, the war was more than half over. Responsibility for the failure to raise sufficient tax revenue may also be placed on the Treasury and the tax committees, each of whom displayed an unseemly narrowness in rejecting out of hand the tax proposals of the other.

In developing reconversion policy, Congress turned its attention from immediate war needs to the requirements of the postwar world, and here different standards of judgment were involved. A number of congressional committees worked diligently on plans for reconversion, although the attempt of special committees to coordinate policy was not entirely successful. Congress acted on the theory that the conditions requisite for the operation of a free economy should be reestablished quickly, with the least possible disturbance. In line with this policy, legislation was enacted which provided for the quick termination of war contracts, so that there would be no temptation to retain war contracts for the purpose of continuing profits or maintaining employment. The controversies over public works and unemployment benefits proved to be less meaningful than was believed at the time, for the anticipated economic slump did not occur. On many reconversion questions, such as the continuation of price control and of rationing of scarce capital goods, no decisions could be made until after the war, and yet these decisions greatly affected the nature of the reconversion.

Partisanship and party alignment continued during the war, with partisan decisions being made on many issues, although the actual prosecution of the war or the goal of victory were never partisan issues. One may well ask why partisanship continued when theoretically a war required all partisans to close the gap, forget their differences, and present a united front until victory was achieved. It would be time enough for partisan quarrels to be resumed after victory had been won. This oversimple view fails to take into account the continued requirement for electing officials and the necessity for debate when public officials held varying views on how the nation should be organized for fighting the war.

Partisanship continued as a necessary part of the competition for public office, and no attempt was made, as in Great Britain, to postpone elections until after the war. Elections may serve as an integrating force in society by making major decisions on rulers and policies, but the electoral process itself is rife with partisanship and partisan appeals. Another and equally pertinent reason for partisanship was the conflict which existed between various interests. The answers to questions on how the nation was to be organized for prosecuting the war were not obvious and were frequently controversial. In a legislative assembly, partisanship and party alignment is the customary, prescribed method for conducting debate, developing consent, and securing the necessary support for making the decision.

The Democrats held comfortable majorities in Congress before Pearl Harbor, making it possible for them to enact such prewar legislation as that relating to selective service, lend-lease, and defense priorities without facing overwhelming partisan opposition. However, Democratic control was challenged by the 1942 elections, when the Democrats lost heavily, although they kept a margin sufficient to retain nominal party control. The new Congress was antibureaucratic in attitude and keen on investigations, and the Republican members were stimulated by the prospects of winning the presidential election in 1944. Rep. Joseph Martin, the Minority Leader in the House, showed his skill as a legislative tactician by mobilizing his so-called minority party at the right time and in such numbers that for the next two years the Republicans won more roll-call victories than the Democrats. In the 1944 elections, however, the Democrats won the presidential election, and their increased strength in both Houses gave them firmer control over legislation than they had had in the preceding two years. The charts in Appendix B show how the party battle surged back and forth on the various votes. An indication of the extent of party control over roll-call votes is the frequency with which a party majority is on the winning side of all roll-call votes. In the House, a majority of Democrats were on the winning side of 92 percent of the roll-call votes in 1941; of 87 percent in 1942; of 65 percent in 1943; of 71 percent in 1944; and of 87 percent in 1945. A majority of Republicans were on the winning side of 51 percent of the roll-call votes in 1941; of 86 percent in 1942; of 83 percent in 1943; of 85 percent in 1944; and of 62 percent in 1945. In the Senate a majority of Democrats were on the winning side of 93 percent of the roll-call votes in 1941; of 88 percent in 1942; of 79 percent in 1943; of 79 percent in 1944; and of 85 percent in 1945. A majority of Senate Republicans were on the winning side of 37 percent of the roll-call votes in 1941; of 78 percent in 1942; of 68 percent in 1943; of 69 percent in 1944; and of 60 percent in 1945. The extent of party control over voting can also be shown by the results of party contests, where a majority of one party is pitted against a majority of the other party. The ratio of House Democratic victories to Republican victories was 7:1 in 1941, 1:1 in 1942, 1:2 in 1943, 1:2 in 1944, and 3:1 in 1945. On the Senate side, the ratio of Democratic victories to Republican victories was 9:1 in 1941, 2:1 in 1942, 3:2 in 1943, 3:2 in 1944, and 3:1 in 1945.

OVERSIGHT AND CONTROL

After delegating power to the government agencies, Congress often had feelings of guilt for having done so, and it would frequently denounce the bureaucrats for exercising the power granted them. Some of these attacks were unfair, and Congress might well have exercised greater restraint in the use of hyperbole. However, the basic problem relates to the establishment of confidence between Congress and the government agencies, which can be achieved in part through improved procedures. Far from finishing its work with the enactment of the required war legislation, Congress and its various committees entered into an active examination of administrative decisions. The interest of Congress in how law is administered is of course not new, but the scope of interest was extended with the wide range of activities carried on by the government. The delegation of power in broad terms meant that Congress lacked its traditional method of controlling government action by specific legal prescription, so that, the power having been delegated, Congress began to "work back," as it were, by establishing more specific controls over the government, including in some instances providing a more respectable legal basis for agencies and policies. By the end of the war even consumer subsidies were based on law. The complex pattern of control often varied from agency to agency, and in some cases there was no precise standard of accountability for which an administrator knew he was responsible. In some way, in some fashion, an administrator had to "make his peace" with Congress, which meant pacifying and mollifying those elements in Congress whose support he thought desirable. For Congress's part, hearings and investigations were held, representations were made to the responsible officials, amendments were added to the law, and restrictions were placed in appropriation bills. Congress reasserted its general authority over appropriations by providing that all agencies created by the President had to secure their operating funds from Congress. This annual review gave Congress an opportunity to control policy more specifically, or even, if it wished, to liquidate the agency in question.

Another control was established by placing a specific time limit on legislation, which either permitted Congress to review the legislation during the war period or made certain that the legislation would not extend beyond the war. Some Acts contained a proviso that Congress could terminate the law by its own action (thus averting a possible veto), but no law was actually repealed by this method. Again, some Acts contained provisions that Congress itself, or a committee, should be consulted before the legislation would go into effect. There were also informal understandings not written into the law between agencies and committees on how legislation would be carried out. In addition, there was the unpredictable type of control exercised by investigating committees.

The investigation of the government during a time of war is, of course, no new development, the most remarkable example in modern history being the investigation carried on during the Civil War by the Joint Committee to Investigate the Conduct of the War. This committee acted as a general critic for military activities, including the actual conduct of battles and campaigns, and among other things it visited battlefields, gave advice, and asked generals for explanations. In all, the committee went beyond what would now be considered the most useful scope of congressional inquiry, but it should be noted that the army of the 1860s lacked a general staff to plan and coordinate military action. Neither the First nor the Second World War offered a parallel to this extraordinary congressional foray into military strategy and tactics.

During the First World War, the marked improvements in the organization of the Army made the investigation of military activities less inviting than was the case in the Civil War. Nor did Congress carry on any major investigations on the domestic front, although after the war the investigation of war frauds by the Graham Committee led to reforms in accounting procedures and to the establishment of the General Accounting Office.

In contrast, Congress conducted more than a hundred investigations during the Second World War, exploring many aspects of war policy but falling short of investigating the actual conduct of the war. This propensity of Congress to investigate was due in part to the magnitude of the war effort and to its impact on a wide variety of American life. The war created many dislocations and maladjustments, and those most affected often sought to better their position by persuading Congress to investigate the cause of their grievance. An investigation is often particularistic, being concerned, for instance, with an event, or an agency, or a policy, or a commodity, and it can be used to direct a spotlight on particular grievances. And grievances could be quickly called to the attention of Congress by organized groups through techniques developed in the preceding decade—mass letter-writing campaigns, floods of telegrams, advertising, and the visitation of delegations. The press and radio were able to acquaint the public with such administrative difficulties as rubber shortages, rationing troubles, or wage disputes, so that it was not difficult for vexatious administrative problems to be blown up into national issues for which investigations could be demanded. Moreover, the failure to regularize the communications process between government agencies and Congress meant that investigations were used to find facts or debate policies when less dramatic forms of reporting and debate might have been sufficient.

In looking for causes of investigations, one must also recognize the relationship between the creation of investigating committees and the competition for political power. Investigations may enhance the prestige of committee members, and especially of the chairman, the notable example during the war being Senator Harry S. Truman. Inasmuch as investigations may influence elections, partisans are continually advocating the creation of investigating committees or hoping to exploit them for partisan advantage after they are created. It might seem that the majority party could, if it wished, prevent the authorization of investigations, and that it would wish to forestall investigations that would embarrass the Administration or adversely affect the elections. However, the control of investigations by the majority party is more difficult than it might appear. With the minority party continually pressing for more investigations, the support of a few dissidents from the majority party is enough to set an investigation going. During the war, new investigations were created from time to time as events and the requirements of politics seemed to dictate, such as the Smith Committee (to investigate acts in which the government exceeded its authority), the committee to investigate grade labeling by the OPA, and the committee to investigate the seizure of Montgomery Ward. Moreover, some of the regular standing committees wished to carry on investigations so that they could keep up with events (and forestall investigations by rival committees), and they were permitted to do so.

The organization and procedures of Congress were designed for periods of relative domestic tranquillity, with full opportunity for public deliberation, and one may well inquire how the internal apparatus of Congress met the test of war. A decentralized committee system has been a characteristic of Congress for a century and a quarter, and during the war period committees continued to play a major role, being used for developing legislation and for exercising supervisory control over the actions of government agencies. Committees flourished in numbers, the Senate having some thirty standing committees and the House almost fifty, and in addition special committees were created from time to time. The committee system as a whole showed considerable strength, demonstrating its greatest usefulness in preparing legislation, and it appeared to maintain the allegiance of most Congressmen, who considered committees the natural and expeditious method for conducting a legislative assembly.

The strength of the committee system lies in the fact that a known group in Congress is responsible for developing policy in specific areas. Committees develop considerable corporate unity and are able to command the sedulous attention of their members on difficult problems for prolonged periods of time. A well-functioning committee which shows concrete results from its efforts can give its members a feeling of satisfaction to reward them for their service. Moreover, the relations established with the government agencies provides the committees with some awareness of and insight into administrative problems and programs.

But the committee system also has weaknesses, some of which were embarrassingly revealed during the war period. The proliferation of committees was sometimes criticized, partly because of the burdens placed on more active members, and there was some support for the movement to reduce the number of standing committees. (This was accomplished in 1946.) Another, more pronounced, weakness—and one difficult to remedy—was the shortcoming of committees as instruments for coordinating policy. The making of fiscal policy is an excellent example of the lack of coordination, with congressional committees considering separately the interrelated problems of taxing, spending, borrowing, and controlling prices. The malady was again demonstrated when Congress considered reconversion legislation for the postwar period. Special committees were created to coordinate the actions of the several legislative committees, but when the coordination was not successful one more legislative step was added to an already complex procedure.

Jurisdictional conflicts between the committees vitiated some of the benefits of standing committees. For instance, several committees with different theories of labor relations claimed jurisdiction over labor legislation, and it is perhaps not going too far to say that this intercommittee conflict diminished the role of Congress in developing a wartime labor policy. On investigating matters, two or more committees might investigate the same subject and reach different conclusions on what the department concerned was expected to do. If a particular subject was of special concern to a wide public, the number of congressional committees which become interested might increase proportionately, and it is remembered that Mr. Donald Nelson found that he had to discuss the rubber shortage with some seventeen different congressional committees.

The wartime debates in Congress were similar to those held in more normal times, the same rules of procedure being followed, and although the debate was uneven from topic to topic, the bulk of the legislation was fully considered, explained, questioned, and defended, and the legislators were aware of the significance of their action. As in peacetime, some of the debate was petty, personal, and irrelevant, and, on the part of a few, even vulgar. The curious House practice of allowing members to revise and extend their remarks places an irrevocable blemish on the records of the debate; one cannot be sure that the words which appear in the official record were actually spoken on the floor, and the record itself becomes padded with banalities and irrelevancies.

The debate on military strategy and, to a degree, on foreign policy, merits special comment. Congress has never relied on debate as a method of reaching a consensus on policy in those areas where legislation cannot be specific. The result is that the degree of influence of Congress in such areas is uneven, and it is greatest when it is acting on some concrete proposal. In the debates on such measures as the UNRRA agreement and the United Nations treaty, there was a persistent fear that someone, somehow, intended to prevent Congress from having a voice in the peace settlement and, more, that the United States would be committed to policies which Congress had no part in making. The debate on foreign policy frequently seemed more concerned with possible slights to congressional authority than with the nature of the world we were, or would be, living in. One reason for this continued suspicion was the uncertain nature of the commitments we would be required to make, but another reason, relating to the political system itself, was the lack of a positive understanding on the respective functions of the President and of Congress in making postwar commitments.

In the area of military policy, Congress showed considerable faith in the decisions of the Joint Chiefs of Staff, a faith due in part to the considerable respect it had for General George C. Marshall, the Army Chief of Staff. Congress tended to refrain from expressing publicly its feelings, attitudes, and basic interests in military strategy, and the few open debates on the subject were largely inconclusive. It was anomalous that Congress as a whole should know no more about the progress of the war than the informed reader of the daily press. Reference was occasionally made in the debates to contemporary military events, but military affairs as such were rarely the subject of sustained debate. It would be incorrect to infer that Congress lacked interest in military affairs; rather, it feared that debate might cause definite harm by creating suspicions or doubts or by injecting partisan considerations, and in many cases it lacked the information necessary for debate. Moreover, there was the possibility that military information, revealed in confidence to a committee, might be referred to inadvertently and so reach the ears of the enemy. However, Congress was occasionally restless when it was not given information which some of its members thought it was entitled to receive, such as the extent of damage at Pearl Harbor; the Darlan episode and our relations with the Free French; the military position in India; the possibility of securing Siberian bases; the threat to the Pacific coast from the Japanese occupation of several islands in the Aleutians; the pledge of unconditional surrender; and the possibility that secret agreements were made at the various military-political conferences. If in any future war there are serious military reverses, or if there is not a general acceptance of the broad strategy of the war, one might expect Congress to be more vocal in debating military strategy than it was in the Second World War.

The Senate held one secret session at which it heard reports from the five Senators who had recently returned from an inspection of the war fronts. Secrecy was not preserved, and a garbled version of the debate soon reached the press. The failure of this session shows that discipline is required if Congress is to be given secret information; by failing to control its more talkative members, Congress relinquished an opportunity of being more fully informed. A case can be made for the proposition that the failure to inform Congress of major decisions and significant developments in the military-political sphere of action may lead to an erosion of confidence between the President and Congress.

The war period marked a development in the use of consultations by departments and committees. There is no extensive public record of this interesting development, but available evidence shows that consultations were frequently used to establish clearer understanding between Congress and the agencies. In the early period of price control, to use one example, Congress was uneasy over the operations of the price agency, and the price administrators, in turn, felt that congressional criticism was often hostile and unfair. A *modus vivendi* was eventually worked out in which regular consultations were established between the OPA and members of the appropriate congressional committees. To cite another example, frequent consultations were held between Mr.

Donald Nelson, the chairman of the War Production Board, and the Truman Committee, which acted as a sympathetic critic of the agency and helped to create the public confidence enjoyed by the agency throughout the war. In a similar fashion, the Army and Navy established close relations with the relevant congressional committees, and one would gather from statements made on the floor that these committees were kept informed on the progress of the war.

At the close of the First World War, the relations between Congress and the President were strained, and some of the more aggressive Senators supported a resolution to send a Senate committee to the Paris Peace Conference. Although this quixotic move was defeated, the feeling persisted that President Wilson had slighted the Senate in carrying on postwar negotiations and, most irritatingly, had failed to include one or two Senators in the American delegation. During the Second World War, Secretary of State Hull (who had himself been in Congress during the earlier period), was determined to prevent another schism from developing, and as part of a program of conciliation he invited a select group from Congress to participate in the discussions of postwar foreign policy. Members of Congress were also included in the delegations to several international conferences, a practice designed to keep Congress informed and to develop political support for the policy.

RELATIONSHIPS

The relative power of institutions and the relationship among them cannot be permanently fixed by constitutional provisions alone. The function of the electoral college, for instance, has been changed without altering the written constitutional base, and in other times and eras one may note the continuity of institutions after their effective power has ebbed. The Roman Senate continued on into the Empire, although with diminished power, and monarchies which were once powerful have been circumscribed by law and custom. It may therefore be pertinent to inquire whether the extensive authority exercised by government agencies during the war altered the relationship between Congress and the Executive branch, although any final answer is premature, inasmuch as established trends may not be immediately discernible.

Whatever the final verdict, Congress made serious attempts to retain and assert its authority. At the end of the war strong voices demanded that "Congress regain its powers," as the phrase went, and this move had the obvious support of those who wished to remove government controls over the economy. In due time, Congress repealed the emergency grants of power, abolished the war agencies and administrative courts, disassembled the great military machine, and reestablished a free economy. From the legal point of view, Congress may be said to have "regained" the delegated powers and reestablished the constitutional position it enjoyed before the war. It is less demonstrable, however, that an equilibrium of power was reestablished, a doubt which is sustained by the relative positions of strength of the President and the military establishment and by the continued existence of unsolved problems which Congress must face in any future crisis. These relate to the control of delegated power, the allocation of resources, the determination of fiscal policy, and the making of foreign and military commitments.

It seems obvious that the authority of the President was increased during the war, not only as a result of power delegated to him but also as a result of the increasingly significant position of the United States in world affairs. Moreover, the bureaucracy in the White House itself has been expanded and centralized so that the President has closer control over significant governmental decisions. The authority of the military establishment has also increased, and it has been given new responsibilities by virtue of the expanding military commitments and by a series of regional alliances. The voice of military officials is also important in domestic issues affecting defense and in foreign issues.

The increased power of the Executive branch of the government is directly related to the question of how men, money, and material are to be allocated, and these are decisions lying at the heart of the political process. In time of war, with many aspects of society controlled by government regulation, centripetal trends develop which make it attractive to centralize control over these decisions in the Executive agencies. No one would argue that it would be desirable for Congress itself to make all decisions of whatever magnitude on allocating resources, but one can argue, I believe, that it would be desirable that basic policy in these areas be laid down by law and that Congress make the decisions on the political adjustments required. One may well ask whether it would not have been more salutary, for instance, to let Congress adjust the respective demands of agriculture and labor than to tolerate a situation where it appeared that the President was the defender of one set of interests and Congress of another; or whether it would not have been better if Congress had established a legal basis for the war agencies, established a labor program, determined policy on subsidies, and debated the nature of our postwar military commitments.

Another problem relates to establishing a stable fiscal policy. In an era of multibillion dollar budgets, Congress is faced with the problem of making intelligent decisions on how these funds are to be spent and revenue raised and of assessing the impact of both on the internal economy. During the war period, military appropriations were often made with little public debate, although the discovery of the Manhattan Project by the Appropriations Committee testifies to the alertness of the committee members. The budget system has deficiencies both as a device of appropriating large amounts and as a means of learning how funds have been spent, and the deficiencies will possibly be accentuated in any future crises requiring vast fiscal outlays. However, it is enough to make the point at this time that fiscal control is deficient without elaborating on the nature of desirable budgetary reform or the possible benefits of a performance audit. The control of large appropriations is closely related to the stability of the internal economy. New procedures might well be considered for bringing together the myriad strands of fiscal policy—spending and taxing, borrowing, subsidizing costs, and controlling prices. The decentralized formulation of policy through committees is not conducive to establishing and maintaining a firm policy on fiscal matters, and the difficulty is enhanced by the dispersal of authority among several agencies in the Executive branch. Under present procedures, it may be difficult to maintain monetary stability for any protracted period of crisis.

The control over foreign and military commitments presents additional problems. During the war period, Congress—and especially the Senate—was beset with fears that the President would commit the United States to policies without the knowledge or consent of Congress. However exaggerated the expression of these fears may have been, it is nevertheless true that the President, or the Secretary of State, or high-ranking military leaders, are sometimes in a position to make significant policy decisions beyond the power of Congress to question. The procedures of Congress were developed for an era of public debates and open diplomacy, with the Senate participating in the formation of foreign policy through its control over treaties. Although the Senate rules permit treaties to be considered in secret, the rule is seldom invoked and in any event is of little value in enabling Congress to cope with foreign policy questions where secrecy is required. Indeed, in many cases significant policy may be made and agreements reached without recourse to treaties. The argument often advanced, that foreign policy or military policy is not the proper sphere for congressional action, is in many ways beside the point, for in one way or another Congress has power to make, influence, or destroy some types of foreign policy, and its control over the purse strings gives it considerable potential authority in this field. Indeed, the whole nature of foreign policy requirements raises at once the question of the most desirable relationship to be established between Congress and the foreign-policy makers and of the type of control Congress is to exercise in situations where a treaty is not called for. These are problems for the future.

Congress survived the stresses and tensions of the war. With victory won, it entered the difficult period of postwar adjustment with the determination to repeal the war powers and to make its voice increasingly heard. Yet if war solves some problems, it creates others—a truism Congress soon discovered when confronted with the burdens, responsibilities, and complexities of the postwar world.

Appendix A

CONGRESSIONAL MEMBERSHIP DURING THE SECOND
WORLD WAR, WITH PARTY CLASSIFICATION

THE MEMBERS OF CONGRESS who served during the Second World War are listed below, together with their party classification. The classificatory system has been developed from an analysis of party-votes, which are defined as those in which a majority of one party is opposed by a majority of the second party. In the preparation of this material, each member was given a score based on the percentage of times he agreed with the majority of his own party in all party-votes, and the scores were then plotted from 100 to zero. The scores were then divided into three groups of roughly the same size, and the members were given the classification of the group in which they fell. Members who cast fewer than twenty party-votes have not been included in the classification.

In general, the members in Group I may be termed strong party supporters; those in Group II, moderate party supporters; and those in Group III, mild party supporters. In a few cases, party support has been so low that members fell within the lowest group of the opposite party. These cases are indicated by the numeral III followed by the party in parentheses. It follows from this analysis that those in Group I tend to vote alike. This is less true of those in Group II. Those in Group III are the least homogeneous in their party-voting, and they do not necessarily think alike on partisan issues. The identifying factor of this group is a common deviation from the party norm. The abbreviation "Inc." (for inconclusive) is used for those who cast fewer than twenty party-votes.

ALABAMA
Democratic Senators
II   Bankhead, John H., Jasper, 1941–45
II   Hill, Lister, Montgomery, 1941–45

ALABAMA (*Continued*)

Democratic Representatives

III	Andrews, George W., Union Springs, 3d, 1944–45
Inc.	Bankhead, Walter W., Jasper, 7th, 1941
III	Boykin, Frank W., Mobile, 1st, 1941–45
II	Grant, George M., Troy, 2d, 1941–45
II	Hobbs, Sam, Selma, 4th, 1941–45
II	Jarman, Pete, Livingston, 5th, 1941–45
III	Manasco, Carter, Jasper, 7th, 1941–45
III	Newsome, John P., Birmingham, 9th, 1943–44
I	Patrick, Luther, Birmingham, 9th, 1941–42, 1945
I	Rains, Albert, Gadsden, 5th, 1945
I	Sparkman, John J., Huntsville, 8th, 1941–45
III	Starnes, Joe, Guntersville, 5th, 1941–44
II	Steagall, Henry B., Ozark, 3d, 1941–43

ARIZONA

Democratic Senators

| I | Hayden, Carl, Phoenix, 1941–45 |
| I | McFarland, Ernest W., Florence, 1941–45 |

Democratic Representatives

| II | Harless, Richard F., Phoenix, At Large, 1943–45 |
| I | Murdock, John R., Tempe, At Large, 1941–45 |

ARKANSAS

Democratic Senators

I	Caraway, Hattie W., Jonesboro, 1941–44
II	Fulbright, J. William, Fayetteville, 1945
III	McClellan, John L., Camden, 1943–45
Inc.	Miller, John E., Searcy, 1941
II	Spencer, Lloyd, Hope, 1941–42

Democratic Representatives

III	Cravens, Fadjo, Fort Smith, 4th, 1941–45
Inc.	Ellis, Clyde T., Bentonville, 3d, 1941–42
	[Fulbright, J. W., Fayetteville, 3d, 1943–44: see classification as Senator]
III	Gathings, E. C., West Memphis, 1st, 1941–45
II	Harris, Oren, El Dorado, 7th, 1941–45
I	Hays, Brooks, Little Rock, 5th, 1943–45
III	Mills, Wilbur D., Kensett, 2d, 1941–45
III	Norrell, W. F., Monticello, 6th, 1941–45

Inc.   Terry, David D., Little Rock, 5th, 1941–42
I   Trimble, James W., Berryville, 3d, 1945

CALIFORNIA

Democratic Senator
I   Downey, Sheridan, Atherton, 1941–45
Democratic Representatives
Inc.   Buck, Frank H., Vacaville, 3d, 1941–42
III   Costello, John M., Hollywood, 15th, 1941–44
I   Douglas, Helen Gahagan, Los Angeles, 14th, 1945
I   Doyle, Clyde, Long Beach, 18th, 1945
III (Rep.)   Elliott, Alfred J., Tulare, 10th, 1941–45
III   Engle, Clair, Red Bluff, 2d, 1944–45
I   Ford, Thomas F., Los Angeles, 14th, 1941–44
Inc.   Geyer, Lee E., Gardena, 17th, 1941
I   Havenner, Franck, San Francisco, 4th, 1945
I   Healy, Ned R., Los Angeles, 13th, 1945
I   Holifield, Chet, Montebello, 19th, 1943–45
I   Izac, Ed. V., San Diego, 20th, 23d, 1941–45
I   King, Cecil R., Los Angeles, 17th, 1943–45
Inc.   Kramer, Charles, Los Angeles, 13th, 1941–42
III   Lea, Clarence F., Santa Rosa, 1st, 1941–45
I   Miller, George P., Alameda, 6th, 1945
I   Outland, George E., Santa Barbara, 11th, 1943–45
I   Patterson, Ellis E., Los Angeles, 16th, 1945
III   Rogers, Will, Jr., Culver City, 16th, 1943–44
II   Sheppard, Harry, Yucaipa, 19th, 1941–45
I   Tolan, John H., Oakland, 7th, 1941–45
I   Voorhis, Jerry, San Dimas, 12th, 1941–45
Republican Representatives
II   Anderson, Jack Z., San Juan Bautista, 8th, 1941–45
II   Carter, Albert E., Oakland, 6th, 1941–44
III   Englebright, Harry L., Nevada City, 2d, 1941–44
Inc.   Ford, Leland M., Santa Monica, 16th, 1941–42
II   Gearhart, Bertrand W., Fresno, 9th, 1941–45
III   Hinshaw, Carl, Pasadena, 11th, 20th, 1941–45
III   Johnson, J. Leroy, Stockton, 3d, 1943–45
I   Johnson, Ward, Long Beach, 18th, 1941–44
III   McDonough, Gordon, Los Angeles, 15th, 1945
I   Phillips, John, Banning, 22d, 1943–45
II   Poulson, Norris, Los Angeles, 13th, 1943–44

CALIFORNIA *(Continued)*

Republican Representatives (Continued)

III   Rolph, Thomas, San Francisco, 4th, 1941–44
III (Dem.) Welch, Richard J., San Francisco, 5th, 1941–45

COLORADO

Democratic Senators

Inc.   Adams, Alva B., Pueblo, 1941
III   Johnson, Edwin C., Denver, 1941–45

Democratic Representatives

Inc.   Lewis, Lawrence, Denver, 1st, 1941–42
Inc.   Taylor, Edward, Glenwood Springs, 4th, 1941

Republican Senator

II   Millikin, Eugene D., Denver, 1942–45

Republican Representatives

II   Chenoweth, J. Edgar, Trinidad, 3d, 1941–45
II   Gillespie, Dean M., Denver, 1st, 1944–45
II   Hill, William S., Fort Collins, 2d, 1941–45
I   Rockwell, Robert F., Paonia, 4th, 1942–45

CONNECTICUT

Democratic Senators

III   Maloney, Francis, Meriden, 1941–44
I   McMahon, Brien, Norwalk, 1945

Democratic Representative

Inc.   Downs, LeRoy, South Norwalk, 4th, 1941–42
Inc.   Fitzgerald, William J., Norwich, 2d, 1941–42
I   Geelan, James P., New Haven, 3d, 1945
I   Kopplemann, Herman P., Hartford, 1st, 1941–42, 1945
Inc.   Maciora, Lucien J., New Britain, At Large, 1941–42
I   Ryter, Joseph F., Hartford, At Large, 1945
Inc.   Shanley, James A., New Haven, 3d, 1941–42
Inc.   Smith, Joseph, Prospect, 5th, 1941
I   Woodhouse, Chase Going, New London, 2d, 1945

Republican Senators

II   Danaher, John A., Hartford, 1941–44
II   Hart, Thomas C., Sharon, 1945

Republican Representatives

II   Compton, Ranulf, Madison, 3d, 1943–44
III   Luce, Clare Booth, Greenwich, 4th, 1943–45
I   McWilliams, John D., Norwich, 2d, 1943–44

III	Miller, William J., Wethersfield, 1st, 1943–44
II	Monkiewicz, B. J., New Britain, At Large, 1943–44
II	Talbot, Joseph E., Naugatuck, 5th, 1942–45

DELAWARE

Democratic Senators

| I | Hughes, James H., Dover, 1941–42 |
| II | Tunnell, James M., Georgetown, 1941–45 |

Democratic Representative

| II | Traynor, Philip A., Wilmington, At Large, 1941–42, 1945 |

Republican Senator

| I | Buck, C. Douglass, Wilmington, 1943–45 |

Republican Representative

| II | Willey, Earle D., Dover, At Large, 1943–44 |

FLORIDA

Democratic Senators

| I | Andrews, Charles O., Orlando, 1941–45 |
| I | Pepper, Claude, Tallahassee, 1941–45 |

Democratic Representatives

III	Cannon, Pat, Miami, 4th, 1941–45
II	Green, Lex, Starke, 2d, At Large, 1941–44
II	Hendricks, Joe, De Land, 5th, 1941–45
II	Peterson, J. Hardin, Lakeland, 1st, 1941–45
II	Price, Emory H., Jacksonville, 2d, 1943–45
III	Rogers, Dwight L., Fort Lauderdale, 6th, 1945
II	Sikes, Robert L. F., Crestview, 3d, 1941–45

GEORGIA

Democratic Senators

| III | George, Walter F., Vienna, 1941–45 |
| II | Russell, Richard B., Winder, 1941–45 |

Democratic Representatives

II	Brown, Paul, Elberton, 10th, 1941–45
II	Camp, A. Sidney, Newnan, 4th, 1941–45
III	Cox, E. E., Camilla, 2d, 1941–45
III	Gibson, John S., Douglas, 8th, 1941–45
III	Pace, Stephen, Americus, 3d, 1941–45
III	Peterson, Hugh, Ailey, 1st, 1941–45
I	Ramspeck, Robert, Atlanta, 5th, 1941–45
III	Tarver, Malcolm, Dalton, 7th, 1941–45

GEORGIA (*Continued*)
Democratic Representatives (*Continued*)

II	Vinson, Carl, Milledgeville, 6th, 1941–45
III	Whelchel, Frank, Gainesville, 9th, 1941–44
III	Wood, John S., Canton, 9th, 1945

IDAHO
Democratic Senators

III	Clark, D. Worth, Pocatello, 1941–44
Inc.	Gossett, Charles C., Nampa, 1945
I	Taylor, Glen H., Pocatello, 1945

Democratic Representative

II	White, Compton I., Clarksford, 1st, 1941–45

Republican Senator

I	Thomas, John, Gooding, 1941–44

Republican Representative

II	Dworshak, Henry C., Burley, 2d, 1941–45

ILLINOIS
Democratic Senator

II	Lucas, Scott W., Havana, 1941–45

Democratic Representatives

Inc.	Arnold, Laurence F., Newton, 23d, 1941–42
Inc.	Barnes, James M., Jacksonville, 20th, 1941–42
Inc.	Beam, Harry P., Chicago, 4th, 1941–42
I	Dawson, William L., Chicago, 1st, 1943–45
I	Douglas, Emily Taft, Chicago, At Large, 1945
I	Gordon, Thomas S., Chicago, 8th, 1943–45
I	Gorski, Martin, Chicago, 4th, 1943–45
II	Kelly, Edward A., Flossmoor, 3d, 1943–45
Inc.	Kocialkowski, Leo, Chicago, 8th, 1941–42
I	Link, William W., Chicago, 7th, 1945
Inc.	McKeough, Raymond S., Chicago, 2d, 1941–42
Inc.	Maciejewski, Anton F., Cicero, 6th, 1941–42
Inc.	Mitchell, Arthur W., Chicago, 1st, 1941–42
II	O'Brien, Thomas J., Chicago, 6th, 1943–45
I	Price, Melvin, East St. Louis, 22d, 1945
I	Resa, Alexander J., Chicago, 9th, 1945
I	Rowan, William A., Chicago, 2d, 1943–45
I	Sabath, Adolph J., Chicago, 5th, 1941–45

Inc.   Schaefer, Edwin M., Belleville, 22d, 1941
II   Schuetz, Leonard W., Chicago, 7th, 1941–43
Republican Senator
I   Brooks, C. Wayland, Chicago, 1941–45
Republican Representatives
I   Allen, Leo E., Galena, 13th, 1941–45
II   Arends, Leslie C., Melvin, 17th, 1941–45
II   Bishop, C. W. (Runt), Carterville, 25th, 1941–45
I   Busbey, Fred E., Chicago, 3d, 1943–44
I   Chiperfield, Robert B., Canton, 15th, 1941–45
I   Church, Ralph E., Evanston, 10th, 1943–45
I   Day, Stephen A., Evanston, At Large, 1941–44
II   Dewey, Charles S., Chicago, 9th, 1941–44
II   Dirksen, Everett M., Pekin, 16th, 1941–45
I   Heidinger, James V., Fairfield, 24th, 1941–44
I   Howell, Evan, Springfield, 21st, 1941–45
I   Johnson, Anton J., Macomb, 14th, 1941–45
I   Johnson, Calvin D., Belleville, 22d, 1943–44
I   McMillen, Rolla C., Decatur, 19th, 1944–45
II   Mason, Noah M., Oglesby, 12th, 1941–45
II   Paddock, George A., Evanston, 10th, 1941–42
II   Reed, Chauncey W., West Chicago, 11th, 1941–45
I   Simpson, Sid, Carrollton, 20th, 1943–45
Inc.   Stratton, William G., Morris, At Large, 1941–42
II   Sumner, Jessie, Milford, 18th, 1941–45
I   Vursell, Charles W., Salem, 23d, 1943–45
I   Wheat, William H., Rantoul, 19th, 1941–43

INDIANA

Democratic Senators
I   Jackson, Samuel, Fort Wayne, 1945
III   Van Nuys, Frederick, Indianapolis, 1941–43
Democratic Representatives
Inc.   Boehne, John W., Evansville, 8th, 1941–42
Inc.   Larrabee, William H., New Palestine, 11th, 1941–42
III   Ludlow, Louis, Indianapolis, 11th, 12th, 1941–45
II   Madden, Ray, Gary, 1st, 1943–45
Inc.   Schulte, William T., Hammond, 1st, 1941–42
Republican Senators
I   Capehart, Homer E., Indianapolis, 1945
Inc.   Jenner, William E., Bedford, 1944

INDIANA (*Continued*)
Republican Representatives
I   Gillie, George W., Fort Wayne, 4th, 1941–45
I   Grant, Robert A., South Bend, 3d, 1941–45
I   Halleck, Charles A., Rensselaer, 2d, 1941–45
I   Harness, Forest A., Kokomo, 5th, 1941–45
I   Johnson, Noble J., Terre Haute, 6th, 1941–45
III   LaFollette, Charles M., Evansville, 8th, 1943–45
I   Landis, Gerald W., Linton, 7th, 1941–45
I   Springer, Raymond S., Connersville, 10th, 1941–45
I   Wilson, Earl, Bedford, 9th, 1941–45

IOWA
Democratic Senators
III   Gillette, Guy M., Cherokee, 1941–44
Inc.   Herring, Clyde L., Des Moines, 1941–42
Democratic Representatives
Inc.   Harrington, Vincent F., Sioux City, 9th, 1941–42
Inc.   Jacobsen, William S., Clinton, 2d, 1941–42
Inc.   Narey, Harry, Spirit Lake, 9th, 1942
Republican Senators
II   Hickenlooper, Bourke, B., Cedar Rapids, 1945
II   Wilson, George A., Des Moines, 1943–45
Republican Representatives
II   Cunningham, Paul, Des Moines, 5th, 6th, 1941–45
II   Dolliver, James I., Fort Dodge, 6th, 1945
II   Gilchrist, Fred C., Laurens, 6th, 8th, 1941–44
I   Gwynne, John W., Waterloo, 3d, 1941–45
II   Hoeven, Charles B., Alton, 8th, 1943–45
I   Jensen, Ben F., Exira, 7th, 1941–45
II   LeCompte, Karl M., Corydon, 4th, 5th, 1941–45
II   Martin, Thomas E., Iowa City, 1st, 1941–45
II   Talle, Henry O., Decorah, 2d, 4th, 1941–45

KANSAS
Democratic Representative
Inc.   Houston, John M., Wichita, 5th, 1941–42
Republican Senators
II   Capper, Arthur, Topeka, 1941–45
II   Reed, Clyde M., Parsons, 1941–45

Republican Representatives

II	Carlson, Frank, Concordia, 6th, 1941–45
I	Cole, Albert M., Holton, 1st, 1945
I	Guyer, U. S., Kansas City, 2d, 1941–42
II	Hope, Clifford R., Garden City, 5th, 7th, 1941–45
I	Lambertson, William P., Fairview, 1st, 1941–44
I	Rees, Edward H., Emporia, 4th, 1941–45
I	Scrivner, Errett P., Kansas City, 2d, 1943–45
II	Winter, Thomas D., Girard, 3d, 1941–45

KENTUCKY

Democratic Senators

I	Barkley, Alben W., Paducah, 1941–45
III	Chandler, Albert B., Versailles, 1941–45

Democratic Representatives

II	Bates, Joe B., Greenup, 8th, 1941–45
III	Chapman, Virgil, Paris, 6th, 1941–44
III	Chelf, Frank L., Lebanon, 4th, 1945
III	Clements, Earle C., Morganfield, 2d, 1945
II	Creal, Edward W., Hodgenville, 4th, 1941–43
I	Gregory, Noble J., Mayfield, 1st, 1941–45
III	May, Andrew J., Prestonsburg, 7th, 1941–45
II	O'Neal, Emmet, Louisville, 3d, 1941–45
I	Spence, Brent, Fort Thomas, 5th, 1941–45
II	Vincent, Beverly M., Brownsville, 2d, 1941–44

Republican Senator

Inc.	Stanfill, William A., Hazard, 1945

Republican Representatives

II	Carrier, Chester O., Leitchfield, 4th, 1943–44
II	Robsion, John M., Barbourville, 9th, 1941–45

LOUISIANA

Democratic Senators

I	Ellender, Allen J., Houma, 1941–45
III	Overton, John H., Alexandria, 1941–45

Democratic Representatives

II	Allen, A. Leonard, Winnfield, 8th, 1941–45
Inc.	Boggs, Hale, New Orleans, 2d, 1941–42
II	Brooks, Overton, Shreveport, 4th, 1941–45
III	Domengeaux, James, Lafayette, 3d, 1941–45
III	Hebert, F. Edward, New Orleans, 1st, 1941–45

LOUISIANA (*Continued*)
Democratic Representatives (*Continued*)
III   Larcade, Henry D., Jr., Opelousas, 7th, 1943–45
III   McKenzie, Charles E., Monroe, 5th, 1943–45
I   Maloney, Paul H., New Orleans, 2d, 1943–45
Inc.   Mills, Newt V., Monroe, 5th, 1941–42
III   Morrison, James H., Hammond, 6th, 1943–45
Inc.   Plauche, Vance, Lake Charles, 7th, 1941–42
Inc.   Sanders, Jared Y., Jr., Baton Rouge, 6th, 1941–42

MAINE
Republican Senators
I   Brewster, Ralph O., Dexter, 1941–45
II   White, Wallace H., Jr., Auburn, 1941–45
Republican Representatives
II   Fellows, Frank, Bangor, 3d, 1941–45
II   Hale, Robert, Portland, 1st, 1943–45
Inc.   Oliver, James C., South Portland, 1st, 1941–42
III   Smith, Margaret Chase, Skowhegan, 2d, 1941–45

MARYLAND
Democratic Senators
III   Radcliffe, George L., Baltimore, 1941–45
III   Tydings, Millard E., Havre de Grace, 1941–45
Democratic Representatives
III   Baldwin, H. Streett, Towson, 2d, 1943–45
Inc.   Byron, Katherine, Williamsport, 6th, 1941–42
Inc.   Byron, William D., Williamsport, 6th, 1941
Inc.   Cole, William P., Jr., Towson, 2d, 1941–42
I   D'Alesandro, Thomas, Jr., Baltimore, 3d, 1941–45
III   Fallon, George H., Baltimore, 4th, 1945
Inc.   Meyer, John A., Baltimore, 4th, 1941–42
Inc.   Roe, Dudley G., Sudlersville, 1st, 1945
II   Sasscer, Lansdale G., Upper Marlboro, 5th, 1941–45
II   Ward, David J., Salisbury, 1st, 1941–44
Republican Representatives
II   Beall, J. Glenn, Frostburg, 6th, 1943–45
III   Ellison, Daniel, Baltimore, 4th, 1943–44

MASSACHUSETTS
Democratic Senator
III   Walsh, David I., Clinton, 1941–45

Democratic Representatives

Inc.	Casey, Joseph E., Clinton, 3d, 1941–42
Inc.	Connery, Lawrence J., Lynn, 7th, 1941
III	Curley, James M., Boston, 11th, 1943–45
Inc.	Eliot, Thomas H., Cambridge, 9th, 1941–42
Inc.	Flaherty, Thomas A., Boston, 11th, 1941–42
Inc.	Healey, Arthur D., Boston, 11th, 1941–42
II	Lane, Thomas J., Lawrence, 7th, 1942–45
I	McCormack, John W., Boston, 12th, 1941–45
III	Philbin, Philip J., Clinton, 3d, 1943–45

Republican Senators

II	Lodge, Henry Cabot, Jr., Beverly, 1941–44
III	Saltonstall, Leverett, Chestnut Hill, 1945
I	Weeks, Sinclair, West Newton, 1944

Republican Representatives

III	Bates, George J., Salem, 6th, 1941–45
II	Clason, Charles R., Springfield, 2d, 1941
II	Gifford, Charles L., Cotuit, 15th, 1941–45
I	Goodwin, Angier L., Melrose, 8th, 1943–45
II	Herter, Christian A., Boston, 10th, 1943–45
II	Heselton, John W., Deerfield, 1st, 1945
II	Holmes, Pehr G., Worcester, 4th, 1941–45
II	Martin, Joseph W., Jr., North Attleboro, 14th, 1941–45
II	Rogers, Edith Nourse, Lowell, 5th, 1941–45
Inc.	Tinkham, George Holden, Boston, 10th, 1941–42
II	Treadway, Allen T., Stockbridge, 1st, 1941–44
II	Wigglesworth, Richard B., Milton, 13th, 1941–45

MICHIGAN

Democratic Senator

Inc.	Brown, Prentiss M., St. Ignace, 1941–42

Democratic Representatives

I	Dingell, John D., Detroit, 15th, 1941–45
I	Hook, Frank E., Ironwood, 12th, 1941–42, 1945
II	Lesinski, John, Dearborn, 16th, 1941–45
II	O'Brien, George D., Detroit, 13th, 1941–45
II	Rabaut, Louis C., Grosse Point Park, 14th, 1941–45
I	Sadowski, George G., Detroit, 1st, 1943–45
Inc.	Tenerowicz, Rudolph G., Hamtramck, 1st, 1941–42

Republican Senators

II	Ferguson, Homer, Detroit, 1943–45
II	Vandenberg, Arthur H., Grand Rapids, 1941–45

MICHIGAN (*Continued*)

Republican Representatives

II	Bennett, John B., Ontonagon, 12th, 1943–44
II	Blackney, William W., Flint, 6th, 1941–45
II	Bradley, Fred, Rogers City, 11th, 1941–45
II	Crawford, Fred L., Saginaw, 8th, 1941–45
I	Dondero, George A., Royal Oak, 17th, 1941–45
II	Engel, Albert J., Muskegon, 9th, 1941–45
I	Hoffman, Clare E., Allegan, 4th, 1941–45
I	Jonkman, Bartel J., Grand Rapids, 5th, 1941–45
II	Michener, Earl C., Adrian, 2d, 1941–45
II	Shafer, Paul W., Battle Creek, 3d, 1941–45
II	Wolcott, Jesse P., Port Huron, 7th, 1941–45
I	Woodruff, Roy O., Bay City, 10th, 1941–45

MINNESOTA

Democratic Representatives

I	Gallagher, William J., Minneapolis, 3d, 1945
I	Starkey, Frank T., St. Paul, 4th, 1945

Republican Senators

II	Ball, Joseph H., St. Paul, 1941–45
Inc.	Nelson, Arthur E., St. Paul, 1942
II	Shipstead, Henrik, Miltona, 1941–45

Republican Representatives

II	Andersen, H. Carl, Tyler, 7th, 1941–45
I	Andresen, August H., Red Wing, 1st, 1941–45
III	Gale, Richard P., Mound, 3d, 1941–44
III	Hagen, Harold C., Crookston, 9th, 1945
III	Judd, Walter H., Minneapolis, 5th, 1943–45
I	Knutson, Harold, St. Cloud, 7th, 1941–45
II	Maas, Melvin J., St. Paul, 4th, 1941–44
II	O'Hara, Joseph P., Glencoe, 2d, 1941–45
III	Pittenger, William A., Duluth, 8th, 1941–45
Inc.	Youngdahl, Oscar, Minneapolis, 5th, 1941–42

Farmer-Labor Representatives

Inc.	Buckler, R. T., Crookston, R.F.D., 9th, 1941–42
	[Hagen, Harold C., Crookston, 9th, 1943–44: see classification as Republican]

MISSISSIPPI

Democratic Senators

II	Bilbo, Theodore G., Poplarville, 1941–45
I	Doxey, Wall, Holly Springs, 1941–42
II	Eastland, James O., Ruleville, 1941, 1943–45
Inc.	Harrison, Pat, Gulfport, 1941

Democratic Representatives

III	Abernethy, Thomas G., Okolona, 4th, 1943–45
Inc.	Collins, Ross A., Meridian, 5th, 1941–42
III	Colmer, William M., Pascagoula, 6th, 1941–45
	[Doxey, Wall, Holly Springs, 2d, 1941: see classification as Senator]
Inc.	Ford, Aaron Lane, Ackerman, 4th, 1941–42
III	McGehee, Dan R., Meadville, 7th, 1941–45
III	Rankin, John E., Tupelo, 1st, 1941–45
III	Whitten, Jamie L., Charleston, 2d, 1942–45
III	Whittington, William M., Greenwood, 3d, 1941–45
III	Winstead, Arthur, Philadelphia, 5th, 1943–45

MISSOURI

Democratic Senators

II	Briggs, Frank P., Macon, 1945
III (Rep.)	Clark, Bennett Champ, University City, 1941–44
I	Truman, Harry S., Independence, 1941–44

Democratic Representatives

III	Bell, C. Jasper, Blue Springs, 4th, 1941–45
III	Cannon, Clarence, Elsberry, 9th, 1941–45
II	Carnahan, A. S. J., Ellsinore, 8th, 1945
II	Cochran, John J., St. Louis, 13th, 1941–45
III	Duncan, Richard M., St. Joseph, 3d, 1941–42
Inc.	Nelson, William L., Columbia, 2d, 1941–42
Inc.	Romjue, Milton A., Macon, 1st, 1941–42
Inc.	Shannon, Joseph B., Kansas City, 5th, 1941–42
III	Slaughter, Roger C., Kansas City, 5th, 1943–45
II	Sullivan, John B., St. Louis, 11th, 1941–42, 1945
Inc.	Williams, Clyde, Hillsboro, 8th, 1941–42
II	Zimmerman, Orville, Kennett, 10th, 1941–45

Republican Senator

II	Donnell, Forrest C., Webster Groves, 1945

MISSOURI (*Continued*)

Republican Representatives

I	Arnold, Wat, Kirksville, 1st, 1943–45
I	Bennett, Marion T., Springfield, 6th, 1943–45
Inc.	Bennett, Philip A., Springfield, 6th, 1941–42
I	Cole, William C., St. Joseph, 3d, 1943–45
I	Elmer, William P., Salem, 8th, 1943–44
II	Miller, Louis E., St. Louis, 11th, 1943–44
I	Ploeser, Walter C., St. Louis, 12th, 1941–45
I	Schwabe, Max, Columbia, 2d, 1943–45
I	Short, Dewey, Galena, 7th, 1941–45

MONTANA

Democratic Senators

I	Murray, James E., Butte, 1941–45
III	Wheeler, Burton K., Butte, 1941–45

Democratic Representatives

Inc.	D'Ewart, W. A., Wilsall, 2d, 1945
II	Mansfield, Mike, Missoula, 1st, 1943–45
II	O'Connor, James F., Livingston, 2d, 1941–45

Republican Representative

Inc.	Rankin, Jeannette, Missoula, 1st, 1941–42

NEBRASKA

Democratic Representatives

Inc.	Coffee, Harry B., Chadron, 5th, 1941–42
Inc.	McLaughlin, Charles F., Omaha, 2d, 1941–42

Republican Senators

I	Butler, Hugh A., Omaha, 1941–45
I	Wherry, Kenneth S., Pawnee City, 1943–45

Republican Representatives

I	Buffett, Howard H., Omaha, 2d, 1943–45
Inc.	Copeland, Oren S., Lincoln, 1st, 1941–42
II	Curtis, Carl T., Minden, 1st, 4th, 1941–45
II	Miller, A. L., Kimball, 4th, 1943–45
II	Stefan, Karl, Norfolk, 3d, 1941–45

Independent Senator

III (Rep.)	Norris, George W., McCook, 1941–42

NEVADA

Democratic Senators
[Bunker, Berkeley, Las Vegas, 1941–42: see Classification as Representative]
Inc. Carville, Edward P., Reno, 1945
III McCarran, Pat, Reno, 1941–45
II Scrugham, James G., Reno, 1943–45
Democratic Representatives
III Bunker, Berkeley, Las Vegas, At Large, 1945
Inc. Scrugham, James G., Reno, At Large, 1941–42
II Sullivan, Maurice J., Reno, At Large, 1943–44

NEW HAMPSHIRE

Republican Senators
I Bridges, Styles, Concord, 1941–45
III Tobey, Charles W., Temple, 1941–45
Republican Representatives
II Adams, Sherman, Lincoln, 2d, 1945
Inc. Jenks, Arthur B., Manchester, 1st, 1941–42
II Merrow, Chester E., Center Ossipee, 1st, 1943–45
II Stearns, Foster, Hancock, 2d, 1941–44

NEW JERSEY

Democratic Senators
II Smathers, William H., Margate, 1941–42
II Walsh, Arthur, South Orange, 1943–44
Democratic Representatives
I Hart, Edward J., Jersey City, 14th, 1941–45
I Norton, Mary T., Jersey City, 13th, 1941–45
Inc. Sutphin, William H., Matawan, 3d, 1941–42
II Wene, Elmer H., Vineland, 2d, 1941–44
Republican Senators
II Barbour, W. Warren, Locust, 1941–43
I Hawkes, Albert W., Montclair, 1943–45
II Smith, H. Alexander, Princeton, 1945
Republican Representatives
I Auchincloss, James C., Rumson, 3d, 1943–45
II Canfield, Gordon, Paterson, 8th, 1941–45
III Case, Clifford P., Rahway, 6th, 1945
II Eaton, Charles A., Watchung, Plainfield, 5th, 1941–45
III Hand, T. Millet, Cape May City, 2d, 1945

NEW JERSEY (*Continued*)

Republican Representatives (Continued)

II	Hartley, Fred A., Jr., Kearny, 10th, 1941–45
II	Kean, Robert W., Livingston, 12th, 1941–45
II	McLean, Donald H., Elizabeth, 6th, 1941–45
Inc.	Osmers, Frank C., Jr., Haworth, 9th, 1941
II	Powers, D. Lane, Trenton, 4th, 1941–45
II	Sundstrom, Frank L., East Orange, 11th, 1943–45
III	Thomas, J. Parnell, Allendale, 7th, 1941–45
III	Towe, Harry L., Rutherford, 9th, 1943–45
Inc.	Vreeland, Albert L., East Orange, 11th, 1941
III	Wolverton, Charles A., Merchantville, 1st, 1941–45

NEW MEXICO

Democratic Senators

II	Chavez, Dennis, Albuquerque, 1941–45
I	Hatch, Carl A., Clovis, 1941–45

Democratic Representatives

II	Anderson, Clinton P., Albuquerque, At Large, 1941–45
II	Fernandez, Antonio, Santa Fe, At Large, 1943–45

NEW YORK

Democratic Senators

II	Mead, James M., Buffalo, 1941–45
I	Wagner, Robert F., New York City, 1941–45

Democratic Representatives

II	Barry, William B., St. Albans, 2d, 4th, 1941–45
Inc.	Beiter, Alfred F., Williamsville, 41st, 1941–42
I	Bloom, Sol, New York City, 20th, 1941–45
I	Buckley, Charles A., New York City, 23d, 25th, 1941–45
I	Burchill, Thomas F., New York City, 15th, 1943–44
I	Byrne, William T., Loudonville, 28th, 32d, 1941–45
I	Capozzoli, Louis J., New York City, 13th, 1941–44
II	Celler, Emanuel, Brooklyn, 8th, 13th, 1941–45
I	Cullen, Thomas H., Brooklyn, 1941–44
I	Delaney, James J., Long Island City, 6th, 1945
I	Delaney, John J., Brooklyn, 7th, 1941–45
I	Dickstein, Samuel, New York City, 12th, 19th, 1941–45
Inc.	Edelstein, M. Michael, New York City, 14th, 1941
I	Fay, James H., New York City, 16th, 1943–44

I	Fitzpatrick, James M., New York City, 24th, 1941–44
I	Gavagan, Joseph A., New York City, 21st, 1941–43
I	Heffernan, James J., Brooklyn, 5th, 11th, 1941–45
II	Kennedy, Martin J., New York City, 18th, 1941–44
Inc.	Kennedy, Michael J., New York City, 15th, 1941–42
I	Keogh, Eugene J., Brooklyn, 9th, 1941–45
I	Lynch, Walter A., New York City, 22d, 23d, 1941–45
II	Merritt, Matthew J., Malba, At Large, 1941–44
II	O'Leary, James A., West New Brighton, 11th, 1941–43
II	O'Toole, Donald L., Brooklyn, 8th, 13th, 1941–45
II	Pfeifer, Joseph L., Brooklyn, 3d, 8th, 1941–45
Inc.	Powell, Adam C., New York City, 22d, 1945
I	Quinn, Peter A., New York City, 26th, 1945
I	Rabin, Benjamin J., New York City, 24th, 1945
I	Rayfiel, Leo F., Brooklyn, 14th, 1945
Inc.	Roe, James A., Flushing, 4th, 1945
II	Rogers, George F., Rochester, 40th, 1945
I	Rooney, John J., Brooklyn, 4th, 1944–45
Inc.	Schwert, Pius L., Buffalo, 42d, 1941
I	Somers, Andrew L., Brooklyn, 6th, 10th, 1941–45
I	Torrens, James H., New York City, 21st, 1944–45

Republican Representatives

II	Andrews, Walter G., Buffalo, 40th, 42d, 1941–45
III	Baldwin, Joseph Clark, New York City, 17th, 1941–45
III	Bennett, Augustus W., Balmville, 29th, 1945
II	Buck, E. B., Staten Island, 11th, 16th, 1944–45
II	Butler, John C., Buffalo, 42d, 44th, 1941–45
Inc.	Cluett, E. Harold, Troy, 29th, 1941–42
II	Cole, W. Sterling, Bath, 37th, 39th, 1941–45
Inc.	Crowther, Frank, Schenectady, 30th, 1941–42
III	Culkin, Francis D., Oswego, 32d, 1941–43
II	Douglas, Fred J., Utica, 33d, 1941–44
II	Elsaesser, Edward J., Buffalo, 43d, 1945
I	Fish, Hamilton, Garrison, 26th, 1941–44
I	Fuller, Hadwen C., Parish, 35th, 1944–45
II	Gamble, Ralph A., Larchmont, 25th, 1941–45
I	Gwinn, Ralph W., Bronxville, 27th, 1945
I	Hall, Edwin Arthur, Binghamton, 34th, 37th, 1941–45
II	Hall, Leonard W., Oyster Bay, 1st, 2d, 1941–45
II	Hancock, Clarence E., Syracuse, 35th, 36th, 1941–45

NEW YORK (*Continued*)

Republican Representatives (*Continued*)

II	Kearney, Bernard W., Gloversville, 30th, 31st, 1943–45
II	Kilburn, Clarence E., Malone, 31st, 34th, 1941–45
II	Latham, Henry J., Queens Village, 3d, 1945
II	LeFevre, Jay, New Paltz, 27th, 30th, 1943–45
III	Mruk, Joseph, Buffalo, 41st, 1943–44
II	O'Brien, Joseph J., East Rochester, 38th, 1941–44
Inc.	Pheiffer, William T., New York City, 16th, 1941–42
I	Reed, Daniel A., Dunkirk, 43d, 45th, 1941–45
Inc.	Rockefeller, Lewis K., Chatham, 27th, 1941–42
II	Sharp, Edgar A., Patchogue, 1st, 1945
Inc.	Simpson, Kenneth F., New York City, 17th, 1941
II	Stanley, Winifred, Buffalo, At Large, 1943–44
II	Taber, John, Auburn, 36th, 38th, 1941–45
II	Taylor, Dean P., Troy, 29th, 33d, 1943–45
III	Wadsworth, James W., Geneseo, 39th, 41st, 1941–45

American Labor Representative

I (Dem.)	Marcantonio, Vito, New York City, 18th, 20th, 1941–45

NORTH CAROLINA

Democratic Senators

III (Rep.)	Bailey, Josiah W., Raleigh, 1941–45
III	Hoey, Clyde R., Chelby, 1945
III (Rep.)	Reynolds, Robert R., Asheville, 1941–44

Democratic Representatives

III	Barden, Graham, A., New Bern, 3d, 1941–45
II	Bonner, Herbert C., Washington, 1st, 1941–45
II	Bulwinkle, Alfred L., Gastonia, 10th, 11th, 1941–45
II	Burgin. W. O., Lexington, 8th, 1941–45
II	Clark, J. Bayard, Fayetteville, 7th, 1941–45
II	Cooley, Harold D., Nashville, 4th, 1941–45
II	Doughton, Robert L., Laurel Springs, 9th, 1941–45
III	Durham, Carl T., Chapel Hill, 6th, 1941–45
III	Ervin, Joe W., Charlotte, 10th, 1945
I	Folger, Alonzo D., Mount Airy, 5th, 1941
I	Folger, John H., Mount Airy, 5th, 1941–45
II	Kerr, John H., Warrenton, 2d, 1941–45
I	Morrison, Cameron, Charlotte, 10th, 1943–44
I	Weaver, Zebulon, Asheville, 11th, 12th, 1941–45

NORTH DAKOTA

Democratic Senator
Inc.   Moses, John, Hazen, 1945
Republican Senators
III (Dem.)   Langer, William, Bismarck, 1941–45
 II   Nye, Gerald P., Cooperstown, 1941–44
 II   Young, Milton R., Berlin, 1945
Republican Representatives
III (Dem.)   Burdick, Usher L., Williston, At Large, 1941–44
III   Lemke, William, Fargo, At Large, 1943–45
 I   Robertson, Charles R., Bismarck, At Large, 1941–42, 1945

OHIO

Democratic Senator
Inc.   Huffman, James W., Columbus, 1945
Democratic Representatives
Inc.   Claypool, Harold K., Chillicothe, 11th, 1941–42
 II   Crosser, Robert, Cleveland, 21st, 1941–45
Inc.   Davis, Jacob E., Waverly, 6th, 1941–42
 II   Feighan, Michael A., Cleveland, 20th, 1943–45
III   Gardner, Edward J., Hamilton, 3d, 1945
Inc.   Harter, Dow W., Akron, 14th, 1941–42
Inc.   Holbrock, Greg, Hamilton, 3d, 1941–42
 I   Huber, Walter B., Akron, 14th, 1945
Inc.   Hunter, John F., Toledo, 9th, 1941–42
Inc.   Imhoff, Lawrence E., St. Clairsville, 18th, 1941–42
 I   Kirwan, Michael J., Youngstown, 19th, 1941–45
Inc.   Secrest, Robert T., Caldwell, 15th, 1941–42
Inc.   Sweeney, Martin L., Cleveland, 20th, 1941–42
 II   Thom, William R., Canton, 16th, 1941-42, 1945
Inc.   Young, Stephen M., Cleveland, At Large, 1941–42
Republican Senators
 II   Burton, Harold H., Cleveland, 1941–45
 I   Taft, Robert A., Cincinnati, 1941–45
Republican Representatives
Inc.   Baumhart, A. D., Jr., Vermilion, 13th, 1941–42
 II   Bender, George H., Cleveland Heights, At Large, 1941–45
 II   Bolton, Frances P., Lyndhurst, 22d, 1941–45
 II   Brehm, Walter E., Logan, 11th, 1943–45
 I   Brown, Clarence, Blanchester, 7th, 1941–45

OHIO (*Continued*)
Republican Representatives (*Continued*)

I	Carson, Henderson H., Canton, 16th, 1943–44
I	Clevenger, Cliff, Bryan, 5th, 1941–45
I	Elston, Charles H., Cincinnati, 1st, 1941–45
I	Griffiths, P. W., Marietta, 15th, 1943–45
II	Hess, William E., Cincinnati, 2d, 1941–45
II	Jeffrey, Harry P., Dayton, 3d, 1943–44
I	Jenkins, Thomas A., Ironton, 10th, 1941–45
I	Jones, Robert F., Lima, 4th, 1941–45
II	Lewis, Earl R., St. Clairsville, 18th, 1943–45
I	McCowen, Edward O., Wheelersburg, 6th, 1943–45
I	McGregor, J. Harry, West Lafayette, 17th, 1941–45
II	Ramey, Homer A., Toledo, 9th, 1943–45
II	Rowe, Edward, Akron, 14th, 1943–44
I	Smith, Frederick C., Marion, 8th, 1941–45
II	Vorys, John M., Columbus, 12th, 1941–45
I	Weichel, Alvin F., Sandusky, 13th, 1943–45

OKLAHOMA

Democratic Senators

I	Lee, Josh, Norman, 1941–42
II	Thomas, Elmer, Medicine Park, 1941–45

Democratic Representatives

III	Boren, Lyle H., Seminole, 4th, 1941–45
Inc.	Cartwright, Wilburn, McAlester, 3d, 1941–42
III (Rep.)	Disney, Wesley E., Tulsa, 1st, 1941–44
III	Johnson, Jed, Anadarko, 6th, 1941–45
Inc.	Massingale, Sam C., Cordell, 7th, 1941
II	Monroney, A. S. Mike, Oklahoma City, 5th, 1941–45
III	Nichols, Jack, Eufaula, 2d, 1941–43
Inc.	Rogers, Will, Oklahoma City, At Large, 1941–42
III	Stewart, Paul, Antlers, 3d, 1943–45
III	Stigler, William G., Stigler, 2d, 1944–45
II	Wickersham, Victor, Mangum, 7th, 1941–45

Republican Senator

I	Moore, E. H., Tulsa, 1943–45

Republican Representatives

II	Rizley, Ross, Guymon, 8th, 1941–45
I	Schwabe, George B., Tulsa, 1st, 1945

OREGON
Democratic Representative
Inc.   Pierce, Walter M., La Grande, 2d, 1941–42
Republican Senators
II   Cordon, Guy, Roseburg, 1944–45
II   Holman, Rufus C., Portland, 1941–44
II   McNary, Charles L., Salem, 1941–44
III   Morse, Wayne, Eugene, 1945
Republican Representatives
III   Angell, Homer D., Portland, 3d, 1941–45
II   Ellsworth, Harris, Roseburg, 4th, 1943–45
III   Mott, James W., Salem, 1st, 1941–45
II   Stockman, Lowell, Pendleton, 2d, 1943–45

PENNSYLVANIA
Democratic Senators
I   Guffey, Joseph F., Pittsburgh, 1941–45
I   Myers, Francis J., Philadelphia, 1945
Democratic Representatives
I   Barrett, William A., Philadelphia, 1st, 1945
Inc.   Boland, Patrick, Scranton, 11th, 1941–42
Inc.   Boland, Veronica, Scranton, 11th, 1942
I   Bradley, Michael J., Philadelphia, 3d, 1941–45
I   Eberharter, Herman P., Pittsburgh, 31st, 32d, 1941–45
Inc.   Faddis, Charles I., Waynesburg, 25th, 1941–42
Inc.   Flannery, J. Harold, Pittston, 12th, 1941
I   Flood, Daniel J., Wilkes-Barre, 11th, 1945
I   Furlong, Grant, Donora, 25th, 1943–44
I   Granahan, William T., Philadelphia, 2d, 1945
II   Green, William J., Philadelphia, 5th, 1945
Inc.   Haines, Harry L., Red Lion, 22d, 1941–42
I   Hoch, Daniel K., Reading, 13th, 14th, 1943–45
Inc.   Holland, Elmer, Pittsburgh, 33d, 1942
I   Kelley, Augustine B., Greensburg, 27th, 28th, 1941–45
Inc.   McArdle, Joseph A., Pittsburgh, 33d, 1941
II   McGlinchey, Herbert J., Philadelphia, 6th, 1945
I   McGranery, James P., Philadelphia, 2d, 1941–43
I   Morgan, Thomas E., Fredericktown, 24th, 1945
Inc.   Moser, Guy L., Douglassville, 14th, 1941–42
I   Murphy, John W., Dunmore, 10th, 11th, 1943–45
I   Myers, Francis J., Philadelphia, 6th, 1941–44

PENNSYLVANIA (*Continued*)

Democratic Representatives (*Continued*)

Inc.	Sacks, Leon, Philadelphia, 1st, 1941–42
I	Scanlon, Thomas E., Pittsburgh, 16th, 30th, 1941–44
II	Sheridan, John Edward, Philadelphia, 4th, 1941–45
Inc.	Smith, Francis R., Philadelphia, 5th, 1941–42
II	Snyder, J. Buell, Perryopolis, 23d, 24th, 1941–45
II	Walter, Francis E., Easton, 20th, 21st, 1941–45
II	Weiss, Samuel A., Glassport, 31st, 33d, 1941–45
I	Wright, James A., Carnegie, 32d, 34th, 1941–44

Republican Senator

II	Davis, James J., Pittsburgh, 1941–44

Republican Representatives

I	Brumbaugh, D. Emmert, Claysburg, 22d, 23d, 1944–45
I	Campbell, Howard E., Pittsburgh, 29th, 1945
II	Corbett, Robert J., Bellevue, 30th, 1945
I	Ditter, J. William, Ambler, 17th, 1941–43
II	Fenton, Ivor, Mahanoy City, 12th, 13th, 1941–45
III	Fulton, James G., Dormont, 31st, 1945
II	Gallagher, James, Sr., Philadelphia, 1st, 1943–44
II	Gavin, Leon H., Oil City, 19th, 20th, 1943–45
II	Gerlach, Charles L., Allentown, 8th, 9th, 1941–45
I	Gillette, Wilson D., Towanda, 14th, 15th, 1941–45
II	Graham, Louis E., Beaver, 25th, 26th, 1941–45
I	Gross, Chester H., Manchester, 21st, 22d, 1943–45
Inc.	Jarett, Benjamin, Farrell, 20th, 1941–42
I	Kinzer, Roland, Lancaster, 9th, 10th, 1941–45
II	Kunkel, John C., Harrisburg, 18th, 19th, 1941–45
I	McConnell, Samuel K., Penn Wynne, 16th, 17th, 1944–45
II	Miller, Thomas Byron, Plymouth, 12th, 1942–44
II	Pracht, C. Frederick, Philadelphia, 5th, 1943–44
Inc.	Pratt, Joseph M., Philadelphia, 2d, 1943–44
I	Rich, Robert F., Woolrich, 15th, 16th, 1941–42, 1945
I	Rodgers, Robert L., Erie, 28th, 29th, 1941–45
Inc.	Rutherford, Albert G., Honesdale, 15th, 1941
II	Scott, Hugh D., Jr., Philadelphia, 7th, 1941–44
I	Simpson, Richard M., Huntingdon, 17th, 18th, 1941–45
I	Tibbott, Harve, Ebensburg, 26th, 27th, 1941–45
II	Troutman, William I., Shamokin, At Large, 1943–44
III	Van Zandt, James E., Altoona, 23d, 1941–43
I	Wolfenden, James, Upper Darby, 7th, 8th, 1941–45

RHODE ISLAND
Democratic Senators

III (Rep.)	Gerry, Peter G., Providence, 1941–45
I	Green, Theodore Francis, Providence, 1941–45

Democratic Representatives

II	Fogarty, John E., Harmony, 2d, 1941–45
I	Forand, Aime J., Cumberland, 1st, 1941–45

SOUTH CAROLINA
Democratic Senators

Inc.	Byrnes, James F., Spartanburg, 1941
Inc.	Hall, Wilton E., Anderson, 1944
III (Rep.)	Johnston, Olin D., Spartanburg, 1945
Inc.	Lumpkin, Alva M., Columbia, 1941
II	Maybank, Burnet R., Charleston, 1941–45
Inc.	Peace, Roger C., Greenville, 1941
III (Rep.)	Smith, Ellison D., Lynchburg, 1941–44

Democratic Representatives

II	Bryson, Joseph R., Greenville, 4th, 1941–45
III	Fulmer, Hampton P., Orangeburg, 2d, 1941–44
II	Hare, Butler B., Saluda, 3d, 1941–45
II	McMillan, John L., Florence, 6th, 1941–45
I	Richards, James P., Lancaster, 5th, 1941–45
II	Riley, John J., Sumter, 2d, 1945
III	Rivers, L. Mendel, North Charleston, 1st, 1941–45

SOUTH DAKOTA
Democratic Senator

II	Bulow, William J., Beresford, 1941–42

Republican Senators

I	Bushfield, Harlan J., Miller, 1943–45
II	Gurney, Chan, Yankton, 1941–45

Republican Representatives

II	Case, Francis, Custer, 2d, 1941–45
II	Mundt, Karl E., Madison, 1st, 1941–45

TENNESSEE
Democratic Senators

III	McKellar, Kenneth, Memphis, 1941–45
II	Stewart, Tom, Winchester, 1941–45

TENNESSEE (*Continued*)

Democratic Representatives

I	Cooper, Jere, Dyersburg, 8th, 9th, 1941–45
II	Courtney, Wirt, Franklin, 6th, 7th, 1941–45
I	Davis, Clifford, Memphis, 9th, 10th, 1941–45
Inc.	Earthman, Harold H., Murfreesboro, 5th, 1945
II	Gore, Albert, Carthage, 4th, 1941–45
II	Kefauver, Estes, Chattanooga, 3d, 1941–45
I	McCord, Jim, Lewisburg, 5th, 1943–44
III	Murray, Tom, Jackson, 8th, 1943–45
Inc.	Pearson, Herron, Jackson, 17th, 1941–42
I	Priest, J. Percy, Nashville, 5th, 6th, 1941–45

Republican Representatives

II	Jennings, John, Jr., Knoxville, 2d, 1941–45
II	Reece, B. Carroll, Johnson City, 1st, 1941–45

TEXAS

Democratic Senators

II	Connally, Tom, Marlin, 1941–45
Inc.	Houston, Andrew Jackson, La Porte, 1941
III	O'Daniel, W. Lee, Fort Worth, 1941–45
Inc.	Sheppard, Morris, Texarkana, 1941

Democratic Representatives

II	Beckworth, Lindley, Gladewater, 1941–45
II	Combs, J. M., Beaumont, 2d, 1945
III	Dies, Martin, Orange, 2d, 1941–44
III	Fisher, O. D., San Angelo, 21st, 1943–45
III	Gossett, Ed., Wichita Falls, 13th, 1943–45
II	Johnson, Luther A., Corsicana, 6th, 1941–45
I	Johnson, Lyndon B., Johnson City, 10th, 1941–45
III	Kilday, Paul J., San Antonio, 20th, 1941–45
III	Kleberg, Richard M., Corpus Christi, 14th, 1941–44
III	Lanham, Fritz G., Fort Worth, 12th, 1941–45
III	Lyle, John E., Corpus Christi, 14th, 1945
II	Mahon, George H., Colorado City, 19th, 1941–45
II	Mansfield, Joseph J., Columbus, 9th, 1941–45
I	Patman, Wright, Texarkana, 1st, 1941–45
II	Patton, Nat, Crockett, 2d, 1941–44
III	Pickett, Tom, Palestine, 7th, 1945
III	Poage, W. R., Waco, 11th, 1941–45

Inc.	Rayburn, Sam, Bonham, 4th, 1941–45
III	Russell, Sam M., Stephenville, 17th, 1941–45
Inc.	South, Charles L., Coleman, 21st, 1941–42
III	Sumners, Hatton W., Dallas, 5th, 1941–45
II	Thomas, Albert, Houston, 8th, 1941–45
II	Thomason, R. Ewing, El Paso, 16th, 1941–45
III (Rep.)	West, Milton H., Brownsville, 15th, 1941–45
III	Worley, Eugene, Shamrock, 18th, 1941–45

UTAH
Democratic Senators

I	Murdock, Abe, Beaver, 1941–45
I	Thomas, Elbert D., Salt Lake City, 1941–45

Democratic Representatives

I	Granger, Walter K., Cedar City, 1st, 1941–45
I	Robinson, J. W., Provo, 2d, 1941–45

VERMONT
Republican Senators

III	Aiken, George B., Putney, 1941–45
III	Austin, Warren R., Burlington, 1941–45

Republican Representative

II	Plumley, Charles A., Northfield, At Large, 1941–45

VIRGINIA
Democratic Senators

III (Rep.)	Byrd, Harry Flood, Berryville, 1941–45
Inc.	Glass, Carter, Lynchburg, 1941–45

Democratic Representatives

II	Bland, Schuyler Otis, Newport News, 1st, 1941–45
III	Burch, Thomas G., Martinsville, 5th, 1941–45
II	Daughton, Ralph H., Norfolk, 2d, 1945
III	Drewry, Patrick H., Petersburg, 4th, 1941–45
I	Flannagan, John W., Bristol, 9th, 1941–45
I	Gary, J. Vaughan, Richmond, 3d, 1945
III	Harris, Winder R., Norfolk, 2d, 1941–44
III	Robertson, A. Willis, Lexington, 7th, 1941–45
III	Satterfield, Dave E., Richmond, 3d, 1941–44
III	Smith, Howard W., Alexandria, 8th, 1941–45
III	Woodrum, Clifton A., Roanoke, 6th, 1941–45

WASHINGTON
Democratic Senators

II	Bone, Homer T., Tacoma, 1941–44
I	Magnuson, Warren G., Seattle, 1945
I	Mitchell, Hugh B., Everett, 1945
I	Wallgren, Mon C., Everett, 1941–44

Democratic Representatives

II	Coffee, John M., Tacoma, 6th, 1941–45
I	DeLacy, Hugh, Seattle, 1st, 1945
Inc.	Hill, Knute, Prosser, 4th, 1941–42
I	Jackson, Henry, M., Everett, 2d, 1941–45
Inc.	Leavy, Charles H., Spokane, 5th, 1941–42
	[Magnuson, Warren G., Seattle, 1st, 1941–44: see Classification as Senator]
I	Savage, Charles R., Shelton, 3d, 1945
Inc.	Smith, Martin F., Hoquiam, 3d, 1941–42

Republican Representatives

II	Holmes, Hal, Ellensburg, 4th, 1943–45
II	Horan, Walter F., Wenatchee, 5th, 1943–45
II	Norman, Fred, Raymond, 3d, 1943–44

WEST VIRGINIA
Democratic Senators

I	Kilgore, Harley M., Beckley, 1941–45
Inc.	Neely, Matthew M., Fairmont, 1941
II	Rosier, Joseph, Fairmont, 1941–42
Inc.	Shott, Hugh Ike, Bluefield, 1942

Democratic Representatives

I	Bailey, Cleveland, Clarksburg, 3d, 1945
Inc.	Edmiston, Andrew, Weston, 3d, 1941–42
II	Hedrick, E. H., Beckley, 6th, 1945
Inc.	Johnson, George W., Parkersburg, 4th, 1941–42
II	Kee, John, Bluefield, 5th, 1941–45
I	Neely, Matthew M., Fairmont, 1st, 1945
Inc.	Ramsay, Robert L., Follansbee, 1st, 1941–42
III	Randolph, Jennings, Elkins, 2d, 1941–45
III	Smith, Joe, Beckley, 6th, 1941–44

Republican Senator

| I | Revercomb, Chapman, Charleston, 1943–45 |

Republican Representatives

| I | Ellis, Hubert S., Huntington, 4th, 1943–45 |

II   Rohrbough, Edward G., Glenville, 3d, 1943–44
I   Schiffler, Andrew C., Wheeling, 1st, 1943–44

WISCONSIN
Democratic Representatives
I   Biemiller, Andrew J., Milwaukee, 5th, 1945
I   Dilweg, LaVern, Green Bay, 8th, 1943–44
I   McMurray, Howard J., 5th, 1943–44
III   Wasielewski, Thad F., Milwaukee, 4th, 1941–45
Republican Senator
II   Wiley, Alexander, Chippewa Falls, 1941–45
Republican Representatives
Inc.   Bolles, Stephen, Janesville, 1st, 1941
I   Byrnes, John W., Green Bay, 8th, 1945
I   Henry, Robert K., Jefferson, 2d, 1945
Inc.   Johns, Joshua L., Algoma, 8th, 1941–42
II   Keefe, Frank B., Oshkosh, 6th, 1941–45
I   Murray, Reid F., Ogdensburg, 7th, 1941–45
III   O'Konski, Alvin E., Mercer, 10th, 1943–45
II   Smith, Lawrence H., Racine, 1st, 1941–45
II   Stevenson, William H., La Crosse, 3d, 1941–45
Inc.   Thill, Lewis D., Milwaukee, 5th, 1941–42
Progressive Senator
III (Dem.) LaFollette, Robert M., Madison, 1941–45
Progressive Representatives
Inc.   Gehrmann, Bernard J., Mellen, 10th, 1941–42
III (Rep.) Hull, Merlin, Black River Falls, 9th, 1941–45
III (Dem.) Sauthoff, Harry, Madison, 2d, 1941–44

WYOMING
Democratic Senators
II   O'Mahony, Joseph C., Cheyenne, 1941–45
III   Schwartz, H. H., Casper, 1941–42
Democratic Representative
Inc.   McIntyre, John J., Douglas, At Large, 1941–42
Republican Senator
I   Robertson, Edward V., Cody, 1943–45
Republican Representative
II   Barrett, Frank A., Lusk, At Large, 1943–45

Appendix B

THE SCATTER DIAGRAMS on Charts 1 and 2 show how each member of Congress (Senator or Representative) voted on party-votes during the period from December, 1941, through August, 1945. Party-votes are defined as those in which a majority of one party is opposed by a majority of the second party. The diagram includes only those Senators who cast more than twenty party-votes and those Representatives who cast more than thirty party-votes. Each member has been given two scores, one showing the degree of affinity with his own party when in the majority and one with the opposition party when in the majority. These scores are plotted on the diagram, the Republican axis being horizontal and the Democratic axis vertical. The members clustering around the party axis have been placed in Group I as strong party supporters. Those further removed are placed in Group II (moderate party supporters) and in Group III (mild party supporters).

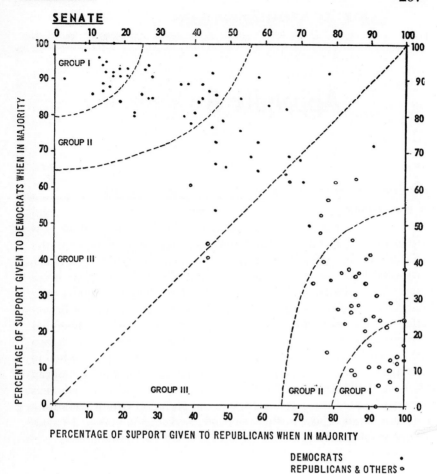

CHART 1

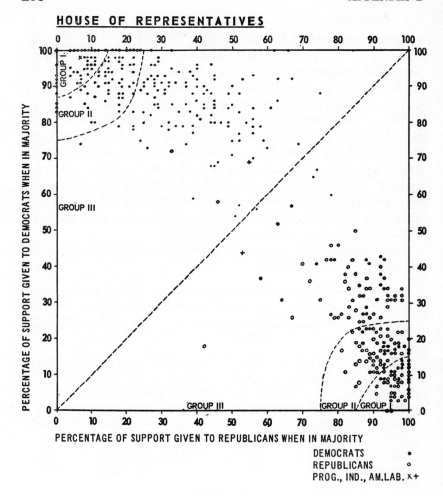

CHART 2

PARTISAN ALIGNMENT ON ALL VOTES, 1941–45

CHARTS 3 and 4 show the percentage of each party supporting the winning side in every roll-call vote. In 1941 and 1942 the Democrats in each House were in almost complete control of the voting, although occasionally the solid line dips down when the Republicans temporarily assumed control. The effects of the close election of 1942 are readily apparent in the voting in the House; the Republicans were in the majority on most votes—sometimes with some Democratic support. The Democratic loss in the 1942 elections was not so great in the Senate, and the Senate Democrats were more persistently successful in 1943 and 1944 than were their House colleagues. In 1945, the House Democrats, with their increased majorities, were once again able to assert greater control over the voting.

The following table indicates the percentage distribution of party strength for all roll-call votes.

	Democrats Only in Majority	Bipartisan, but Greater Democratic Support	Bipartisan Unanimous	Bipartisan, but Greater Republican Support	Republicans Only in Majority
1941					
HR	48.75	17.5	3.75	22.5	7.5
Senate	63.2	13.7	7.4	8.4	7.4
1942					
HR	13.9	16.6	15.3	41.7	12.5
Senate	22.3	21.6	9.6	35.1	11.7
1943					
HR	16.5	14.3	8.8	25.3	35.1
Senate	32.0	18.5	2.5	26.0	21.0
1944					
HR	15.4	17.0	10.7	27.7	29.2
Senate	31.6	15.3	3.1	28.6	21.4
1945					
HR	37.5	30.6	1.4	18.0	12.5
Senate	39.4	29.8	1.0	16.3	13.5

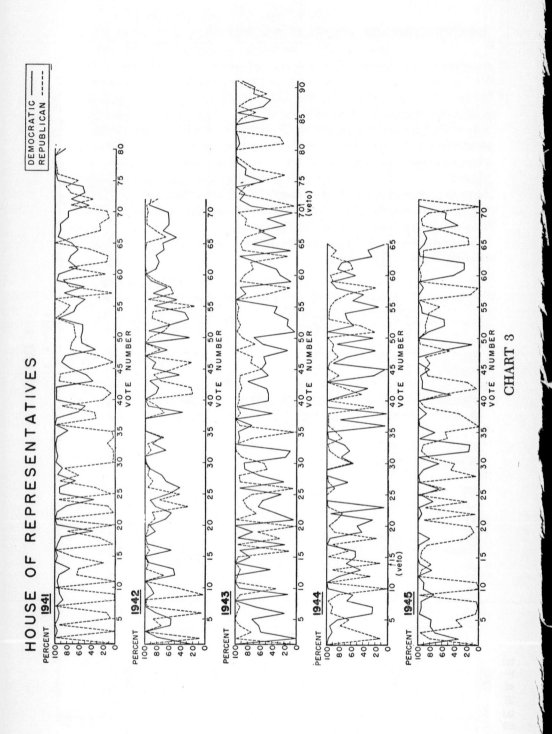

HOUSE OF REPRESENTATIVES

DEMOCRATIC ———
REPUBLICAN -----

CHART 3

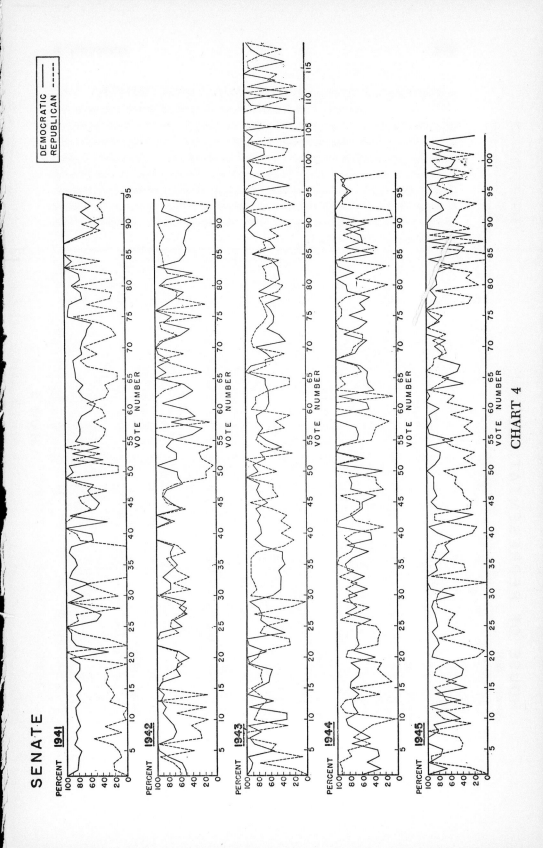

CHART 4

PERCENTAGE OF PARTY COHESION ON ALL VOTES, 1941–45

CHARTS 5 and 6 show the degree of party cohesion on all roll-call votes, arranged according to the decreasing degree of cohesiveness. The horizontal axis shows the number of votes; the vertical axis, the percentage of party cohesion on each vote. In general, there is a higher degree of party cohesion in the House than in the Senate and greater cohesion among the Republicans than among the Democrats. Following the 1944 election, however, there was an increased degree of Democratic cohesion, with the Democrats outstripping the Republicans in the Senate.

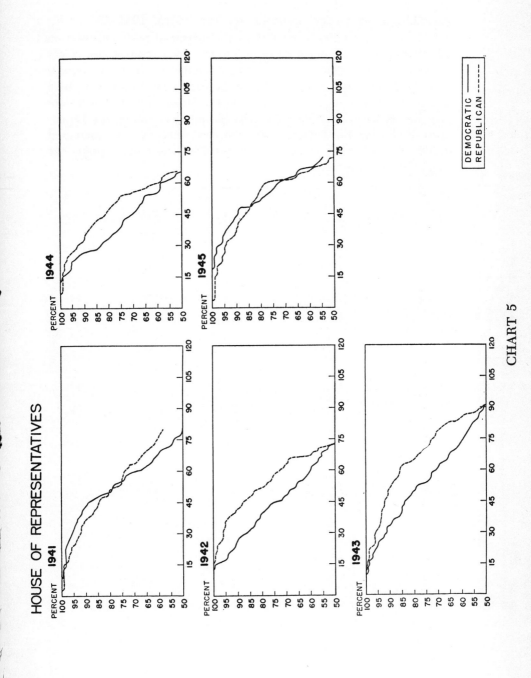

HOUSE OF REPRESENTATIVES

CHART 5

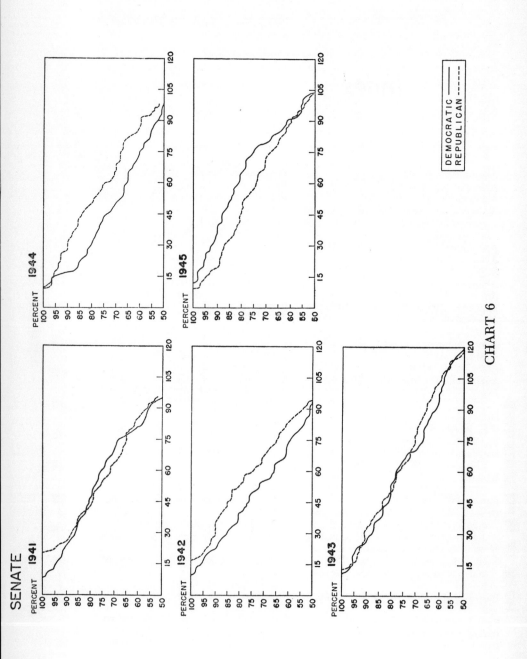

SENATE

PERCENT **1941**

PERCENT **1942**

PERCENT **1943**

PERCENT **1944**

PERCENT **1945**

DEMOCRATIC ———
REPUBLICAN ------

CHART 6

Index

Acknowledgments

THIS VOLUME was prepared at the suggestion of the Committee on War Studies of the Social Science Research Council of New York. For assistance in preparing the manuscript I am indebted to the Committee on Research Funds of the Graduate School of Northwestern University.

R. Y.